CW01083592

Ditherington Mill and the Industrial Revolution

Ditherington Mill and the Industrial Revolution

Edited by Colum Giles and Mike Williams

With contributions from Paul Belford, Ron Fitzgerald, Colum Giles,
Paul Murray Thompson, Tom Swailes, Barrie Trinder,
Ian West, Mike Williams and John Yates

Published by Historic England, The Engine House, Fire Fly Avenue, Swindon SN2 2EH
www.HistoricEngland.org.uk

Historic England is a Government service championing England's heritage and giving expert, constructive advice, and the English Heritage Trust is a charity caring for the National Heritage Collection of more than 400 historic properties and their collections.

First published 2015

ISBN 978-1-84802-118-1

British Library Cataloguing in Publication data
A CIP catalogue record for this book is available from the British Library.

Historic England holds an unparalleled archive of 12 million photographs, drawings, reports and publications on England's places. It is one of the largest archives in the UK, the biggest dedicated to the historic environment, and a priceless resource for anyone interested in England's buildings, archaeology, landscape and social history. Viewed collectively, its photographic collections document the changing face of England from the 1850s to the present day. It is a treasure trove that helps us understand and interpret the past, informs the present and assists with future management and appreciation of the historic environment.

For more information about images from the Archive, contact Archives Services Team, Historic England, The Engine House, Fire Fly Avenue, Swindon SN2 2EH; telephone (01793) 414600.

Brought to publication by Sarah Enticknap, Publishing, Historic England.
Typeset in Charter Regular ITC 9.5pt

Copyedited by Jenny Lawson
Indexed by Sue Vaughn
Page layout by Pauline Hull
Printed in Belgium by DeckersSnoeck

CONTENTS

FOREWORD

Ditherington Mill is rightly celebrated as having, in the form of its Spinning Mill of 1796–1800, the first building in the world with an internal iron frame. Its highly innovative structure provided a fireproof environment for industrial processes and is a predecessor of the technologies that today pepper our cities with skyscrapers. Around the Spinning Mill other early buildings have also survived, which together make the complex a remarkable example of a textile mill from the new generation of steam-powered factories that were changing the face of Britain at the close of the 18th century. The conversion to a maltings in 1897 gave the mill a new lease of life and added further significant buildings to the Shrewsbury skyline. When malting ceased in 1987 the future of the site became an issue of great concern, not only to students of industrial architecture but also to local people who had worked in the maltings or for whom the site had become a familiar landmark in their everyday lives.

The search for a new use for the mill has been protracted and heavily influenced by fluctuating economic conditions. It has, however, drawn together a range of public- and private-sector agencies committed to finding a way not only to preserve and enhance the mill's historic fabric and character, but also to enable it once more to play a significant role in the life of Shrewsbury. Partnership working between Historic England, Shropshire Council, funding agencies, private-sector developers and the local community – represented principally by the Friends of the Flaxmill Maltings – is the key to identifying a sustainable scheme of renewal for the mill.

Historic England believes that a detailed understanding of Ditherington Mill's past should be a cornerstone of its future conservation and adaptation. Since its closure, archaeologists and historians have examined every aspect of this internationally significant industrial site. This research has investigated the innovative technologies employed to create the factory's buildings and has cast light on the people – some of national renown, others now all but forgotten – responsible for the mill's construction and operation. The story which has emerged is a rich one and is summarised in this book, the publication of which is a further demonstration of a collective commitment to securing the site's future.

Sir Laurie Magnus
Chairman, Historic England

PROLOGUE

The Flax Mill at Ditherington in Shrewsbury is one of the world's great buildings, singular in the origin and evolution of its design, in its pioneering use of structural iron, in its influence and its survival. Today, at last, it is gaining the respect and attention it deserves. This book pulls together the threads of what we know so far, in tribute to one of the outstanding symbols of Britain's emergence as the first industrial nation. Among the pantheon of noble buildings it is one of the least known, such that for much of its life it stood virtually forgotten. Brought again to light in 1950 by the distinguished American architectural historian Turpin Bannister, subsequent analysis and research have revealed again its pioneering attributes.

My first visit to the Flax Mill was on a brilliant sunny day in September 1962. With light flooding the spectacular interior it was an astonishing experience, one of those transcendental moments that for me was to determine irrevocably the future of a lifetime's interest in the great age of industry. Subsequently, I have accompanied many people to share in the

Fig 0.1
Interior of the Spinning Mill in 1962, when new research was revealing for the first time the seminal importance of the building.
[© Neil Cossons]

mill's appeal, although never the intense luminescence of that September day. Most of them have been from overseas, scholars and connoisseurs whose discerning judgement drew them inescapably to this most ground-breaking of places. Without exception they have been overwhelmed, yet perplexed that a building of such magnitude could be overlooked for so long.

In this respect the Flax Mill says much about our wider perspectives on the Industrial Revolution and the material evidence of its formative years. The seminal importance of the fire-resistant Spinning Mill contrasts with the relative obscurity of its progenitors. There is no single heroic virtuoso whose name has become synonymous with its design and construction, which in itself reflects the power and substance of the personal connections that gave such potency to the Midlands Enlightenment in the second half of the 18th century. In Charles Bage, however, was a man whose links with William Strutt in Derbyshire, John Marshall and Matthew Murray of Leeds, as well as Matthew Boulton and James Watt, defined him as a critical figure of the new industrial world, this at a decisive moment in the construction of spinning mills and the application of steam to power them in place of water. His contribution is undoubted. The genius of the 1796 Spinning Mill is in its empirical brilliance at a time when there were many who still subscribed to the criticisms suffered by John Smeaton for using so brittle and unreliable a material as cast iron for his millwork.

In this book, for the first time, the creative elegance of the Ditherington Spinning Mill is celebrated. The thought and care we now put into ensuring the mill's future will be the measure of how seriously as a nation we regard its dignity and stature as one of the most seminal of symbols of Britain's Industrial Revolution and the birth of the modern world. Adaptation from flax mill to maltings was surprisingly benign in its effects and we are the beneficiaries of that. Today, the building deserves not only the very best that contemporary research and conservation science can deliver but in deciding its future the same spirit of determination and inventive inspiration that was reflected in its construction over 200 years ago.

Sir Neil Cossons

ACKNOWLEDGEMENTS

This study of Ditherington Mill is the result of a collaboration between authors specialising in a range of different subjects and involved researching a great variety of historical information. The analysis of the site by investigators from Historic England's Assessment Team West began in 2000, when parts of the iron frame were being newly exposed, and this built on earlier work by the staff of the Royal Commission on the Historical Monuments of England and an exceptional range of previously published material. The editors would like to thank the staff of the Historic England West Midlands office, in particular the managers of the Ditherington Flax Mill project: Andrew Patterson, John Yates and Tim Johnston. This publication project has been overseen by Keith Falconer, Chris Smith, John Cattell, Barry Jones, Allan Brodie and Peter Herring, and the book has been brought to publication by Robin Taylor and Sarah Enticknap of the Historic England Publishing Department. Photography is by James O Davies, Peter Williams and Steven Baker. On-site survey is by Nigel Fradgley and Mike Williams, with additional research by Rebecca Lane. Publication drawings are by Allan Adams and Phillip Sinton. Initial text editing was undertaken by Olivia Horsfall-Turner. Comments on the final draft were provided by Mark Watson of Historic Scotland and by Penny Ward, Joanna Layton and Alan Mosley of the Friends of the Flaxmill Maltings. Additional comments were provided by Nick Hill of the Historic England East Midlands Office. The documentary sources used in the book are widely dispersed in archives and record offices around the country. In particular the authors and editors would like to thank the staff of Shropshire Archives, The Leeds University Library, Birmingham Library Services, the Central Library of Sheffield, Warwickshire County Record Office, the West Yorkshire Archives Service and the Leodis archive of the Leeds Library and Information Service. The credits and copyright for the archive images used in the book are stated in the captions.

EDITORIAL NOTES

Measurements are given in metric units except in cases citing documents using imperial units and where imperial measurements clearly have more relevance to the subject matter (for example, in the dimensions of structural members in Ditherington's iron-framed buildings). All modern survey drawings use metric scales.

Abbreviations
BPP: British Parliamentary Papers
BWC: Boulton and Watt Collection, The Library of Birmingham
ESJ: *Eddowes Salopian Journal*
LULSC: Leeds University Library, Special Collections, MS200
SA: Shropshire Archives
SC: *Shrewsbury Chronicle*
SJ: *Shropshire Journal*
UBD: *Universal British Directory*
VCH: Victoria History of the Counties of England

Conventions
'Flax' and 'linen': 'flax' is used as a term to describe the plant and its processing (flax dressing, flax spinning, etc). Mills are described as flax mills (unless the particular mill under discussion is a weaving mill) as this is the substance that is being processed. 'Linen' is used to describe the products (yarn, thread, cloth) and the industry as a whole.

'Marshalls': continuity in the story of Ditherington Mill in its life as a flax mill is provided by the Marshall family, ever present through three generations and through a number of partnerships, the most important of which in relation to Ditherington was with the brothers Benjamin and Thomas Benyon and Charles Bage. For ease of reference, the term 'Marshalls' is used to describe the company. The term 'Marshall' is restricted to reference to John Marshall, founder of the company.

Building names: names of most of the buildings within Ditherington Mill are taken from documents in the Marshall business archive, Leeds University Library. The name applied to the principal building, the Spinning Mill, was not used as a descriptive term by the company: instead, plans label it simply as 'Mill'. 'Spinning Mill', although not fully descriptive of its function in the flax factory, is used in this book as a term of convenience to distinguish it from the term 'mill', which can be applied to the site as a whole. It is also worth remarking that the factory seems to have lacked a consistent name in its life as a flax mill. It is shown on maps as 'flax mill', is described by the historian W G Rimmer as Castle Foregate Mill (although as far as can be determined without any historical references to this name), was often referred to in trade directories simply by its address ('St Michael's Street' in 1835, 'the Factory, Castle Foregate' in 1868) and in this book is called Ditherington Mill, again without any strong historical evidence. On conversion to a maltings, the site came to be known as 'the Shropshire Maltings'.

Surveyed drawings
The book includes many surveyed drawings of the historic iron frames. In most cases substantial parts of these structures remained hidden from view at the time of recording; in particular, those in the Spinning Mill and the Cross Building were encased within thick concrete floors. Some of the drawings are therefore reconstructions, based on the small sections of the frames that have been exposed for structural testing, and will require updating as more of the frames are exposed.

Ditherington Mill: an introduction

COLUM GILES

Ditherington Mill is one of the primary monuments of what is conveniently labelled as the British 'Industrial Revolution'.[1] It is not located in any of the areas that are today regarded as the country's great historic industrial heartlands – the coal-mining north east, the textile-manufacturing areas of Lancashire, the metal-working Black Country – but instead in Shropshire, a largely agricultural county, and more specifically in Shrewsbury, a county town of timber-framed streets and gracious Georgian townhouses. Nevertheless, the mill is linked to crucial developments in engineering, the textile industry and business practices that drove the nation's economy forward at an ever-faster pace in the late 18th and early 19th centuries. Its location in Shrewsbury may seem idiosyncratic to modern eyes, but is explained by the area's important role in the early stages of the Industrial Revolution and by strong personal ties that attracted investment to the town. This book tells the story of the mill, how and why it came to be built and how the characters involved in its history first produced an outstanding and pioneering industrial building and later ran a business of great importance both to the town and to the wider industrial scene.

The mill was built by a partnership of local and Yorkshire entrepreneurs for the processing of flax into linen yarn and thread. Building commenced in 1796 and production began in 1797. The initiative behind its construction came from Shrewsbury merchants Thomas (1762–1833) and Benjamin (1763–1834) Benyon, who some years earlier had entered into partnership with John Marshall of Leeds (1765–1845), a flax merchant and manufacturer and one of the most important pioneers of the factory system. At first the partnership operated from a mill in Holbeck, Leeds, but the Benyons used their position as majority stakeholders in the business to build a new mill in their home town. This was apparently against Marshall's wishes

and, one would think, against business logic, for Shrewsbury and Shropshire were remote from the country's main centres of textile production. The partnership clearly suffered from internal stresses and in 1804 the Benyons left to set up rival factories in both Leeds and Shrewsbury. Thereafter Marshall, and in time his sons and grandsons, ran Ditherington Mill in tandem with the Leeds operation until the failure of the business in 1886. The Ditherington complex was later converted for use as a maltings (Fig 1.1). The mill's significance will be summarised briefly in this introductory chapter and explored in greater detail in the remainder of the book.[2]

The Spinning Mill of 1796–1800 was designed by Charles Bage (1751–1822), a partner in the firm along with the Benyon brothers and Marshall. It is recognised as the first building in the world successfully to substitute incombustible materials – namely cast and wrought iron and brick – for the timber beams and joists used in industrial structures up to that date (Fig 1.2). It therefore provided what was regarded at the time as the holy grail, an environment that was believed to be 'fireproof'.[3] Later developments, both on the same site and elsewhere, departed in important ways from the structural forms adopted in the Spinning Mill, and these serve to emphasise the building's unique and experimental quality in a period of very rapid change initiated by a network of industrialists. The mill is also one of the earliest surviving factories to have been powered entirely by steam engines. While this is more the result of an accident of survival rather than representing a genuinely pioneering development, it nevertheless contributes to our overall assessment of the mill's significance today. Furthermore, the story of the development of steam power on the site brings into sharp focus the battle between the leading engine makers of the period – Boulton and Watt of Soho, Birmingham, who at the time were protected by important patents – and

Fig 1.1
The monumental c 1810 Engine House at the south end of the Spinning Mill. The wooden structure is a hoist tower dating from the conversion into a maltings in the 1890s. [DP163705]

Fig 1.2
Cast-iron columns and
beams in the Spinning Mill,
the first building in the
world with an internal
iron frame.
[DP163697]

upstart rival manufacturers attempting to cut into the growing market for the engines which were powering the fast-growing economy.

Two further aspects of the mill's history confer significance. Ditherington exemplifies both the development of a factory system on a large scale and the rapid and continued change to machines and production techniques necessitated by invention and shifting markets. The building of the mill represented a considerable investment in the factory system – that is, a large workforce operating under supervision. Documentary evidence demonstrates how the mill evolved and adapted to changing external business conditions in a savagely competitive environment. Lastly, the mill's story is linked to characters of national significance. The central protagonists were of course John Marshall and his sometime partners the Benyon brothers and Charles Bage, but alongside these are further personalities of national renown: William Strutt of Derby and Belper (1756–1830), cotton spinner and another pioneer of fireproof mill construction; Matthew Boulton (1728–1809) and James Watt (1736–1819), struggling to preserve their technical supremacy; and Matthew Murray (1765–1826), machine engineer of Leeds, who, working for Marshall, patented key innovations

in flax-spinning machinery and who went on to become one of the foremost challengers to Boulton and Watt in the production of steam engines.

The mill's history as a maltings after 1897 is also of historic importance, especially to the people of Shrewsbury who remember the site as a working factory (Fig 1.3).[4] This phase of the mill's life incidentally produced its most eye-catching feature – the 'Jubilee' crown on the 1897 hoist tower over the main building (see Fig 10.10). The mill's time as a maltings is particularly interesting in the way that it shows the process of conversion of buildings for new purposes, although this was quite common at the time and has many parallels in other industrial complexes. The search for new uses in recent years, however, gives a contemporary significance to the site to complement its historic importance. The mill fell into disuse when malting ceased in 1987 and, while the demolition of a complex of such global historic importance was never seriously considered, a long-term conservation programme has to resolve two potentially conflicting demands. On the one hand, features which demonstrate Ditherington's historic character as a pioneering textile mill have to be retained and displayed, and on the other an economically viable and suitable new use for the complex has to be found, for without this even the most sensitive alterations will prove fruitless in guaranteeing its future. The fact that in 2005 the mill was taken into the ownership of English Heritage,

Fig 1.3
The south end of the
Spinning Mill in c 1900,
when it was in use as a
maltings.
[Shropshire Archives
PH/S/13/M/1/11
(BB015973)]

the body responsible for setting standards in the care of the historic environment, provides an added significance to the site and the discussions about its future. It is hoped that the conservation of the mill will help to regenerate the local area and demonstrate the cultural and economic benefits that can result from the retention of buildings which are central to the nation's history (Fig 1.4).

Ditherington Mill: historiography

The importance of Ditherington Mill was already being hailed at the time of its building, when its fireproof construction was regarded as a leap forward in industrial architecture. Its renown quickly faded, however, as new and improved methods of construction were developed and widely applied. Perhaps never entirely forgotten, its place in industrial history awaited rediscovery until the mid-20th century. In 1950 research by the American professor Turpin Bannister established the importance of the site in an international context, which may have led to the first listing of the mill, registered in 1953.[5] A few years later, in 1962, Skempton and Johnson published one of the seminal articles on the history of industrial architecture, demonstrating that Ditherington Mill was the first to achieve a complete internal iron frame and relating its construction to other contemporary developments.[6] The history of the Marshalls firm was comprehensively studied by Professor W G Rimmer in two publications: the first focusing on the Ditherington end of the business and the second providing a fuller coverage of the company but with a strong emphasis on the Leeds mill.[7] Based largely on the Marshall archive, Rimmer's work mainly concerned economic aspects, with few details about the buildings or comparisons with other mills. Nevertheless, it provides a useful insight into how the business was managed by successive generations of the family.

The potential threat to the survival of Ditherington Mill increased when the site became vacant in the 1980s, but this also had the benefit of prompting comprehensive documentary research and a complete reappraisal of the site. This work was undertaken by the Ironbridge Institute (now the Ironbridge International Institute for Cultural Studies) and resulted in new insights into the mill's history.[8] Understanding of Ditherington's place in the development of industrial architecture was increased considerably in the same period through the publication by the Royal Commission on the Historical Monuments of England of studies of historic textile mills in other areas, and a still wider context was provided by a study of early Scottish flax mills.[9] Ditherington's place in engineering history also became clearer through important studies of the uses of cast and wrought iron and the distribution of early fireproof mills.[10] Both specific and general literature, therefore, ensured that Ditherington's history and importance was well known in specialist circles.

Fig 1.4
Ditherington Mill retains an exceptional variety of early industrial buildings, all of which remain well preserved despite the lack of maintenance after the maltings closed in 1987. This view shows the Malt Kiln, Cross Building and Dyehouse. [DP163728]

New research and the conservation project of the early 21st century

New research undertaken after 2000 has continued to add to the body of knowledge about the mill. Various aspects of its history have been investigated independently by students and local groups and have provided a more refined view of Ditherington's local and national contexts. Furthermore, during these years an important opportunity was afforded to advance knowledge of the mill's place in the history of industrial architecture. For the first time in more than a century the removal of later fabric, in particular parts of the concrete floors inserted during the mill's malting phase, made possible the closer study of the structural forms employed in the early buildings. Details of their iron frames were exposed and subsequently recorded by modern survey methods, particularly involving three-dimensional CAD modelling. The result, set out in this book, is a reappraisal of the development of the early fireproof structures on the site, and this has permitted a more refined understanding of the relationship between Ditherington and other fireproof buildings during a crucial period in the evolution of industrial architecture.

The research that is summarised in this book should be considered in a wider context. New investigation could be justified simply on the grounds of the historical importance of the Ditherington site and because so many unanswered questions in the evolution of industrial architecture could be addressed through further study. However, the research has had a more practical application: of informing the long-term conservation project which will, it is hoped, secure the site's future. New investigation and fresh assessments of significance have been key aspects of this much larger project, helping to identify how best to conserve a site of international importance.

Sources

The story of Ditherington Mill is told in this book through evidence from a number of sources. The mill is one of the best documented factories of the period, thanks mainly to the survival of an extensive, albeit partial, archive of material generated by Marshalls and the Marshall family.[11] Of particular importance are the annual inventories of machinery at Ditherington, the earliest dating from 1806. John Marshall also wrote an account of his extensive travels, during which he inspected many mills in different parts of the country, and he recorded his numerous experiments with new machines and products. Another early source of exceptional interest is the surviving correspondence from Charles Bage to William Strutt between c 1796 and 1818.[12] Although only one of the letters dates from the years when Ditherington Mill was being built, the collection clearly indicates the depth of Bage's interest in the developing technologies of structural engineering and textile processes and his awareness of the value of controlled testing in the design of iron structures. The letters include detailed accounts of Bage's thinking on the design of cast-iron columns and roof trusses and on fireproof construction, although they do not mention Ditherington Mill by name. A third source of immense interest and value are the papers contained in the Boulton and Watt collection. These provide crucial evidence for the first steam power system and for the installation of gas lighting at the site: engineering drawings show the nature of early installations, and correspondence between the firm and Marshalls and between company partners and employees illuminates the challenges which Boulton and Watt faced in the years when their protective patents successively expired.

There is a danger, of course, that this wealth of documentation can introduce distortion into our view of the history of the mill and the role of the different characters involved in its development. The survival of such copious documentation for Marshalls highlights how little we know about the other partners in the Ditherington venture, for the Benyon brothers and Bage left little in the way of business or personal papers. The partnership itself can only be assessed through the writings of John Marshall, although much can be surmised from these. The Bage correspondence with Strutt is important, but it is also one-sided and mainly covers the years after the construction of the Spinning Mill at Ditherington; no responses from William Strutt have survived, and there is just a single tantalising glimpse of what might have been a crucial exchange of letters relating to the thinking behind the structural innovations represented by the Spinning Mill. Thus, the respective roles of Bage and Strutt in the development of fireproof construction remain elusive. In the field of steam engine development the same imbalance is found: while Boulton and Watt recorded events and orders in great detail and left a large consolidated archive, evidence for Matthew Murray's business is more dispersed and less complete: we see Murray's sparring with Boulton and Watt only from the defensive actions recorded by the Soho company. Finally, the sources are strongest when dealing with the principal personalities in the great changes that were taking place in industry during this period. The experience of the much larger numbers of people who laboured in mills can only be seen through the eyes of the employers and, fleetingly, in parliamentary inquiries into working conditions in mills. These provide some insight into the lives of the mill hands, but their voices are largely absent from the historical record.

The final source worthy of mention here is the evidence provided by a new survey of the mill's fabric, which fills in the gaps left by the documentary evidence. Documents are generally drawn up with specific purposes in mind, and in the period under review they rarely relate to the construction of a mill's buildings. As such, the evidence for the sequence of construction at Ditherington and the interpretation of individual buildings is found principally in surviving building fabric, the examination of which demands very close attention in the case of a site as important as Ditherington. The evidence for the phased construction of the Spinning Mill is now more substantial as a result of new survey, and examination of the different forms of cast-iron components in the three early fireproof buildings has illuminated a complex story of experimentation, and perhaps also of an unfolding acknowledgement of mistakes, over a 15-year period.

The structure of the book

This book tells Ditherington's story by bringing together a number of strands of research. Previous works have made aspects of the mill's history familiar and formed the starting point for a new study of the complex. What has been added to this is evidence drawn from new fabric survey, fresh research into aspects of the mill's history, such as the housing of a workforce of apprentices, and the fruits of independent investigation into, for example, the installation of gas lighting.[13]

The different parts of this book are a mixture of narrative and thematic discussions. First, the context for Ditherington's construction is set through an examination of the linen industry in Chapter 2. Any discussion of the mill must be informed by an understanding of how the industry developed, both technically, through the application of new and improved machines, and economically, with the development of new products and their distribution across the country. In Chapter 3 the mill's local setting is studied to address the question of why a pioneering factory was built in what, at a superficial glance, might seem an unlikely location. In fact, Shropshire offered a great deal of expertise which was to be harnessed to individual initiative to drive the project forward.

Against this national and local background, the book continues with an account of the building of the mill in Chapter 4. The characters in its development, each with a particular role to play, are introduced and the construction of the site is explained in detail. The development of one building in particular – the Spinning Mill – is complex, but an understanding of how it took its completed form is crucial to an assessment of the overall site's significance.

The next section comprises four thematic chapters on technical and management aspects which influenced the original design of the mill, governed its day-to-day operation and secured its place in industrial history. The iron-framed construction of the factory's early buildings, described in Chapter 5, is undoubtedly the mill's most important facet, but the design of the frame was closely related to the installation of steam power and the arrangement of processes and machinery, a story explained in Chapter 6. Research has indicated that structure, power and processes were central themes for the designers of Ditherington Mill, a very early demonstration of the appreciation of the particular requirements of industrial buildings which later gave rise to a specialist industrial architectural profession. Chapter 7 is devoted to a study of the management of change within the mill over the course of its life as a flax factory; of particular importance is the evidence for the investment in new machinery and the relationship of the Ditherington enterprise to the firm's Leeds mill. Chapter 8 describes the installation of a gas lighting system and its subsequent history, involving first a resort to a public supply and later the construction of a new private gas plant.

Chapter 9 brings together the evidence for the mill's workforce, studying issues such as recruitment, child labour, the provision made for housing (particularly in relation to the accommodation for apprentices) and working conditions in the mill. The history of the mill in its life as a maltings is studied in Chapter 10, which outlines the structural changes made to the complex to accommodate its new function. Finally, the story of the mill is brought up to date in Chapter 11 through an account of how it has fared since it ceased operation as a maltings – a story culminating in a flagship restoration project.

What has emerged from this research is a new understanding of Ditherington Mill, in both its own evolution and its context within the history of the textile industry and that of structural engineering. Our assessment of its importance, at least as far as this is reflected in formal measures of protection, remains unaltered: the Spinning Mill, Cross Building and Flax Warehouse are listed at Grade I, the grade indicating the highest level of special interest and importance; two other buildings on the site are listed at Grade II*; and two further buildings at Grade II. Perhaps the greatest gain in understanding which has resulted from new research relates to the clearer realisation of Ditherington's place in the development of mill construction in the late 18th and early 19th centuries, and of the experimental nature of the structural forms which the mill's early buildings employed in their iron frames. While Ditherington did have antecedents, specifically in William Strutt's work in Derbyshire, the Spinning Mill of 1796–1800 was the first use of a cast-iron framed interior, and included new methods of joining the components together. Both elsewhere, in Strutt's later buildings in Derbyshire and in towns such as Manchester and Leeds, and at Ditherington itself, lessons were learned from the experience of constructing the first mill on the Shrewsbury site, for some of its features were not repeated. The story of iron-framed, fireproof construction during this period can be seen more clearly, therefore, not as an achievement gained in a single dramatic project, but rather as a succession of trials and independent initiatives undertaken before a settled form was reached in the great improvements to cast-iron structures developed by Eaton Hodgkinson and William Fairbairn in the 1830s.

Ditherington Mill, however, is important not just as a pioneering work of structural engineering. Its story illuminates many critical aspects of economic, social and technological history during a time of rapid change. The establishment of a mill in a location without a strong tradition of factory working; investment in new sources of power; technological innovation leading to improvements in the working environment; the workings of partnerships and investment in newly developed machinery; the organisation of production; the housing of a workforce; and the adaptability of industrial buildings to new uses: all are exemplified at Ditherington. The multi-faceted nature of the mill's significance is explored in the following chapters and explains why such efforts have been made to protect the site and to adapt it for a new era.

2

The linen industry in Great Britain: history, products, processes and location

BARRIE TRINDER AND MIKE WILLIAMS

Linen manufacturing – that is, the production of linen yarns and cloth – was not, in quantitative terms, the most prominent sector of the British economy during the Industrial Revolution, but on every measure except size it was comparable with other parts of the textile industry. It made use of new forms of manufacturing technology driven by steam power. It was also one of the first industries to use new forms of employment structure. It came to be organised on a factory basis, which involved the necessity to recruit employees, to train them in appropriate skills and to impose new patterns of work discipline. Examination of the linen industry provides enlightening insights into the motivations of leading manufacturers, their sources of capital and the dynamics of partnerships. The objective of this chapter is to examine linen manufacturing in Great Britain in the 18th and 19th centuries by describing its products, the processes involved in their production, the progress of mechanisation and the distribution of the industry and its various specialisms. The chapter will thus provide a context within which the mill at Ditherington can be understood and its significance better appreciated.

Flax

Flax (*Linum usitatissimum*) is a plant grown for a number of purposes. When processed, its long, tough stalks can be used to make linen yarn which can either be woven to make fabric or twisted to make linen thread. Linen yarn was used to make many types of fabric in the 18th century. Products ranged from the finest-quality cloth – the cambrics, lawns, hollands and damask used for the apparel, bedding and table napkins of the wealthy – to canvas, sacking and tarpaulins. Sailcloth was particularly important in the 18th and early 19th centuries, and was also made from linen yarn. Medium grades of linen yarn were used for tenting fabric, towelling and the rough-backed huckaback fabric used for many mundane household purposes. Some linen fabrics were derived from hemp, another plant crop: hempen sheets, pillowcases and napkins are itemised in many probate inventories of this period. Much of the yarn that was produced commercially was used in such mixed-fibre fabrics as fustian (combined with wool or cotton) and druggets and linsey woolsey (both of which combined linen and wool). Linen thread was also an important product of the industry, and was used in the production of leather goods, lace and clothing.

The economics of the linen industry were strongly influenced by the methods of cultivation of the flax plant and its distinctive characteristics as a textile fibre. Flax requires deep, well-drained soils and benefits from wet springs and hot, dry summers – conditions more prevalent in parts of central and eastern Europe than in Britain.[1] There were typically two crops every year, with the second also providing seed. Flax had to be rotated with other crops, which in England typically meant that it could only be produced every five to seven years from the same land.[2] The growing of flax was particularly labour intensive. Each crop was sown by hand from fresh seed, frequent weeding was needed during its growing life and the mature plants were harvested by pulling rather than cutting. The flax was then stacked for air-drying in the field (Fig 2.1) and then retted (soaked) in water to soften the hard outer stem. In the 18th century the subsequent processing of the crop also involved a great deal of manual labour, which was a significant factor in the cost of production. The first stages were breaking and scutching, manual or mechanical processes by which the hard outer casings of the flax plants were loosened and removed to extract the useful fibre.[3] The particular sequence of processes varied widely in different

growing areas. The resulting stems of fibre, usually about 750mm long, were bundled for export as the 'rough flax' that was received at the factories.

Heavy reliance on imports and the varying proportion of 'line' and 'tow' (see below) in the flax crops could affect the cost of the raw material and have a significant effect on the profitability of a flax factory. John Marshall's astute management of the stocks of raw material maintained the competitiveness of his mills during volatile trading conditions in the 1790s and during the Napoleonic Wars (between c 1793 and c 1814). The mills at both Leeds (the company's principal base of operations) and Ditherington were built with flax warehousing which was extended significantly in the first decade of the 19th century, at one point containing sufficient flax for up to a year's production at Leeds.[4] At Ditherington, flax consumption between 1815 and 1822 was typically around seven to eight tons (6.4 to 7.3 tonnes)

per week.[5] Flax factories in other areas also had relatively large warehouses, in part because the supply of both imported and home-grown flax could be unpredictable from year to year.

Processes in the early flax factories and the progress of mechanisation

The arrangement of processes in a factory and the accommodation of machinery were primary considerations in the design of textile mill buildings (Fig 2.2). In a flax mill, the layout of the factory reflected variations in the type of flax being worked and the particular quality – fine or coarse – of the products. The finer yarns and threads sold for the highest prices and many of the improvements in machinery were directed towards the production of higher value goods. To this end, successive innovations allowed finer yarns to be spun and enabled lower-grade flax to be used to produce fine yarns. There were also important developments made in machines which reduced the consumption of raw flax for the same output.

The precise control required for successive stages of production was one reason for the rigid nature of employment in a mill, and the specialised language of flax processes was part of the daily routine of the operatives. Linen yarns were measured using different terminology to that employed in the manufacture of other textiles. The 'count' of linen yarn was specified as the number of units of 300 yards (274m), known as a 'lea', that could be spun from a pound (450g) of flax; a twelve lea yarn, for example, comprised 12 × 300 yards spun from one pound of flax. After spinning, the yarn was wound into 'hanks' of 3,600 yards (3,292m).

The machines used in early textile factories were simpler and of quite different appearance to those in use by the mid-19th century. The

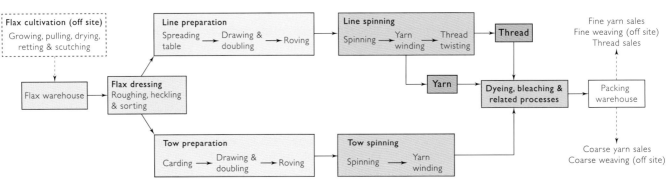

early machines were of heavy wooden construction, comprising a rectangular framework of posts and pegged rails, with working parts moved by a combination of simple iron gearing, levers and wooden pulleys. The wooden machines were sometimes referred to as 'frames', and the term remained in use after the introduction of improved cast-iron framed machinery. Because a specialist textile-machine-making industry was slow to develop, a distinctive feature of many of the most successful early textile firms was that they often built their own machinery, the larger mills including both woodworking and engineering departments for this purpose.

Flax dressing: roughing, heckling and sorting

The initial stages in yarn production were entirely manual processes before the mid-1790s. They concerned the cleaning of the rough flax, followed by its separation into long and short fibres, both obtained from the same plant but in different proportions according to the variety of flax and the growing conditions in any given year. The processes involved in flax dressing were often grouped together in a heckling department, frequently located in a workshop which, for convenience, was sited close to or within a flax warehouse.[6] Since these preparatory stages produced large amounts of dust and waste they were commonly located away from rooms containing powered machinery.[7]

The first of the flax dressing processes was roughing, in which handfuls of flax were straightened and cleaned by manually drawing them through sets of metal spikes fixed to a bench, thus removing unwanted material (Fig 2.3). This was followed by heckling itself, which separated the long fibre (line) from the short fibre (tow). Line was used for spinning finer yarns and for thread-making and was much more valuable; tow was used for coarser yarns and heavier cloths. The heckling process was similar to roughing and involved drawing the flax through finer spikes of different lengths. The spikes (or 'heckles') were mounted on wooden benches, often fixed along the side walls to provide good lighting. The process was carried out in stages, each stage using finer heckles to extract finer grades of tow. Heckling remained a manual operation for at least two decades after the introduction of powered spinning machinery, limiting the development

of factory production well into the 19th century. It was an arduous occupation, dominated by men, which was crucial to the profitability of a mill; good hecklers could obtain a higher proportion of the valuable line fibres, although this required more time and increased labour costs.[8] The hecklers were highly skilled and organised, noted for their resistance to mechanisation, and commanded high wages. They were paid separately from the other mill operatives, even when heckling was based on the mill premises, and retained their independence in some areas until well into the 1820s.[9]

Heckling machines were introduced and patented in 1809 by John Hives of Leeds, then one of John Marshall's principal partners, and appear from that year in the inventories of both the Ditherington and Leeds mills.[10] The patent was challenged by Marshall's former employee, Matthew Murray, who was later credited with the invention of the machines.[11] Heckling machines were initially used in small numbers alongside manual hecklers, but had replaced them within a decade. The machines comprised a large, narrow cylinder, powered by line shafting, with heckles mounted around its circumference. Handfuls of flax were hung from brackets above the cylinder and combed by the revolving heckles. The line remained in the bracket, the tow was pulled out into the heckles and waste dropped down into the base of the machine (Fig 2.4). The tow was then taken off the cylinder by a mechanism at the back of the machine. Heckling machines were installed in groups, each with successively finer heckles to produce a different grade of tow, in a similar method of working to that used by the hand

Fig 2.3
The first stage of heckling involved roughing: manually drawing the fibre through spikes to clean out the waste. [Reproduced courtesy of the Bridport Museum Trust (DP000599)]

Preparation: drawing and doubling

After heckling, the separated line and tow fibre passed through different sets of machinery for preparation and spinning – processes that had become mechanised by the end of the 18th century. In a flax-spinning mill, preparation involved the production and gradual refinement of a sliver of the raw fibre. Two or more slivers were doubled together, and the doubled sliver was drawn further to remove irregularities. This combination of doubling and drawing was similar to that used for other textiles such as wool and cotton. In flax mills the sequence was typically

Fig 2.4
A heckling machine of the early 19th century, when heckling was chiefly an occupation for women and children.
[Leeds University Library Special Collections MS200/44, 20 (DP163785)]

hecklers. At the end of the process the line and the different grades of tow were sorted and transferred to different groups of preparation machines.[12] The early heckling machines were mostly restricted to the larger mills of Marshall and his associates, where they were hidden from public view but had immediate benefits for the business.[13] They were mainly tended by boys and girls, who were paid far less than adult male hecklers, and were said to consistently produce a higher proportion of line than the old manual process.[14] At first, smaller firms did not have access to the new machines and were disadvantaged by their continued reliance on manual hecklers.

b

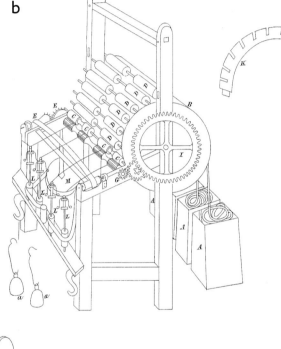

Figs 2.5a and 2.5b
The original flax-processing machine patented by John Kendrew and Thomas Porthouse in 1787.
[Sheffield Libraries (DP157072 and DP157074)]

a

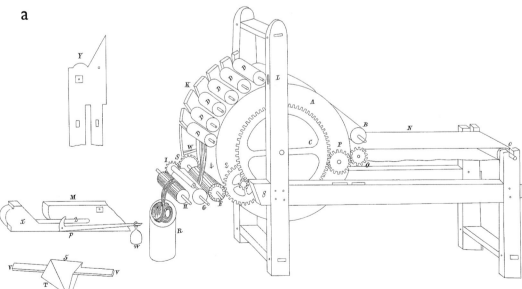

repeated three or four times to produce a sliver of the required weight and consistency. This was given a slight twist to form a 'roving', and was then transferred to the spinning machines.

In 1787 John Kendrew, an optician, and Thomas Porthouse, a watchmaker, both of Darlington, patented a 'mill or machine upon new principles for spinning yarn from hemp, tow, flax or wool' (Figs 2.5a and 2.5b). Their patent described a system for both preparation and spinning, and it acknowledged that some parts of the machines were similar to those developed by Richard Arkwright for spinning cotton.[15] To perform the drawing operation, the Kendrew and Porthouse machine had a wooden cylinder revolving on a horizontal shaft, with a series of smaller rollers resting on its upper edge (in appearance much like a carding machine). The 1787 patent specified the use of leather covering for the rollers to avoid damaging the fibre. The heckled flax was initially arranged on a table next to a conveyor and formed into a sliver by hand in a process known as spreading. The conveyor passed the sliver around the large cylinder, where it was compressed by the weight of the smaller rollers. At the rear of the machine the sliver was pulled off and passed between two pairs of drafting rollers, the second pair rotating faster to give the required amount of draft, and then loosely coiled into cans. These were used to transfer the sliver to similar subsequent drawing machines, set up with rollers of different weights and without the spreading tables, to be doubled and drafted further.

The flax machinery patented by Kendrew and Porthouse was of great significance, paving the way for the introduction of factory methods in the linen industry, but numerous improvements were needed before it could work successfully on a large scale. Along with his engineer Matthew Murray, John Marshall spent several years experimenting and improving the machines, and Murray patented improved types of drawing and spinning machines in 1790 and 1793 (Figs 2.6a and 2.6b).[16] The 1790 patent was aimed at improving the preparation and spinning of line flax and included a drawing mechanism utilising a pair of touching conveyors in place of the earlier rollers. Murray's machines were installed in Marshall's newly built Leeds mill in 1791 and 1795, and were said to be commercially successful from 1793.[17] It is likely that Murray's success gave Marshall and his partners confidence that con-

a

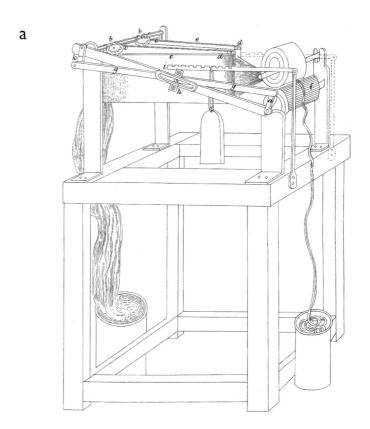

b

Fig 2.6a and 2.6b
Improved flax machinery patented by Matthew Murray in 1790 and 1793, which was developed in partnership with John Marshall. [Sheffield Libraries (DP157159 and DP157160)]

Fig 2.7
Early 19th-century flax-roving machinery, shown in cross section on the left and front elevation on the right.
[From Gray 1819, © The British Library Board, G70085-76]

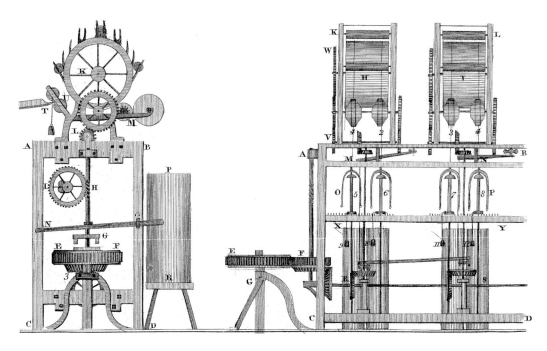

struction of a new mill at this point would prove to be a profitable investment.

The shorter fibres of tow flax could not be drafted as much as line and had to be prepared for spinning using a different sequence of machinery. The heckled tow was initially fed into a carding engine, a modified version of the machines used in other textile industries, after which the slivers were drafted and doubled in a similar way to line flax. Matthew Murray's 1793 patent concerned an improved type of carding engine for preparing tow, and following its introduction Marshall's mills could efficiently process the full range of fibre obtained from raw flax.

The final stage of both line and tow preparation involved the further drafting of the slivers and giving them a limited amount of twist to form the roving; the twist enabled the roving to be wound onto bobbins for mounting on to

the spinning machines. Early roving frames were similar to cylinder drawing frames, but produced more draft and added twist using a spindle-and-flyer mechanism similar to contemporary spinning machines (Fig 2.7). Different roving frames were dedicated for use with slivers of either line flax or the various grades of tow flax.

One of the major developments in flax machinery in the early 19th century was the introduction of new types of preparation machinery that enabled a wider range of raw flax to be used for spinning the finer grades of yarn, which sold at a premium. The most important innovation was the gill frame for drawing and roving (Figs 2.8a and 2.8b). The technique combined drawing with a process of combing the fibre and was first patented in 1795, but underwent significant improvement

Figs 2.8a and 2.8b
Gill-drawing machinery, as patented by Sellers and Standage in 1795 and Hall in 1814. This represented a major improvement in flax preparation.
[Sheffield Libraries (DP157043 and DP157127)]

a   b

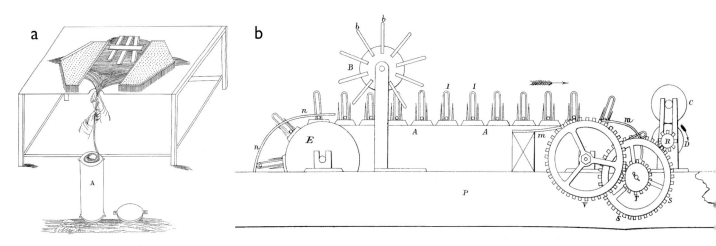

in the early 19th century.[18] The gill machines that were finally adopted in the industry used a system of fine pins mounted on moving belts to lightly comb the slivers during drafting; this enabled coarser grades of flax to be drafted further, producing a finer roving. The increased output of gill frames had a similar effect on flax mills to that of the earlier introduction of heckling machines, altering the sequence of production so that the whole system of machinery could produce the more profitable finer yarns. The result was that by the 1820s flax mills might contain a variety of preparation machines of different dates suited to different types of flax.

Spinning and twisting

The Kendrew and Porthouse machinery was patented to spin 'yarn from hemp, tow, flax or wool', but the spinning process itself remained similar to that used in the earlier cotton-spinning machinery of Richard Arkwright. The roving produced by the preparation processes was drafted further, using pairs of drafting rollers, and to produce the finished yarn a twist was applied with a spindle-and-flyer mechanism, similar to that used on Arkwright machines and some earlier types of spinning wheels. The amount of draft and twist was adjusted to suit the greater length of flax fibres. Wooden-framed spinning

frames of about 30 spindles each, probably incorporating Marshall and Murray's improvements but still respecting the original 1787 patents, were installed at the Leeds mill between 1791 and 1796, and the original Ditherington spinning machines in 1797 would have been of similar appearance. In the early 19th century spinning machines began to be made with cast-iron frames (Fig 2.9), but for existing mills it was cheaper and more practical to upgrade components rather than replacing a complete set of machines. Older mills retained wooden-framed machinery until at least the 1820s, when some of the earlier wooden machines at Ditherington were still being replaced.

The next major advance that affected the whole linen industry was the introduction of wet spinning from the mid-1820s. This technique was patented by James Kay, a millowner from Preston, Lancashire, in 1825, but was in fact a development of several earlier concepts and was intended to accompany the introduction of gill-roving machinery.[19] The use of a sponge fixed to the spinning frames to wet the slivers, reducing yarn breakages during drafting, had been mentioned in Matthew Murray's patent of 1791, but the most important precursor to Kay's machine formed part of the system invented by Philippe de Girard in France and patented in Britain in 1814, which was the first to use a trough of water

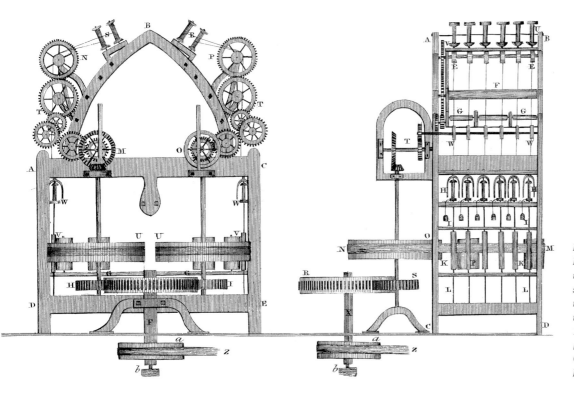

Fig 2.9
Iron-framed spinning machinery, with the spindles arranged in two rows along each side, was introduced from the early 19th century.
[From Gray 1819, © The British Library Board, G70085-77]

in the spinning frames to wet the rovings.[20] The wet-spinning technique in Kay's patents further refined the wetting of the flax, including the use of hot water, through which the rovings were passed immediately prior to drafting (Fig 2.10). This enabled the roving to be drafted further, complementing the benefits of the gill frames mentioned above and allowing the production of finer counts of both line and tow yarns; a wider range of flax could, therefore, now be used to make thread. Wet spinning was recognised as a great improvement, but involved completely replacing the existing machines, along with the associated shafting, and installing a hot water system in the spinning rooms. For existing mills, the introduction of wet spinning was therefore associated with an extensive overhaul of their machinery and power system.

After spinning, the yarn was transferred onto winding (or reeling) frames and wound into bundles (or 'skeins') of a specific length measured in hanks. Winding frames were relatively lightweight, often located in the top storey, and could be hand-powered or driven by shafting (Fig 2.11). The yarn was wound around an open drum made of wooden slats, which could be collapsed to enable the hanks of yarn to be removed. The circumference of the drum was such that a given number of rotations would wind on a single hank. Some specialised mills like Ditherington included a further major group of twisting machines for combining two or more yarns into thread. Since thread was made from fine yarns, these twisting frames were sited in a room or floor with good access to the line-spinning room.

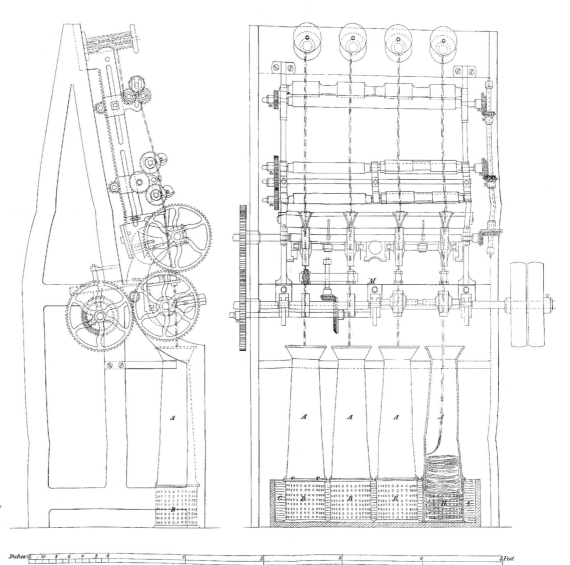

Fig 2.10
Wet spinning, shown here in James Kay's patent of 1825, was combined with gill drawing in a major overhaul of machinery at Ditherington in the 1820s and 1830s. [Sheffield Libraries (DP157114)]

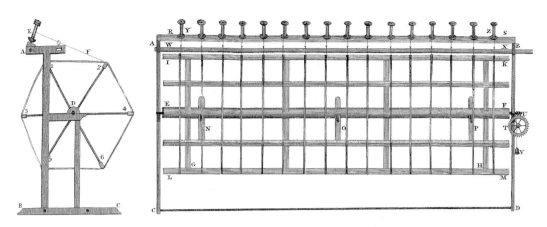

*Fig 2.11
Winding (or reeling)
machines were used to
measure fixed lengths of
yarn for sale or further
processing in the mill.
[From Gray 1819, © The
British Library Board,
G70085-80]*

Weaving

The handloom weaving of linens, canvas and mixed-fibre fabrics such as fustian was an important part of the traditional flax industry in many areas, but had become less common in factories by the early 19th century. Linen weaving was greatly affected by the rise of the cotton industry, which could produce vast quantities of light fabrics at lower prices, and by the falling demand for heavy canvas. At Leeds, large numbers of handloom weavers around the town were supplied with yarn by Marshalls mill, but cloth made up only about a third of the firm's output in the mid-1790s,[21] and out-working seems to have been far less significant in Shrewsbury. The development of a mechanically powered loom had begun in the 1780s and powerlooms were being used by a few innovative cotton manufacturers before 1820. They were, however, not widely successful in the cotton industry until the late 1820s.[22] Charles Bage experimented with producing linen with powerlooms in a weaving factory in Kingsland, Shrewsbury, after his split from John Marshall.[23] In 1818 he corresponded with William Strutt on the potential commercial benefits of powerlooms and on the difficulties he was encountering in making them work efficiently.[24] Take-up of powerlooms in the linen industry was gradual from the 1830s; in Scotland, '1836 must be regarded as the real starting point for the powerloom in Dundee', and in Ireland the development was even further delayed, with only 50 powerlooms being in operation in Northern Ireland in 1850, rising to over 4,000 by 1862.[25] In England, a powerloom weaving mill was built in Barnsley in 1845, but it operated in a town which still had over a thousand handloom weavers in 1874.[26]

The finishing of yarn and cloth; bleaching and dyeing

Bleaching was an essential process which added to the strength and quality of linen yarn and cloths, and by the late 18th century bleachers had acquired a significant influence on the pre-factory industry. Traditional bleaching methods were highly developed but required a great deal of time, effectively delaying the sale of finished goods. In some areas bleachers had acquired a similar central role to the clothiers of the woollen industry. They organised production by putting out spinning and weaving to cottage-based workers, bleaching yarn and cloth at their own works and then trading the finished products at the cloth markets. In the more productive flax areas, such as the northern counties of Ireland, the development of consolidated bleachworks in the mid-18th century represented an early form of the factory system, pre-dating factories built for spinning and weaving.[27] John Marshall recognised the importance of bleaching and its potential to both limit output and increase prices, and therefore set up his own bleaching facilities at Leeds and at Hanwood, near Shrewsbury, thus avoiding any controlling influence by independent bleachers.

Traditional bleaching methods involved boiling the yarn or cloth in an alkaline solution (known as lye, usually made from some kind of vegetable ash), thorough washing and outdoor tentering, soaking in an acid solution and finally further washing and tentering. The whole process was repeated several times, and could take up to six months. Potash was often used to make the lye, but was being replaced by various forms of chlorine from the late 18th century.[28] Buttermilk was traditionally used as a mild acid, but sulphuric acid, then known as vitriol, was being manufactured from the 1740s and was soon adopted by the more progressive bleachers. The use of chemicals, together with refinements in the washing and tentering processes, dramatically reduced the time required for bleaching. In the early 19th century, further developments included the introduction of scouring (or washing) machines, and the use of specially designed 'stoves' with perforated floors and heating systems permitting year-round drying of yarn and cloth.

Dyeing was less widespread than bleaching in the linen industry but was important in the production of coloured thread, for which the Marshalls firm became renowned. In the period when John Marshall was establishing his flax factories, dyeing was mechanically less complex than spinning or weaving, but still had to be precisely controlled to ensure colours were reproduced consistently. It usually comprised two stages: first the fibre, yarn or cloth was boiled in vats containing a solution of dyestuff, and this was followed by a separate treatment in vats containing a mordant to fix the colour. Other vats and winches might be used for washing and wringing, although dyeing remained a largely manual process in the early 19th century. It is likely that only natural dyestuffs would have been used at Ditherington, since synthetic dyes were not widely available until the end of the 19th century.

The linen trade in the 18th century: locations and specialisms

The manufacture of linen had ancient origins and was established in some areas of the British Isles in the medieval period, but the industry grew substantially between the Restoration of the monarchy in 1660 and 1850. Early in this period much of the demand for linens was met by substantial imports, but by 1770 a prosperous English manufacturing industry had developed.[29] Specialist producers in several areas provided goods for national markets, which were sustained after 1757 by freely imported yarns and protected by duties on imported linen fabrics.[30]

One of the most important centres of linen production in England in the late 18th century was Darlington. Earlier, in the 1720s, Daniel Defoe had observed that linen bleaching was a prosperous part of the town's trade. In 1753 John Julius Angerstein noted the use of 'a stamp mill for softening flax', doubtless a scutch mill, and observed that because flax could not be grown successfully in the region, manufacturers used raw materials imported from Holland to make fabrics for women's petticoats, sheets and tablecloths, as well as coarse cloths and waistcoating. Darlington was also the scene of the first modestly successful attempts to mechanise flax spinning, with Kendrew and Porthouse producing yarn from flax in a watermill that Kendrew used for his patent process for grinding glass. In the 1790s it was observed that Darlington's principal manufactures were linen and woollen cloth, 'the former of which exceeds almost any town in England'. Of the twelve mills on the River Skerne in or near the town, three were used for spinning yarn. Eight linen manufacturing businesses were located in Darlington, as well as two heckle-making and two flax-dressing concerns.[31]

The linen industry also flourished in several parts of the West Riding of Yorkshire. Linen cloth manufacture was the principal trade of Knaresborough and adjacent areas in Nidderdale. More than a thousand pieces measuring 20 yards by 35 inches (18.3m by 0.89m) were being made weekly in the town and its neighbouring areas in the 1790s. There were 20 linen manufacturers in Knaresborough, including Ralph Dearlove, partner of John Marshall's father, as well as three flax dressers and a dyer. When contemplating the development of his business in the late 1790s John Marshall noted the existence of mechanised flax-spinning mills at Beverley (East Riding) and Conisbrough. He took a particular interest in the Ripon mill of a Mr Coates, who had copied his spinning frames, and the Bingley mill of Sedgewick & Co, where 3,000 spindles were worked by a waterwheel.[32] In the south of the county, as indicated above, a considerable linen-weaving industry developed in and around Barnsley.

Linen manufacturing employed many people in the towns and surrounding areas of present-day Cumbria. For many decades Kendal was renowned for its trade in linsey woolsey, and in 1753 Angerstein observed women at Egremont spinning linen yarns. Ulverston was celebrated in 1815 for the manufacture of canvas. In the late 1790s John Marshall was aware of the flax-spinning mill of Parker Waithman & Co at Yelland near Lancaster. When he passed through the Lake District in 1800 he carefully noted six manufacturers of Osnabrug (a coarse linen cloth that takes its name from Osnabruck

Fig 2.12
Barracks Mill in
Whitehaven, a pioneering
factory in the Cumbria flax
industry, was built in 1809
with an internal iron
framework notably similar
to those of the slightly later
Flax Warehouse and Cross
Building at Ditherington.
[DP044299]

in Lower Saxony) in Whitehaven, a thread manufacturer at nearby Henningham, a spinning mill with 1,500 spindles at Egremont, six makers of linen fabrics and three of thread in the Maryport area, four similar businesses at Cockermouth, seven in the Wigton area and six at Carlisle. On 8 September he hoped to see spinning frames for tow at Benson & Braithwaite's premises near Ambleside but was told 'they never let anyone in the mill'. In 1809 Joseph Bell and John Bragg built Barracks Mill in Whitehaven for flax spinning, and the main building there – five-storeyed, iron-framed, and steam-powered – had similarities with the fireproof flax mills built by Marshall and his former partners at Leeds and Ditherington (Fig 2.12). Flax spinning ceased at the mill after only a few years.[33]

Linen yarns were used in great quantities in the Manchester region in the 18th century, but chiefly in mixed fabrics using a cotton warp and a linen weft. Pococke observed at Manchester in 1750 that there was 'a great manufacture here of linen and cotton which for spinning and reeling employs most of the country round', and that Stockport was involved in the production of 'Manchester linen'. Whatley noted in the following year that Manchester goods included ticking, tapes and linen cloth, and that the town's fustian had been famous for 150 years.

In the 1750s much of the region's linen was made from hemp and flax from St Petersburg, imported through Preston. In the second half of the 18th century the linen industry in the region was largely eclipsed by the rapid growth of cotton manufactures. One of the largest of the region's textile factories, the Salford Twist Mill of *c* 1800, was designed for flax spinning but was actually used for cotton production, which is perhaps an indication of the diminished importance of linen in the Manchester region. Elsewhere in south Lancashire, the town of Warrington – where in the 1720s Defoe observed a market for huckaback used for table linen that realised a turnover of £500 per week – remained a significant centre for the manufacture of coarse cloths.[34]

There was also a considerable trade in flax and hemp fabrics and yarn in Nottinghamshire and Lincolnshire, which benefited from the proximity of ports that traded with the Netherlands and the Baltic. In 1799 Arthur Young observed that large quantities of hemp sacking were made at Gainsborough, and that much flax spinning and linen weaving took place around Normanby and Barton on Humber.[35]

Specialist linen-producing areas were also found in the south of England in the 18th century. One of the areas where manufacturing was most firmly based was around Bridport in Dorset. Pococke in 1750 and Shaw in 1788 remarked that Bridport was a centre for the production of twine, cables, sailcloth and other coarse fabrics, and that manufacturers prospered because hemp and flax could be grown successfully as commercial crops in the surrounding countryside.[36]

Much linen production in Britain was linked only loosely with the mainstream of commerce. In many areas families grew crops of hemp and flax on marginal plots of land, which they harvested, retted, scutched, heckled, carded and spun, and took the resultant yarn to 'custom weavers', who produced fabrics that could be used for clothing, towels and bedclothes. The first phases of preparation might be carried out by specialist flax dressers, some of them itinerants. John Marshall observed at Dumfries in 1800 that 'the country people grow a patch of flax from one quarter to an acre and dress it, spin it, weave it and bleach it all in their own families'. George Eliot's Silas Marner was an archetypal custom weaver, and in *The Mill on the Floss* Mrs Tulliver reflects, as the contents of her home are sold, that she herself had spun the yarn for her best tablecloths, the fabric for which was woven by Job Haxey who had delivered the piece on his back.[37] This subsistence production of linen was widely practised in Shropshire. Detailed studies of the Coalbrookdale Coalfield area have revealed evidence of domestic spinning in 20 per cent of 1,372 probate inventories taken between 1660 and 1764; many of these inventories also list stocks of flax. The proportion is similar in other parts of the county. In 1776 Arthur Young stated that every farmer in Shropshire grew about two acres (0.8ha) of hemp, and every cottager all he could spare from potatoes and beans. Custom weaving in the county continued on an increasingly reduced scale in the 19th century, as it did in other parts of the Midlands, but it appears to have been wholly divorced from commercial-scale production. The landowner Edward Harries insisted in 1795 that Shropshire spinners did not spin 'for manufactures', that is, for selling in distant markets.[38]

In Scotland, as in England, linen manufactures benefitted from government encouragement. A Board of Trustees for Manufactures was established in 1727 to promote industry in the country, and the linen trade received more assistance than any other industry.[39] Most production was centred on bleachfields and on water-powered mills such as the Lintmill (or scutch mill) of Boyne, 13km east of Banff. Nevertheless, there were moves towards the concentration of production long before the mechanisation of spinning and weaving. 'Factories', which were entirely hand-driven, worked flax and hemp in Cromarty and Banff as well as in lowland Scotland, where there was a particular concentration in the eastern counties. The 'Muckle House' at Spittalfield, near Caputh, Tayside, was a five-bay, two-storey building that served as a focus for a domestic manufacturing system that involved, among others, weavers living in single-storey cottages located around the adjacent green. The building was used as a spinning school, one of several supported by the Board of Trade and Manufactures.[40] The first mechanised flax-spinning mill in eastern Scotland was established at Inverbervie, Kincardineshire, in 1787, followed by other water-powered mills at Douglastown, Angus, in 1789 and Kinghorn, Fife, in 1792. Grandholm Mill in Aberdeen (established in 1793–4), was largest, with a seven-storey main building, and the first steam-assisted mill in Dundee was working by 1793.[41]

Linen was made in many parts of Ireland and from 1696 Irish merchants were able to export linen to England free of duties. Production was fostered by the Board of Trustees of the Linen Manufacturers of Ireland, which was established in 1711. The Board built the White Linen Hall in Dublin in 1728. Much of the trade to England passed through Chester, where Pennant noted in 1771 that as many as 2,000 boxes and packs of cloth, containing up to 25,000 pieces, might arrive for the Midsummer and Michaelmas fairs, in addition to 300 boxes imported through Liverpool. In 1778 a New Linen Hall was built by Irish linen merchants in Dublin to accommodate the growing trade.[42] Arthur Young observed in 1780 that linen manufactures were 'the great staple of the kingdom'. He described the processing on small farms in Co Armagh of flax imported from Riga, Königsberg (Kaliningrad) and St Petersburg. He remarked on the 'manufactory' at Ballymote, Co Sligo, on the estates of William, 2nd Earl and 1st Marquess of Lansdowne (1737–1805), which was developed from 1774 around a beetling mill (used to finish linen cloth) and a bleachworks, and processed fabrics produced from 90 looms. At Blarney near Cork he visited the complex set up in 1745 by Major James St John Jefferyes (1734–96) that produced cotton, woollen and linen fabrics and transformed an accumulation of mud huts into a village of 90 cottages, many built for weavers. The manufacturing system here centred around a scutch mill and a bleach-works serving 130 weavers and finishing the cloth. Fine linens as well as cotton fabrics were printed within the complex. Like other observers, Young deplored the spread of manufacturing into the countryside where wages were low, thus delaying the take-up of mechanisation.[43]

The linen industry in the 19th century

The gradual development of larger manufacturing units in the linen industry, the application of power to the spinning process from 1787 and the improved technology and managerial expertise introduced by John Marshall resulted in an increase in the manufacture of yarn. Imports of yarn fell from 17,000 tons (15,400 tonnes) in 1771 to only 1,000 tons (900 tonnes) in 1830, while imports of raw flax increased from 12,000 tons (11,000 tonnes) in 1787 to 50,000 tons (45,000 tonnes) by 1830. Exports of linen cloth increased. Prior to 1790 the total never exceeded 12,000 yards (10,972m) but through the 1820s the level did not fall below 24,000 yards (21,945m). A total of 100,000 yards (91,440m) was attained for the first time in 1849 and exports never fell below that level during the remainder of the 19th century. In 1864 a total of 200,000 yards (182,880m) was exported, but competition from abroad, particularly Belgium, constrained subsequent growth.[44]

By the middle decades of the 19th century the main centres of British linen production were in Scotland and Ireland rather than in England. There was large-scale growth at Dundee in the 1820s and 1830s, confirming William Brown's prediction in 1821 that the passion for improvement among Scots flax spinners would enable them to overtake their English competitors within a decade. This was the period when Dundee became one of Europe's principal textile cities, producing heavy linen from flax and increasingly, after a slump in the 1840s drove down margins, the cheaper and coarser jute substitute.[45] In 1847 the Scottish linen industry gave employment to 45,837 people throughout the country: in Ayrshire, Aberdeenshire (where there were 1,600 in the city of Aberdeen alone), Banff, Berwick, Edinburgh, Elgin, Dunfermline, Dundee, Arbroath, Kincardine, Perthshire and Wigtown.[46]

In the north of Ireland the growth of mechanised flax spinning was delayed by the cheapness of hand labour and, according to John Marshall, by the Corn Laws, which encouraged many farmers to grow grain instead of flax.[47] While in the early years of his business Marshall bought an appreciable proportion of his raw flax in Ireland, in the late 1820s he was exporting large quantities of yarn to its linen weavers. Irish cotton manufacturers faced severe difficulties after the withdrawal of protective tariffs in 1824, and as knowledge spread of the wet-spinning process many of them turned to factory-based flax spinning.[48] The focus of Irish linen manufacture moved emphatically from Dublin to Ulster from the late 18th century. Linen Halls were built in Newry in 1783 and in Belfast two years later, while Dublin's Linen Board was closed in 1828, reflecting the decline of trade flowing through the city.[49] It was in the north of Ireland that most large-scale, wet-spinning flax factories were introduced. By 1831 the Irish flax and linen industry employed 135,303 people, comfortably more than half of the 197,057 who worked in the industry in the United Kingdom, while Ulster was responsible for much of the total of British exports for the rest of the century.[50]

In England, by contrast, the census of 1831 showed that only 15,917 people were engaged in linen manufacture. There was a cluster of mills in the Bridport area, some sailcloth production around other seaports, a presence in Co Durham centred on Darlington, and there was continuing production of mixed fabrics at Kendal. Well over half the total employed – some 9,867 – were in Yorkshire. Of these, some lived in York, Ripon and Nidderdale, and new mills were built in Pateley Bridge, Bishop Thornton, Whitby and York.[51] By this date, however, the Yorkshire industry was concentrated in Leeds and Barnsley. Although continuing to be dominated by woollen manufacture, by 1820 Leeds had become 'the principal town in England for flax spinning' where 30 years earlier the industry had been of negligible importance.[52]

The foundation of the Leeds flax-spinning industry was an array of small, unspectacular firms that, at least for a time, provided a nursery for new talents. The Scot William Brown observed such mills in 1821: 'they are old, irregular looking houses seemingly much disfigured with alteration and additions. Some of

Fig 2.13
John Marshall's extensive mill complex in Leeds in c 1850, in the period when it became integrated with the production of the firm's thread at Ditherington. In the foreground is Temple Mill and the mill offices, built in an Egyptian style in 1838–43. Beyond them are the earlier multi-storeyed mills noted by William Brown.
[Courtesy of Leeds Library and Information Service]

the smaller ones are even made out of a range of old dwelling houses'. He excepted from this description the premises of John Marshall and the Benyons (Fig 2.13). Several other substantial complexes were built in the town in the 1820s and 1830s, including those of Atkinson and Hives, former partners of John Marshall, and John Wilkinson. Brown calculated in 1821 that 14 firms in Leeds operated 19 flax mills and utilised steam engines producing 565 horsepower. In 1836, 64 of the 152 flax mills in England were located in the West Riding of Yorkshire, 34 of them in Leeds. The town's flax mills employed an average of 200 people, while the average elsewhere in the West Riding was 66, and that in south-west England 31.[53]

There was an increasing tendency in Yorkshire in the 1820s and 1830s for flax spinners to twist their yarn into thread, for which there was growing demand from manufacturers of footwear, saddlery, carpets, lace and clothing. By 1834, 23 spinning concerns in Leeds produced thread as well as yarn, and two of Knaresborough's seven flax-spinning companies were so involved.[54] Although there were several integrated mills in Yorkshire both spinning and weaving to produce linen cloth, Barnsley was the principal centre in the county for weaving linen fabrics. Many of the town's weavers worked in their own homes, but there were several substantial factories, such as Hope Mill, which originated as a mill for finishing linen cloth, and the steam-powered Taylor's Mill of 1845, built by a family who had been involved in linen weaving for four generations. Barnsley was supplied with its yarn from Leeds and other centres of flax spinning.[55]

The linen industry in Yorkshire, of which Ditherington Mill must be regarded as a detached part, steadily declined in the third quarter of the 19th century. Woodfield Mill at Bishop Thornton ceased to be used for flax spinning soon after 1830 and High Mill in the same parish was converted to silk spinning by 1871. Castleton Mill at Wortley was used principally for woollens from the 1860s, and the Lawrence Street Mill in York was adapted for comb making after 1872. The Benyons' mill at Holbeck in Leeds closed when the company went bankrupt in 1861, and John Wilkinson's Hunslet Mill was adapted for woollen manufacturing from the early 1870s.[56] This left Marshalls as the sole large producer of linen yarns and thread in Yorkshire. By this stage the Leeds mill's production was closely integrated with that of its sister mill in Shrewsbury and the company was facing growing difficulties in a market that was now increasingly international in scope. In that market, the English linen industry was falling behind its competitors in both Britain and Europe.[57]

3

Shrewsbury in the 18th and 19th centuries: industry and culture

BARRIE TRINDER

Ditherington Mill occupies a unique position in the history of the British textile industry and in the development of iron structures, but it has also played an influential role in the history of Shrewsbury. Its construction was closely related to the long history of industry in Shropshire, without which a mill of such scale and innovatory nature could not have been envisaged.

Within a county in which Coalbrookdale and Ironbridge are rightly celebrated for their influence on technological history, Shrewsbury was the principal cultural centre and a thriving commercial and thoroughfare town (Fig 3.1). This made it possible to generate capital for investment in such a large enterprise as Ditherington Mill. This chapter examines the mill's

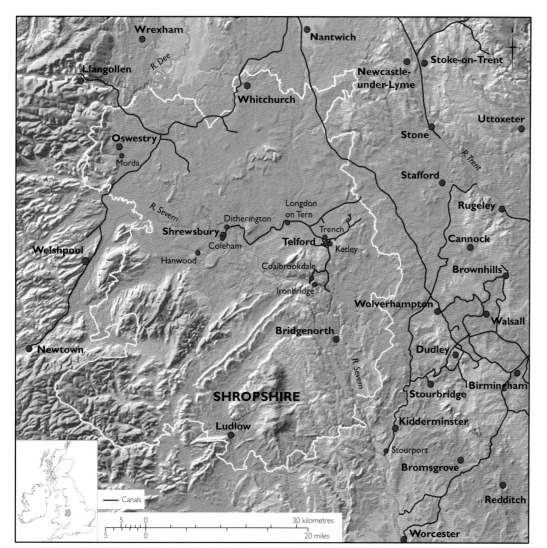

Fig 3.1
The construction of the first iron-framed mill at Shrewsbury reflected the town's strong connections with pioneering industrialists and merchants in the surrounding region. Ironbridge and Coalbrookdale lie a few miles downstream from the town, and the River Severn was a busy commercial waterway.
[90m SRTM Topography data courtesy of the CGIAR, http://srtm.csi.cgiar.org]

local and regional contexts by describing the economic and cultural climate in the town and the wider area. It shows how the mill contributed to the growth of Shrewsbury's northern suburbs and illustrates how through its longevity – first as a flax-spinning factory and later as a maltings – it became a significant element in the town's economy.

Shrewsbury's industry in the 18th century

Shrewsbury in the 1790s was among the 50 largest towns in England. In 1801 its population was just under 15,000 – smaller than that of Chester, Leicester, Exeter or York, rather larger than that of Derby, Oxford, Preston, Wolverhampton and Worcester, but only about a quarter the size of that of Leeds. It was more populous than most county towns and larger than any town in Wales. Its population grew in the late 18th century, rising to its 1801 figure from just over 8,000 in 1750, according to a survey by John Leigh that appears to be reasonably accurate. Shrewsbury therefore grew by about

80 per cent over 50 years, a considerably faster rate than the figure of between 40 and 50 per cent that is usually reckoned to have been the rate of growth in England and Wales during that period.[1]

That this was a prosperous time in Shrewsbury is confirmed by architectural evidence. Two substantial inns, many town houses in the classical style, three new or largely new parish churches, two bridges over the River Severn and a new shire hall were built between 1750 and 1800 (Fig 3.2). Most traces of medieval fortifications were obliterated except for the castle, which was adapted to serve as a salon intended to radiate political influence and as the residence of the county surveyor. The high street was realigned and the suburbs, which in 1750 extended no further than they had in the late Middle Ages, began to grow. In 1790 the *Shrewsbury Chronicle* commended the 'rapid progress of improvement in the town', and hoped that new houses would 'render the long-allowed pleasantest town in the kingdom one of the handsomest'.[2]

This prosperity had several origins. Henry Skrine observed in 1798 that Shrewsbury was

Fig 3.2
Shrewsbury as seen from the south in the early 19th century. A Severn trow carrying goods moves upstream in the foreground. [Artist: Henry Burn, Shrewsbury Museum, image sy1179 (DP164598)]

'the great frontier town of England towards North Wales … many families of North Wales make it their winter residence'. From the 1750s the turnpiking of roads had made it easier for gentry families from Wales and Shropshire to trade and enjoy recreation in Shrewsbury, where there were ample professional and retail facilities to cater for their needs. The town acted as a regional social centre: in 1835, as well as a new racecourse, there was a theatre, a subscription library and a newsroom.[3] The town's inhabitants in 1786 included more than a dozen lawyers, the same number of clergy, and at least seven doctors. Shrewsbury had drapers, grocers and ironmongers, but also traders supplying goods and services unobtainable in any town to the west nearer than Dublin, including six peruke (wig) makers, four shops selling china, two dancing masters, two sculptors, an engraver, a drawing master, a portrait painter, a barometer maker and an astronomer.[4]

Road improvements in the mid-18th century stimulated Shrewsbury's development as a town of thoroughfare. Direct stagecoach services to London began in the 1750s but it was not until the early 1770s that a coach proprietor claimed to be able to reach the capital within 24 hours. The development of coaching was due largely to Robert Lawrence (1749–1806), landlord of the Raven hotel and later of the Lion, who began services to Holyhead in 1779. By 1786 there were 15 weekly departures from Shrewsbury to London, 6 to Holyhead, 3 to Bristol and 3 to Chester. In the late 1790s these were augmented by summer services to Aberystwyth and Barmouth for the bathing season, and in the following decade the Chester coaches were extended to run to Manchester and Liverpool. In 1786 there were twice-weekly stage wagons to London and to Chester, and one each to Birmingham, Manchester, Stafford, Newport (Shropshire), Brecon, Welshpool, Nantwich and Oswestry.[5]

For several centuries much of Shrewsbury's trade had been carried by barges on the River Severn, and some wine and groceries still arrived in the town by river in the 1790s. The density of traffic on the Severn between Coalbrookdale and Shrewsbury increased between 1815 and 1830, but the growth was largely in bulk cargoes, particularly bricks and imported timber, while most goods consigned for shops arrived in the town by road in the 1820s.[6] Two canals were authorised by Act of Parliament in 1793 to serve the town, but only the Shrews-

bury Canal was actually built. Following a route from Trench, on the northern edge of modern Telford, to Shrewsbury it was an extension of the tub boat canal system that had developed in the Coalbrookdale Coalfield since the 1760s and initially had no connection with the national waterways system. It was opened to Berwick Wharf, about 4km east of Shrewsbury, in 1796 and the final stretch, opened in January of the following year, took a great loop on the east side of the town and then turned to the south to terminate near the castle.[7] The wharf in Shrewsbury became the focus of the coal trade, although expectations that the opening of the canal would reduce the price of fuel were not realised. The route of the canal seems to have been altered to run alongside the site of Ditherington Mill, which was being built at the same time. The original map of the proposed route showed it close to the east side of the main turnpike road that runs past the mill site, but the canal was actually built further to the west, running parallel with the full length of the main block of the mill (Fig 3.3). The change of plan may have been initiated by the Benyon brothers, who as well as being partners in the

Fig 3.3
The proposed route of the Shrewsbury Canal, shown here, was shifted to the west to run directly alongside the newly built mill complex at Ditherington. The site of the mill is marked as 'The lands of John Mytton Esq'.
[Shropshire Archives DP289]

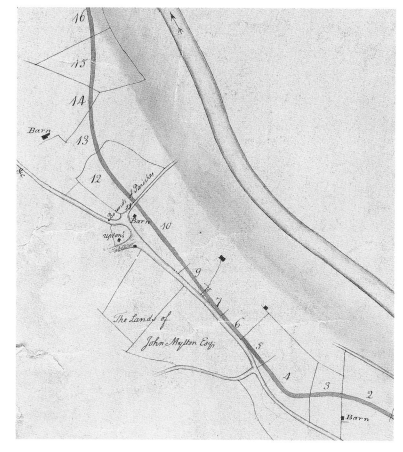

mill company were also among the promoters of the canal. Since the canal was originally the only source of water for the mill's steam plant its construction was probably a key factor in enabling the mill to be built at this location. The Shrewsbury Canal was part of an isolated system until 1835 when the Wappenshall branch of the Birmingham and Liverpool Junction Canal at last linked it with the national canal network.[8]

The latter part of the 18th century is sometimes called the 'Shropshire Enlightenment'. It was a time when several men of outstanding ability were active in Shrewsbury and its surrounding areas. Appointed headmaster of Shrewsbury school at a time when its reputation had diminished, Dr Samuel Butler (1774–1839) increased the number of pupils from about 20 in 1798 to 295 by 1832. Charles Bage sent his sons to the school in the 1820s. Thomas Telford (1757–1834) made his home at the town's castle, the property of his patron William Pulteney, from 1786–7 and developed a local reputation as an architect before becoming engaged with the completion of the Shrewsbury and Ellesmere canals and gaining international renown as a civil engineer. In 1796 William Hazledine (1763–1840) established a foundry in Coleham, just across the river from the town, from which he supplied castings for many of Thomas Telford's bridges (Fig 3.4). He became one of the principal iron- and coalmasters in the region and the owner of many properties in Shrewsbury. The physician Robert Darwin (1766–1848), son of the polymath Erasmus Darwin (1731–1802), settled in Shrewsbury in 1786 and in 1797 constructed the house on The Mount where his son Charles, the world-famous scientist, was born in 1809. Robert Darwin had many wealthy patients but also prospered by lending money on a large scale, some of it to Charles Bage.[9]

Shrewsbury had links with enlightened members of the gentry such as Joseph Plymley (1759–1838) of Longnor Hall, who was an agricultural improver, developer of turnpike roads and an early campaigner for the abolition of the slave trade. Similarly, Thomas Eyton of Eyton, who suggested that the Longdon-on-Tern Aqueduct should be built of iron; Rowland Hunt (1752–1811) of Boreatton, who made a cultured speech when the Pontcysyllte Aqueduct was opened; and Thomas Kenyon (1780–1851) of Prado, enthusiast for stagecoaching and member of the Holyhead Road Commission, all lent their status to the town. The ironmasters of the Coalbrookdale coalfield, the builder of the Iron Bridge Abraham Darby III (1759–89), Richard (1735–1816) and William (1758–1803) Reynolds, and John Wilkinson (1728–1808), also looked to Shrewsbury as a cultural centre, as did the philosopher Archibald Alison (1757–1839), vicar of Kenley. Local society was connected through various individuals to the broader intellectual life of the Midlands, to the Lunar Society in Birmingham, to the Wedgwoods (the famous pottery manufacturers) in North Staffordshire and to the Strutts (cotton spinners) in Derbyshire. Leading national figures spoke in Shrewsbury: Thomas Clarkson (1760–1846) advocating freedom for slaves, Joseph Lancaster (1778–1838) arguing for schools based on the monitorial system, John Waltire expounding on chemistry, and John Banks (1740–1805), inventor of the elliptical beam for steam engines, discussing engineering. This period of prosperity and intellectual awakening provides the social and cultural context in which the activities of Charles Bage and the brothers Benyon must be placed.

Shrewsbury's historic association with the textile industry was through the trade in Welsh woollen cloth (known as 'webs'), of which the town's Drapers' Company gained control in

Fig 3.4
The memorial bust of William Hazledine, the most successful of Shrewsbury's early ironmasters, whose firm cast the columns and beams for Ditherington Mill. [Courtesy of St Chad's Church, Shrewsbury (DP163745)]

the early 17th century. After they had been purchased by the Drapers, webs were traditionally finished by shearmen in Shrewsbury and then sent to London for export through Blackwell Hall to the poorest parts of Europe and to America, where they were made into garments for slaves. The trade continued throughout the 18th century, but on a diminishing scale. Probate records survive for 29 Shrewsbury clothworkers and shearmen who died between 1660 and 1679, but for only 7 between 1730 and 1749. The frankpledge list of 1709 includes 47 clothworkers, but there are only 21 listed for 1731. The apprenticeship register of the Drapers' Company records that 76 apprentices were indentured in the first half of the century but only 51 in the second, and only 29 in the 50 years after 1780. The historians Hugh Owen and J B Blakeway recalled in 1826 how each Thursday Welshmen wearing blue cloth coats over striped waistcoats had sold cloth to members of the Drapers' Company in the market square, and the end of the market had been signalled by the ascent of the Company in order of seniority into the upper room of the market hall. The last formal market was probably held in 1795, the year after the calamitous bankruptcy of Joshua Blakeway, a member of the Company whose warehouse on St Chad's Hill contained 12,000 yards of Welsh flannels and webs, with 40 quires of paper and 400 ells of hurden cloth used for packing. The Drapers' Company relinquished the lease of the market hall in 1803.[10] Shrewsbury's traditional marketing role declined in part because Welsh weavers began to make flannel instead of the traditional webs, and as markets were established at Welshpool in 1797, Newtown in 1832 and Llanidloes in 1836.

Despite the Drapers' Company's loss of influence, Shrewsbury's wool trade remained substantial and persisted well into the 19th century. A directory of 1786 lists 12 drapers (excluding woollen drapers or those retailing linen) and the poll book for the borough parliamentary election of 1796 includes 14 cloth workers, 22 weavers, 9 shearmen and a clothier. Five merchants in the town dealing with flannel were listed in a directory published in 1834. As late as 1851 Charles B Nicholls was working as a Welsh flannel factor from his residence in Quarry Place, the traditional home of Shrewsbury drapers, and in 1865 a warehouse used for many years for wool and flannel was sold in Frankwell.[11]

The changes in technology in the Welsh woollen industry may have affected Shrewsbury's role in finishing and marketing but it also stimulated manufacturing in the town and its vicinity. A water-powered flannel mill was built in about 1797 by Cook and Mason, powered by a tunnelled canal dug across the isthmus of the horseshoe bend on the River Severn at The Isle, upstream from Shrewsbury. It was in use until the 1820s, at which date an inventory recorded carding and spinning machines, 20 looms and fulling stocks.[12] By 1800 a flannel factory was working in the centre of Shrewsbury, probably at Rowley's Mansion, where there were some handlooms and carding machinery, the latter powered by a chestnut mare. It was still worked by a single horse in 1830. Woollen cloth was also produced and techniques of spinning and weaving were taught to children at the workhouse in Kingsland that had been opened by the Shrewsbury parishes in 1783.[13]

The first purpose-built textile factory in Shrewsbury was completed in 1790. Powis & Hodges invested more than £10,000 in a mill in Longden Coleham close to the confluence of the Severn and the Rea Brook. It consisted of two five-storey ranges, one measuring 33.9m × 12m and the other 31.3m × 12m, and a four-storey block, measuring 13.8m × 12m. The machinery, powered by a small steam engine and a 4.57m-diameter, 2.1m-wide waterwheel, included carding engines, spinning jennies and fulling stocks, as well as handlooms. This was one of the largest woollen mills built in England at that time, but the partners soon went bankrupt. The buildings were offered for sale in 1795 and for a decade were empty or served temporary purposes. The mill was part of a strip of industrial premises developed between 1790 and 1815 between Longden Coleham and Kingsland Lane and the banks of the Severn.[14] The mill passed for a time into the ownership of William Hazledine, but in 1802 it was sold to Charles Hulbert (1778–1857) and adapted for cotton weaving in association with a spinning factory at Llangollen and a print works at Morda near Oswestry. Hulbert built a Gothic villa that he called his 'castle' on the edge of the site near the river. He employed more than a hundred people but he lacked capital and when his proposal to introduce powerlooms provoked Luddite threats he moved, in 1814, to the town centre where he sold cotton fabrics. He disposed of the mill in 1825 and subsequently made his living as an auctioneer, author and publisher.[15]

The growth of Shrewsbury

Medieval suburbs lined all the radial routes out of Shrewsbury beyond the town's bridges. The Castle Foregate, the area beyond the North Gate, lay mostly in the parish of St Mary. The land east of the road as far as New Park Road appears to have belonged before the Reformation to the chantry of the Virgin in St Mary's church. It was divided into regular plots extending about 320m, which from the 1790s were bounded on the eastern side by the terminus wharf of the Shrewsbury Canal. Castle Foregate was by repute a plebeian suburb, although in the mid-18th century it included at least one substantial house (the building that incorporates the present-day Britannia public house) with ornamental gardens. The land on the western side of the road, whose western boundary was the Bagley Brook, formed a detached part of the parish of St Alkmund. Since the Middle Ages most of it had belonged to the Corbets of Moreton Corbet.[16]

The end of the medieval suburb was marked by the Plough public house on the eastern side of the road and the Red Lion on the western side, which lay about 610m south of Marshalls' mill. To the north the only settlement in existence when the factory was built was on the Old Heath, 655m north of the mill entrance, land that belonged to Shrewsbury Corporation outside the borough boundary. In the mid-17th century the settlement included a brickmaker's cottage and an inn with a bowling green. Old Heath in the 1790s consisted of squatter-like cottages within small enclosures. The corporation began to sell its properties in the area in the 1770s, and speculators in the early 19th century, most notably William Hazledine, built terraces of cottages. There were about 130 dwellings on the Old Heath by 1881. Well established in the area during the building of the settlement, brickmaking continued until at least the 1860s, leaving a legacy of pits and waste tips. The community had its own Primitive Methodist chapel of 1844 and its own school.[17]

The open land between Castle Foregate and Old Heath was filled in over the course of a century as this side of Shrewsbury developed as an industrial and residential suburb. The County Gaol, built between 1786 and 1793, was the first significant building beyond the town's medieval limits. Howard Street, leading from Castle Foregate to the River Severn, was laid out at about the same time, and the canal wharf in 1797. The major stimulus to suburban growth, however, was the development of industry and the resulting need for housing. The gasworks was built on the eastern side of St Michael's Street, the continuation of Castle Foregate, in the 1820s, and beyond it canal carrying companies erected warehouses after Shrewsbury was linked to the national network in 1835. The warehouses were succeeded by steam-powered corn mills, adapted for malting by William Jones in the early 20th century. The area now occupied by Primrose Terrace and a

Fig 3.5
The flax mill at Castlefields, south of Ditherington, built in c 1804 by Thomas and Benjamin Benyon and Charles Bage after their split from John Marshall. Most of the site was demolished in the late 1830s.
[Shropshire Archives PH/5/13/C/2/76]

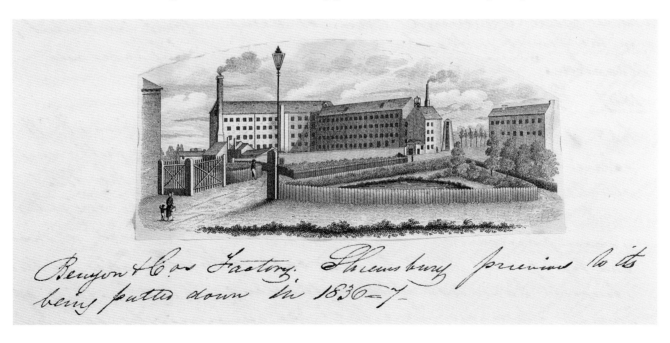

recreation ground was one of Shrewsbury's principal brickmaking areas for much of the 19th century.[18]

Most significant as a stimulus to suburban growth were the construction of Ditherington Mill in the last years of the 18th century and of the nearby Castlefields Mill a few years later (Fig 3.5). The latter was built, 580m south of Ditherington, by the Benyon brothers and Charles Bage, who had agreed that they would end their partnership with John Marshall with effect from July 1804 to set up a parallel business, with factories in Leeds and in Shrewsbury.[19] Between them, Marshalls and the Benyons required a large workforce. The company provided a limited amount of housing near to Ditherington Mill in c 1796 (see Chapter 9), but for the most part development was left in the hands of speculators. Within a decade or so of the completion of Marshalls' mill, four courts lined by more than 60 cramped and insanitary dwellings had been built in the Castle Foregate area, together with 38 houses in two back-to-back terraces behind the Plough public house. One of the courts, built in 1812 and containing 23 houses, was offered for sale in 1819 as accommodation 'well-calculated for small families and near to both the great manufactories'. A commentator in 1825, when the linen industry in the town was near its peak, described the rapid increase of building in the vicinity of Ditherington Mill, yet it was many years before the mill was joined to the end of the medieval suburb of Castle Foregate by an unbroken line of buildings, and the progress of construction in the area that came to be known as Spring Gardens was spasmodic (Fig 3.6). None of the later housing here was built directly by the Marshalls concern. By 1850 Spring Gardens had been filled with more than 130 houses, in addition to the small amount of housing provided earlier by Marshalls. Two terraces south of the mill have been particularly associated with the factory in popular memory, perhaps because William Jones & Sons (the malting company which took over the mill in 1897) owned them from the 1920s, but they had no direct connection with the flax mill. The first originated in the early 19th century as two separate blocks, acquired in 1828 by Robert Davies, a linen weaver who by 1859 had created from them a terrace of six dwellings called Davies' Buildings. A curving terrace of 12 houses known as St Michael's Gardens was built between 1830 and 1850. Hackfield Place, the range of 30

houses south of the mill, was not built until after 1851.[20]

The linen industry in Shrewsbury reached its peak about 1820 when both Ditherington and Castlefields were in full production. The industry had diversified further by this date, for Charles Bage had withdrawn from his partnership with the Benyons in 1815–16. After experimenting with powerlooms for weaving linen he erected a weaving shed on Kingsland Lane, on the other side of Shrewsbury, which was 90ft (27.4m) long and 30ft (9m) wide, with a brick arch roof, 9in (220mm) thick, and which accommodated 30 handlooms and 24 of his newly designed powerlooms, worked by a 4-horsepower steam engine. This was a pioneering, if not entirely successful, use of powerlooms in the linen industry. By 1820 the

Fig 3.6
Hitchcock's 1832 map of Shrewsbury illustrates how the Ditherington and Castlefields mills, along with the Shrewsbury Canal, delineated a new industrial suburb along one of the main roads leading north from the town's historic centre. The Benyons' Castlefields Mill is shown as 'New Factory', Ditherington Mill as 'Old Factory'.
[Shropshire Archives 3073/1]

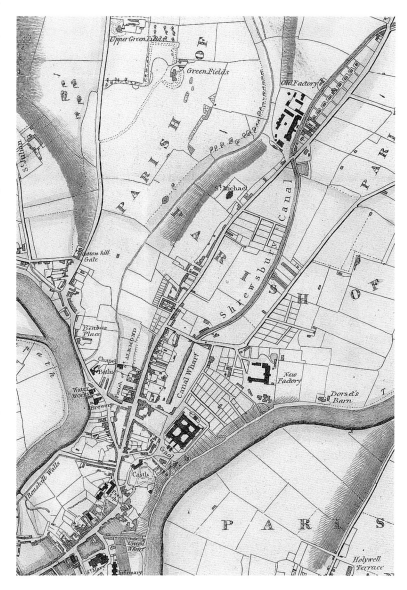

mills at Ditherington and Castlefields were employing at least a thousand people between them, while more than a hundred were working for Charles Bage at his powerloom weaving mill and for some smaller concerns.[21]

Despite these important initiatives, this was to be the zenith of the Shrewsbury flax industry and it faltered thereafter. Bage died on the penultimate day of 1822 and his widow went bankrupt in 1826. His weaving mill became the nucleus of the lead works established by Thomas Burr in 1829.[22] As for the Benyons, Thomas died in 1833 and his brother in the following year. It appears that there was a 'spirit of discord' within the family, with the brothers' wills both stipulating that the mill should be sold rather than inherited by their children.[23] A case on this matter was already proceeding in Chancery before the brothers died and Castlefields Mill was offered for sale in 1831. It was again advertised for sale in October 1833, when its principal product was said to be fine yarns for the Irish market, and again in 1835 and 1836. No one wished to buy the business and the site was eventually sold to a builder. The mill had been demolished by 31 May 1837, except for the fireproof flax warehouse and the apprentice house: the latter was converted into 10 back-to-back houses called Cadran Place, replaced by a block of council flats in 1956.[24]

Closures, first in 1821 of the linen weaving company of Edwin Paddock and Joseph Davies in Coleham, then of Bage's weaving shed and finally of the Benyons' mill, dramatically reduced the scale of the industry in the town, which was said to be one of the causes of the decline in Shrewsbury's population during the 1830s. The surviving flax warehouse of Castlefields Mill was used for a small weaving business by Sacheverell Harwood, then by the Benyons'

former cashier Robert Minns, and later by his widow until the 1870s.[25] With that exception, Marshalls was the only textile manufacturing concern in Shrewsbury after the mid-1830s. Its importance to the town was acknowledged in 1851, when it was described as 'the chief manufactory at the present time in Shrewsbury'.[26]

The flax-spinning enterprise established by the Benyons and John Marshall in Shrewsbury in 1796–7 was one of the most powerful influences on the history of the town in the following century. It provided employment for thousands of workers over the course of its 90 years of operation and therefore contributed markedly to the local economy, but it also had a wider role. Marshalls became a global business, drawing raw materials from at least nine modern European countries and exporting on a large scale to the United States and elsewhere. In the second half of the century the company developed a strong brand image for its 'Shrewsbury thread', using sophisticated means of marketing. No other manufacturing enterprise in Shrewsbury's history – not William Hazledine's foundry, nor Thomas Corbett's agricultural implement works, nor William Jones's maltings, nor the Sentinel Wagonworks – lasted as a family business for so long. The mill was nourished by the intellectual ferment that characterised the Industrial Revolution both in Yorkshire and in the Midlands. While little is known of Charles Bage, there is clear evidence of his links with the Darwins, the Strutts and Thomas Telford. William Hazledine and John Simpson, having made their contributions to Ditherington Mill, went on to build the Pontcysyllte Aqueduct and many other important civil engineering structures. The mill at Ditherington was a building at the heart of Shropshire's role in the Industrial Revolution and put Shrewsbury on the world map.

4

Building the mill

BARRIE TRINDER AND MIKE WILLIAMS

The flax mill at Ditherington was constructed in two main building campaigns, the first following the agreement in 1796 to purchase the site and the second after 1809. The complex was essentially complete by 1812, following the addition of new buildings and rebuilding after a destructive fire. For the rest of the period in which the site operated as a flax mill, structural work was confined to renewal of the power system, involving additions and alterations to the Engine and Boiler Houses, and to the enlargement and rebuilding of the Dyehouse and Stove House. This chapter tells the story of the main characters involved in the mill's construction and of the developing relationship between them in the first years of production. It describes how the mill was built over a 15-year period and looks in more detail at the interpretation of the early fireproof buildings on the site – the Spinning Mill, the Cross Building and the Flax Warehouse. Finally, later developments relating to the site's use as a flax mill are summarised. Significant structural changes to the complex during its life as a maltings after 1897 are discussed in Chapter 10. Understanding the evolution of the flax mill will help to provide essential context for the technical and managerial aspects of the site's history, which will be considered later in the book.

Partners and builders

The central character in the story of the building of Ditherington Mill is John Marshall (Fig 4.1). It is on his brief autobiography of 1828 that we rely for most of the personal information that we have about him, much of it reproduced here.[1] He was born in Leeds in 1765, the son of a draper and merchant who traded in linen. A sickly child, he was brought up until the age of 11 in the nearby village of Rawdon by a maternal aunt, in whose house he was in adult company for most of the time. After attending various schools he began to work for his father at the age of 17 in March 1782. The following year he was made responsible for supervising the construction of a new house and warehouse, a task that gave him a taste for building that he retained throughout his life. His father died in 1787 leaving an estate of about £9,000, the income from which would have allowed him to live comfortably, but he preferred to enter into 'more hazardous schemes', since he had 'an active mind which would have been miserable in idleness'.

Fig 4.1
Portrait of John Marshall
by John Russell, 1802.
[© The University of Leeds
Art Collection]

The consequence of this disposition was the formation in 1785 of a partnership with Samuel Fenton (his late father's partner) and Ralph Dearlove of Knaresborough, 'a linen manufacturer of great probity'. Marshall confessed that his attention 'was accidentally drawn to spinning of flax by machinery', which he judged was 'a thing much wanted by linen manufacturers'. He reflected in 1820 that 'when I began to spin flax by machinery, it was a new and unknown trade'. Unusually for one of the leading entrepreneurs of the Industrial Revolution, John Marshall was conscious of his own motivations and transparent about his ambitions. At the age of just 31 he reflected that he had set up his company 'not with the desire of getting money but with the ambition of distinguishing myself', although he acknowledged that he had been drawn to mechanised flax spinning by the immense profits that had been made by cotton spinning. He recalled that he had longed for 'an employment where there was a field for exer-

tion and improvement, where difficulties were to be encountered and distinction and riches to be obtained by overcoming them', and that the labour and pain he had encountered in business had not altogether been unattended with pleasure. In 1801, 14 years after entering business on his own account, he confessed to a friend who was considering the establishment of a flax mill in Dundalk that 'the obstacles to the first establishment of any new manufacture are greater than any man can imagine who has not experienced them', detailing the construction of machinery and the disciplining of a workforce as the principal difficulties.

The new partnership of Marshall, Fenton and Dearlove quickly leased and adapted a watermill on Meanwood Beck at Scotland, Adel, 6km north of Leeds. In 1791 the partners moved the business to a new mill on Water Lane in Holbeck, just to the south of Leeds. In 1793 the financial crisis triggered by the outbreak of war with revolutionary France (which was to last until 1815) brought the partnership into a crisis that Marshall, with hindsight, regarded as 'the most fortunate event that could have happened for me'. Marshall bought out his partners, borrowed money to cover short-term obligations, and sold off some of the partnership's flax that was in warehouses at Hull. He was soon able to seek new partners to expand his company.[2]

Before the outbreak of war in 1793, Marshall had had financial dealings with the brothers Thomas and Benjamin Benyon, wool merchants of Shrewsbury and fellow Unitarians. They belonged to a minor gentry family with an estate at Ash, near Whitchurch, that passed to their elder brother Samuel Yate Benyon (1758–1822), who followed a legal career in north-west England, becoming a King's Counsel, vice-chancellor to the Duchy of Lancaster and Recorder of Chester. Samuel Benyon studied at the celebrated dissenting academy in Warrington, and it is likely that his brothers were also educated there. The Unitarian minister from Whitchurch conducted Samuel Benyon's funeral in 1822, which suggests that the family maintained their dissenting tradition. The brothers had houses in Quarry Place, the most exclusive residential enclave in Shrewsbury (Fig 4.2), and were certainly wealthy men in the early 1790s when they were trading in the manner of Shrewsbury Drapers, although they were not admitted to the Drapers' Company through apprenticeship and were not among the Drapers listed in a Shrewsbury directory of

Fig 4.2
The former residences of Thomas and Benjamin Benyon at Quarry Place in Shrewsbury.
[DP163733]

1786. The nature of their business is revealed by insurance policies that they took out jointly: in 1790 for flannel worth £300 in a warehouse in Mardol, Shrewsbury, and stock at Dolgellau, and in 1792 for a new warehouse in Shrewsbury. They were recorded in the poll book for the election of 1796 as 'merchants', although by this date they were already partners in John Marshall's flax-spinning company in Leeds.[3]

A partnership between Marshall, with his knowledge of the flax trade and his entrepreneurial approach to business, and the Benyons, who brought much needed capital and creditworthiness to the enterprise, was formed in 1793. A formal agreement was reached giving the Benyons a majority share, with assets at the end of 1795 of £12,889; Marshall's holding was £9,435. The Benyons moved to work in Leeds and gave up their woollen cloth business in Shrewsbury, although they retained their houses in the town. The partners completed a second mill in Leeds in 1795, but it suffered a severe fire on 13 February of the following year. Repairs were soon carried out and it recommenced working on 11 July 1796, but by May of that year the Benyons, with Marshall's reluctant agreement, had decided to erect a factory at Ditherington in Shrewsbury. The partnership was restructured so that Marshall held a dominant share of the concerns in Leeds. Thomas Benyon remained in Yorkshire to oversee his family's interests there, while his brother Benjamin returned to Shrewsbury to manage the new mill at Ditherington.[4]

It was at this point, in June 1796, that Marshall and the Benyons admitted Charles Bage to their partnership. More is known about Bage than about the Benyons, but important aspects of his life remain obscure. He was born at Darley Abbey, near Derby, where for several generations the Bage family had run a paper mill on the River Derwent.[5] He spent his youth at Elford, between Lichfield and Tamworth, at the family's paper mill on the River Tame. When he was aged about 14, his father Robert sold the Elford Mill to raise a share of the capital for a new iron rolling and slitting mill at nearby Wychnor.[6] Such a mill would turn billets of wrought iron into plate and sheet, bar and rod. In partnership with Robert Bage in this enterprise were Samuel Garbett, a Birmingham industrialist and co-founder of the famous Carron Ironworks in Scotland, John Barker and Dr Erasmus Darwin, both of Lichfield. At first the works were not profitable and they were sold in

1783, but there seems little doubt that Charles would have gained familiarity with the practical aspects of the making and working of iron. The elder Bage maintained connections with the industrial community at Darley Abbey, his birthplace, and joined the Derby Philosophical Society in 1788.

Charles Bage was living in Shrewsbury by 1776. He practised as a land surveyor and two of his plans, displaying meticulous draughtsmanship, remain in the Shropshire Archives and the library of Shrewsbury School. By the 1780s he was also trading as a wine merchant and insured premises on Pride Hill, with a liquor store on Roushill, in 1782–3. He became a burgess in 1789, served as mayor in 1807 and designed and built the town's Lancasterian school in 1812.[7] Bage carried out some survey work for the Shrewsbury Canal company and, along with the great civil engineer Thomas Telford (1757–1834), valued the church of St Michael, Madeley, prior to its demolition in 1793. His worth to the Ditherington concern stemmed from his interest in the structural uses of cast iron, an interest probably gained from two sources. First, he knew the ironmasters William and Joseph Reynolds, and the latter passed to him the results of tests on the structural properties of iron carried out during the design of the aqueduct that carried the Shrewsbury Canal over the River Tern at Longdon, 13km from Ditherington. Second, he was probably more closely acquainted with Thomas Telford, who built the Longdon Aqueduct in 1795–6 and was at the same time also designing the iron bridge over the Severn at Buildwas.[8] While John Marshall does not reveal in his autobiography what may have been one of the most cogent reasons for building a mill in Shrewsbury – the presence in the town of a potential partner who had the ability to design a multi-storey building with an internal iron frame – his assessment that Bage was 'possessed of talent and ... cultivated understanding but ... not a man of business' certainly indicates that it was not commercial acumen that brought Bage into the partnership.[9]

Two further figures were involved in the construction of Ditherington Mill. Both were based in Shrewsbury, a fact which serves to emphasise that the town had a considerable body of expertise relevant to the construction of a large building of experimental form. Born in 1763, William Hazledine grew up in the Shropshire iron trade, one of four sons of a millwright (see Fig 3.4). His three brothers established the foundry at Bridgnorth that provided engines for Richard Trevithick (1771–1833) and the castings for the iron bridge at Chepstow. Hazledine was working as a millwright and forge carpenter from premises on Wyle Cop, Shrewsbury, by 1789. He established a foundry in the town centre soon afterwards and in about 1796 moved to an extensive site alongside the Severn at Coleham. Here he cast the iron frame for the mill at Ditherington. Hazledine was acquainted with leading figures in the development of iron for structural purposes: he got to know Thomas Telford through membership of the Salopian Masonic lodge and (after the construction of Ditherington Mill) worked with David Mushet (1772–1847), an ironfounder with a strong interest in the properties of the material. His partnership with Telford developed into one of great significance in the field of bridge building. Hazledine provided the ironwork for Telford's Pontcysyllte Aqueduct in 1802–3 and later worked with Telford on a number of innovative cast-iron bridges. In 1821 he provided the ironwork for Telford's Menai Bridge (1819–26), at that time the longest-span bridge ever built.

Hazledine's work at Ditherington came relatively early in his career but already by 1796 his genius had been recognised. In that year, Telford called him 'the Arch conjuror himself, Merlin Hazledine' and his contribution at Ditherington served to enhance his reputation.

The writer of a guidebook in 1803 lauded the iron frame of the mill:

full many an iron friend whose massive strength
Seems to defy old time's long-threatening stroke.

He added that the pillars and beams 'were cast at Mr Hazledine's foundry in this town'. Within a decade Hazledine had leased the Plas Kynaston estate near Wrexham and set up the ironworks that produced the castings for the Pontcysyllte Aqueduct. He took responsibility for their erection, under the superintendence of his manager, William Stuttle (d 1827). In 1810–11 Hazledine provided an iron frame for a thread mill at Market Drayton, which appears never to have gone into production before it was sold and demolished. After the 1815 peace with France, Hazledine began to work on collieries and the Calcutts ironworks in the Coalbrookdale Coalfield, and became a substantial property owner in Shrewsbury, but he had divested himself of many of his business interests by the time of his death in 1840. He served as mayor of Shrewsbury in 1836 and was prominent in the town's Liberal politics. He was known to contemporaries as 'the great ironfounder', and is commemorated with a bust by Sir Francis Chantrey in St Chad's Church. His career is sparsely documented, and more knowledge of it would add much to our understanding of Ditherington Mill and of other early iron-framed buildings.[10]

The last major figure in the development of the Ditherington complex was John Simpson (1755–1815), who was probably responsible for erecting the mill and certainly provided capital for ancillary buildings off the site (Fig 4.3). Simpson was born in Stenhouse, Midlothian, trained as a mason, and moved to Shrewsbury in 1790 to serve as clerk of works for the new church of St Chad. In 1793 he took over the building business of Jonathan Scoltock, and was certainly well known to Charles Bage by 1796. In 1793, along with Thomas Telford, he provided advice, which was ignored, on the rebuilding of the Welsh Bridge. He built the aqueduct at Chirk and the piers of the Pontcysyllte Aqueduct, repaired the Iron Bridge in 1803, constructed locks on the Caledonian Canal and erected many of Telford's bridges. Like Hazledine, he became the owner of many terraced houses in Shrewsbury. Telford regarded him as 'a treasure of talents and integrity', and his memorial, close to that of Hazledine in St Chad's, records that 'lasting monuments of his skill and ability will be found in the building of this church, which he superintended, the Bridges of Bewdley, Dunkeld, Craigellachie and Bonar, the aqueducts of Pontcysyllte and Chirk, and the locks and basins of the Caledonian Canal'.[11]

The decision to build at Ditherington

The decision by John Marshall and the Benyon brothers to expand their business with the construction of a new mill so far from the company's base of operations in Leeds may seem eccentric. The explanation for this can, to a large extent, be found in the links between the town and the Benyon brothers. John Marshall's autobiographical writings suggest that the decision to build a flax-spinning mill at Ditherington was taken for 'reasons in connexion with him [that is, Benjamin Benyon] which induced me to enter into this plan'. Marshall himself would have preferred to invest capital at Leeds, and he regarded proximity to the east coast, with its convenience for imports from the Baltic, to be a prime advantage for a flax-spinning concern. A mill in Shrewsbury could readily sell tow yarn to carpet makers in Bridgnorth and Kidderminster, but was distant from any significant customers for finer yarns, such as the weavers in Barnsley who bought much of the output of Marshalls' Leeds mill.[12] While many people in Shropshire grew flax to be prepared and spun in their own homes and made into fabrics by custom weavers, the plant was not developed for the local market, local supplies were never a significant factor in the economy of the mill, and there were no local precedents for factory-based flax manufacturing. There were, therefore, no strong commercial reasons for beginning to spin flax in Shrewsbury. The decision to set up there in spite of these disadvantages was probably determined by the majority stake that the Benyons held in 1796–7 in the Leeds mill, and by Benjamin Benyon's wish to return to his native Shropshire. The need for renewal after the destruction by fire of one of the main buildings in the Leeds mill in 1796 may also have opened up the question of where and how new investment might best be directed.

There were, however, some circumstances which did favour investment in Shrewsbury.

First, as described above, the town was not only familiar to the Benyons but it also had a body of expertise, in the form of builders and engineers, capable of undertaking a major project. In terms of infrastructure, the Shrewsbury Canal, which opened a few days before the contract for the land for the mill was completed, promised a reliable supply of coal from the east Shropshire coalfield and provided a source of water for boilers and engines. Furthermore, the projected Shrewsbury line of the Ellesmere Canal, being built to the north, offered the possibility of links to Chester and Merseyside that might deliver coal from North Wales and flax from Ireland, thereby freeing the business from dependence on imports of flax from Europe, which could easily be disrupted in difficult political times. These potential benefits were, however, never realised as the branch to Shrewsbury was not completed. Benjamin Benyon was, unsurprisingly, among the shareholders who called for the line to Shrewsbury to be finished at a special general assembly of the company in 1804, but his influence had no effect.

The development of textile mill architecture in the 18th century

Before turning to a more detailed consideration of the building of Ditherington Mill, it is important to first understand the development of mill architecture in the 18th century. Early in the century, English textile mills, which were most commonly involved in the wool textile industry but also in scutching flax, were small water-powered structures, sometimes timber-framed or brick but more usually of stone and perhaps two or three storeys high. In woollen mills water power was used to work fulling stocks on the ground floor; other processes in the manufacture of woollen cloth took place away from the mill in workshops or the homes of spinners and weavers. The first significant development in mill architecture came with the silk mill at Derby built by brothers John (1693–1722) and Sir Thomas (1685–1739) Lombe in 1721. This was a multi-storey building in which water power turned machines on each of the five floors. The Lombes installed machinery of the type that had been developed in Italy, where water power had been employed since *c* 1500. Sir Thomas received a 14-year patent for the process in 1718. The two lower floors of the mill were occupied by circular silk-throwing machines, six ranged on either side of a water wheel, while the three floors above were each occupied by 36 winding machines. The brick building was rectangular in plan, measuring 33.5m × 12m, with an original height of 17m. It became a celebrated attraction to tourists en route to the sublime landscapes of the Derbyshire Peak district, on a par with the caves at Castleton, and a Portuguese writer in 1730 was able to quote with accuracy the numbers of movements made by the mill's machinery.

Other entrepreneurs set up a similar mill in Stockport after Lombe's patent expired in 1732, and five mills were built in Macclesfield between 1744 and 1753. Silk mills proliferated at a modest rate across England in the second half of the 18th century, most of them no larger than Lombe's original.[13] The Old Mill at Congleton was a conspicuous exception. Constructed by Nathaniel Pattison in 1753, it housed 11 circular throwing machines on the lower floors and winding machinery above. A five-storey brick structure, its 29 bays gave it a length of 74m and two pediments adorned the main elevation. It may be regarded as the next significant building in the development of the textile mill.[14] Only fragments remain.

The next major development in mill architecture was prompted by the application of mechanical power to cotton spinning. This led to the construction of large numbers of mills, many of traditional design, but some showing innovatory features. Water power was effectively employed to operate cotton-spinning machinery at Cromford where Richard Arkwright (1732–92) leased a site on the Bonsall Brook in August 1771. Here he constructed an 11-bay building, 28.5m long and 7.9m wide, that soon became as much of a curiosity among writers of books for tourists as the silk mill at Derby, not for its design or structural features but rather for the novelty of power applied to cotton spinning and for its dramatic intervention in a rugged landscape. This is captured in Joseph Wright's atmospheric painting of the Cromford mills, painted in 1783, showing a five-storey mill, plain and unadorned and lit for night working (Fig 4.4).[15] Arkwright subsequently prospered and invested capital in mills in other parts of Britain. His second factory complex on the River Derwent at Cromford, Masson Mill, built in 1783, was a further significant milestone in the development of the textile mill. Its design reflects a deliberate movement towards conscious architectural style. It is a brick building, while the earlier buildings at Cromford Mill were in gritstone, and its principal elevation has a central section ornamented with Venetian and Diocletian windows and a cupola.[16]

Arkwright's decorative embellishments were, however, the exception in mill architecture of the period. By the time that the new factory at Ditherington was being planned and designed, the overall form and principal stylistic features of mill buildings were utilitarian, designed with practical purposes in mind – access, light, the layout and operation of machinery, the limita-

Fig 4.4
Cromford Mills *by Joseph Wright, 1783. The impact of industry on the surrounding rural landscape is clearly evident in this view of the mill by night.*
[© Bridgeman Images MOU272109]

tions of power. The width of mills was in part governed by structural considerations and in part influenced by the arrangement of the machinery which they were designed to house; it has been suggested, for example, that 'Arkwright-type' mills had a width of 29ft (9m) because this allowed the optimum layout of spinning frames.[17] Height and length were less significant constraints on design: mills could be as long as capital, or the available power, permitted. Arkwright-type mills were commonly three or four storeys high, but could be higher. Five or six storeys were common at large sites such as New Lanark in Lanarkshire, Scotland, in 1786–9, in the largest mills in Manchester in the 1780s, and indeed at Arkwright's own mills in Cromford.[18] Power considerations aside, it was, therefore, essentially capital which limited the size of mills; their basic form and structure – a rectangular multi-storeyed box – could be adapted to suit large and small pockets.

Purchasing the site and building the mill

On 20 September 1796 John Marshall, along with his Shrewsbury partners Thomas and Benjamin Benyon and Charles Bage, agreed with John Mytton of Halston (1768–98)[19] to purchase before 2 February in the following year more than 7 acres (2.8ha) of land adjoining the route of the Shropshire Canal which formed part of Child's Fields, 'for carrying on a large and extensive manufactory'.[20] The partners already occupied the ground, and the document recording the release of the fee which completed the transaction in February 1797 noted that several buildings had already been erected.[21] As early as May 1796 the partners had informed Boulton and Watt that they would be building a mill in Shrewsbury for which they required a steam engine by February of the following year.[22] The mill appears to have gone into production in September 1797, by which time the steam engine had been installed at the south end of the main mill.

The flax-spinning complexes built by John Marshall and his imitators in Shrewsbury and Leeds contained broadly similar types of buildings and appear to have worked in similar ways. The governing factors in planning were the range of processes that needed to be housed, the relationship between the stages of production and the location of the source or sources of power. The site at Ditherington, unconstrained by existing buildings, offered the potential for a rational layout of a new factory – and this is what was achieved. The mill was not, however, built in a single phase but rather incrementally. The main buildings housing the manufacturing processes were constructed between 1796 and 1801 and, following Marshall's split with the Benyons and Bage, a major extension of the site was achieved in a second campaign of construction between 1809 and 1812.

The mill occupied 3 acres (1.2ha) at the south end of the plot that the partnership had purchased; the northern part of the land was never used by the company for industrial purposes, although it may have been bought with future expansion in mind, similar to that which was to occur in Leeds. The buildings were constructed principally from bricks made in the vicinity, where there were numerous brickyards. The primary phase of construction was characterised by the use of 'great' bricks, measuring approximately 100mm × 110mm × 240mm and made of a coarse red fabric. A useful key to dating the buildings is the Flax Warehouse, which was probably completed in 1810 and was constructed with standard bricks measuring 75mm × 90mm × 210mm. Most of the buildings that can be proven by documentary evidence to be older than the Flax Warehouse are made of great bricks, while those that can be shown to have been constructed after 1810 are made of standard bricks.[23]

By 1812 the key episodes in the building of the factory had taken place and the structures of this early period remain largely intact today (Fig 4.5). The site was entered, as today, from the south end, where gates opened into a yard bounded on the south and west by a Packing Warehouse, Stable, Smithy and offices. Immediately ahead lay the operational heart of the factory, the L-shaped complex made up of the five-storeyed Spinning Mill, an imposing 18-bay range built on a north–south axis adjacent to the canal (now filled in), and the Cross Building, a wing of five storeys extending for 12 bays to the west from its north end. At the north and south ends of the Spinning Mill were the Engine Houses, which accommodated the steam engines that provided power to the whole mill. There were two Boiler Houses, one attached to the east side of the southern Engine House, in the narrow space between the Spinning Mill and the canal, and the other attached to the northern Engine House. In the angle between

Fig 4.5
As shown in this site plan,
Ditherington Mill reached
its full extent as a flax
factory in c 1812, following
two main campaigns of
building from 1796 to 1801
and 1809 to 1812.

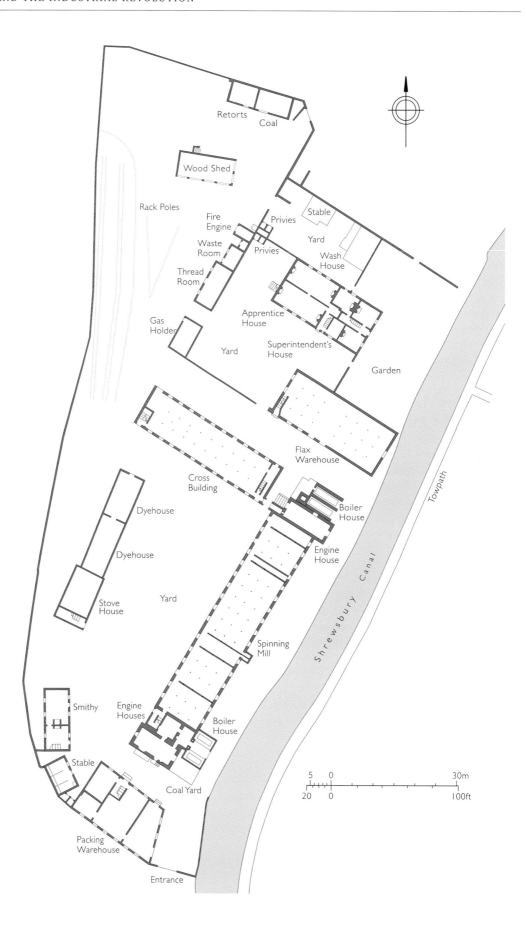

the Spinning Mill and the Cross Building lay the Dyehouse and Stove House, the latter used for drying materials after dyeing. The Dyehouse survives today in its rebuilt form of the 1850s. Beyond the Cross Building was the Flax Warehouse, probably added in 1810, with loading doors in the gable facing the canal, and beyond that the Apprentice House of *c* 1810, originally with a garden for the Superintendent. At the north end of the site were the gasworks, built in 1811, and ancillary buildings associated with the Apprentice House; none of these are extant, but recent excavations have brought parts of them to light once more.

The construction of the Spinning Mill

The largest building in the Ditherington factory complex was the Spinning Mill (Fig 4.6).[24] Construction began in 1796, and a letter of May that year to Boulton and Watt requested 'plans for the Engine House soon as you can as we shall begin of the building immediately', implying that construction of the mill itself was planned and perhaps had begun by this date.[25] Local press reports on 1 September 1797 suggest that the mill was then complete, at least in its first phase, and the engine was certainly

working two months later.[26] The Spinning Mill was designed to house all the main mechanically powered processes in the factory; the other principal mill buildings initially accommodated either hand-powered processes or storage, or were used for the dyeing and drying of products made in the Spinning Mill. The association of the Engine Houses with the Spinning Mill confirms steam power's pivotal role within the factory. The mill was powered in its first years by a steam engine at its south end (this contained the engine supplied by Boulton and Watt in 1797) and a second engine was added in 1800 at its north end.

The Spinning Mill, which was constructed with the same great bricks as the other early buildings at the site, has several external features that distinguish it from other early textile mills and reveal its origins as a pioneering example of factory design. The walls were built with external and internal setbacks, a functional rather than aesthetic feature which progressively reduced the wall thickness in the upper storeys. This feature is rarely seen in later mills. The original fenestration was mostly bricked in during the maltings conversion of the 1890s, but in its original form the mill was distinguished by unusually large windows for the period, creating a well-lit 16-bay interior more typical of a mid-19th century textile mill. The

Fig 4.6
The east elevation of the Spinning Mill in 2002. The wide-gabled bay in the foreground housed the engine installed in 1810 to replace the original Boulton and Watt engine located in the adjacent bay.
[AA022749]

building was 53.94m long and was entered at the south end through a doorway opening into a fireproof stairway; this bay was shared with the first Engine House. With an internal span of about 10.97m, the Spinning Mill was wider than earlier timber-floored mills, particularly those built on the Arkwright model (Fig 4.7). Its proportions heralded one of the main design characteristics of textile mills in the 19th century – a gradual increase in width that was related to improved methods of construction and to the introduction of larger machinery. The roof was very unusual, comprising a series of transverse ridges, one per bay, which sloped down from the centre line to the eaves. No other mill roof of exactly this form is known, and all the later buildings at the site had conventional gabled roofs.

The most striking feature of the interior is the fireproof floor frame, comprising three rows of cruciform cast-iron columns supporting two-piece cast-iron beams and brick-vaulted ceilings. The structure of the mill, which is the most historically significant aspect of the site as a whole, will be considered in detail in Chapter 5. The structure does, however, provide important evidence for the Spinning Mill being developed in two closely consecutive phases of construction, in all likelihood planned from the start.

In its completed form, the building was divided on its lower three floors by a cross wall (Fig 4.8). In the first phase of construction, the eight bays to the south of this wall have irregular widths; tellingly, two of these bays are very narrow, the first against the south wall, the second adjacent to the site of the cross wall. Narrow bays such as these are commonly found in fireproof mills and are designed as stress breakers for the horizontal arch forces where they approached the end walls of the building, as the short bays provided additional strength.[27] Beyond the cross wall, the 10 northern bays have a constant width of about 3.2m. The evidence suggests that the mill of 1796–7 comprised the six full and two short bays to the south of the cross wall and that a 10-bay extension was added to the north very shortly thereafter. The addition must have been built soon after 1797, however, since its iron frame shows few significant differences to that employed in the south end of the mill. It was certainly in existence by 1800, the date of the earliest reference to the north-end engine.[28] The fact that the cross wall did not extend into the upper two storeys, which were therefore always open from end to end, raises the possibility that these floors may themselves have been a later addition, part of the phase of construction which saw the building of the north end of the mill before 1800. Although probably planned from the start, therefore, the mill began its working life as something less than half of its completed form, perhaps because the company wished to begin production at the earliest possible opportunity while at the same time releasing capital for buildings and machinery in stages.

The attention of contemporaries and modern students has focused on the innovatory aspects of Bage's mill, particularly its structure and the way that this related to the layout of power and machinery on each floor. Less attention has been given to more basic elements of the mill's design, and indeed clear evidence is lacking for some aspects of the mill's original form. In contrast to some of the other early textile mills, for example, heating by an external stove was only

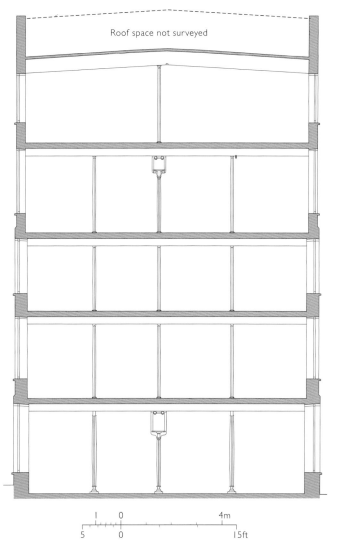

Roof space not surveyed

provided for the manual heckling department in the Cross Building, before it was destroyed by fire, and not for the powered main rooms in the Spinning Mill. There is also little to indicate the nature of the original sanitary arrangements. A plan of 1811 (*see* Fig 8.1) does not show a privy tower of the sort which was becoming common in contemporary cotton mills, and there is nothing in the surviving structure to indicate that privies were provided internally. A privy tower had been added to the Spinning Mill by the middle of the 19th century.

Access to and from the mill is another aspect of original design which appears less than ideal. The main staircase is at the south end of the mill and only a narrow stair in the Cross Building provided access to the upper floors at the north end. It may have been thought that the fireproof nature of the Spinning Mill lessened the likelihood of the need for emergency evacuation, but the movement of bulky goods

to and from the different floors within the mill must have been difficult. One reason for the absence of hoists may have been the distinctive internal organisation of the early flax factories, which at Ditherington resulted in processes being linked horizontally between the Cross Building and the Spinning Mill, rather than vertically between different floors. In the building as a whole, however, the absence of practical features which were becoming common in contemporary mills throws an interesting light on the original design. One might conclude that Bage's approach concentrated more on the innovative structure rather than the mundane aspects of working practice, such as heating, ventilation, sanitation and the movement of goods.

Later phases in the Spinning Mill's development saw the replacement of the early power plant: first, in *c* 1810, a more powerful beam engine was installed in a new Engine House

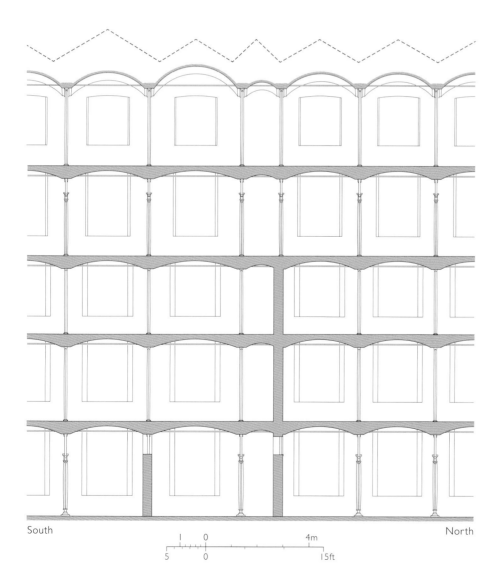

South   North

Fig 4.8
The Spinning Mill, part long section. The former cross wall in the lower three storeys, reconstructed in this drawing, marked the end of the original phase of building and was later used to segregate different processes. It was removed on the conversion of the mill to a maltings.

added at the south end of the mill, and then, in *c* 1820, the northern Engine House was substantially rebuilt to house another new engine (*see* Chapter 6).

Other buildings of the early mill

At right angles to the Spinning Mill a second multi-storeyed building was constructed in the first years of operation. It was probably built by 1799 and was certainly in operation by 1803 (*see* Fig 8.1).[29] Known as the Cross Building, it initially housed hand-powered heckling apparatus and was also used for storage of raw flax and heckled line and tow. The close relationship in functional terms between it and the Spinning Mill explains their proximity, and the large size of the original building reflects the need to keep the main building supplied with heckled flax. It was not, however, built in fireproof form, and in October 1811 it was destroyed by a fire caused by a fault in the newly installed gas-lighting system, which had been part of the overall improvements to the site at that time.[30] The Cross Building's importance to the working of the mill is demonstrated by its immediate rebuilding. The new Cross Building, completed in 1812, was 1.82m wider than its predecessor, and like the Spinning Mill was iron-framed, although with important modifications to the details of the Spinning Mill's fireproof construction (*see* Fig 4.12). It had staircases at either end rising the full height of the building, which was used for heckling and yarn winding. A full-height narrow link block, which may survive from before the fire, provided access to the Spinning Mill, and enabled closer connection between the related processes in the two buildings (*see* Chapter 7).

In the angle between the Spinning Mill and the Cross Building were the Dyehouse and the Stove House. The presence of dyeing facilities was an early and distinctive feature of Ditherington, and the first Dyehouse was built by 1804. The Dyehouse was extended in several phases as it was increasingly used to process material sent from the Leeds mill, and it was completely rebuilt in the early 1850s (Fig 4.9).[31] During the 1850s the internal layout comprised built-in vats arranged in two distinct areas, heated by steam pipes from the Boiler Houses at both ends of the Spinning Mill.[32] A similar range of vats and equipment was described when the site was sold in the 1880s, by which time only 4 of the 19 main dyeing machines were still in use.[33] Prior to the purchase in *c* 1809–10 of a nearby mill at Hanwood and its conversion by 1812 into a bleachworks, bleaching was also undertaken in the Dyehouse.

To the south of the Dyehouse lay a heated Stove House, used to dry the yarn and thread. It was built by 1810 (of great brick) but the surviving building is an extension of 1842–3. Parts of the original Stove House remain attached to the extant structure. An unheated Dry House lay further to the south. An extensive area of racking for open-air drying lay in the yard to the north, and by the mid-century a large Drying Shed had been built.[34]

The yard at the south end of the site, itself an early feature of the factory, still retains some of the ancillary buildings of the flax mill (Fig 4.10). The earliest is the Stable, a small two-storeyed fireproof building of three bays, with brick-vaulted ceilings supported by cast-iron beams which have similar details to those in the Spinning Mill, suggesting a similar date. To the north is the two-storeyed Smithy, shown,

Fig 4.9
East elevation of the Dyehouse. The distinguished treatment of the exterior was continued internally with ornamental details to some of the roof components. [BB92/00176]

Fig 4.10
The Stable (left) and
Smithy. The upper floor of
the Smithy was converted
into offices in the late
19th century.
[DP163732]

like the Stable, on the 1811 plan. South of the Stable lay the Packing Warehouse, built by 1800 but demolished in 1979.[35] This comprised the store and offices where finished goods were prepared for dispatch.

The main operations of the early flax mill were grouped around the yard formed by the buildings at the south end of the site. This makes it likely that the Flax Warehouse, probably built c 1810 to the north of the main working buildings, was not planned at the beginning but was instead part of the mill's expansion after 1809, when machine heckling was introduced to the site and when stockpiling of raw materials provided some guarantee against fluctuating

supplies.[36] With four storeys (plus an attic) and built to a wide plan of nine bays, it was a relatively large warehouse for a textile mill (Fig 4.11). It was built in common brick and lit by fewer and smaller windows than those in the Spinning Mill. The east gable end, which overlooked the canal, included double-width loading doors, and the top storey was linked to the upper floor of the Cross Building by a chain bridge.[37] The iron-framed construction of the Flax Warehouse is of great interest, being very well preserved and notably similar to that of the Cross Building, the two buildings illustrating the rapid development of cast iron as a structural material in the first decade of the 19th

Fig 4.11
The Flax Warehouse of
c 1810, with the 1890s Malt
Kiln adjoining to the right.
[DP163725]

century. Marshall built a similar warehouse at his Leeds mill in 1806, the oldest surviving iron frame in that complex.

The three-storeyed Apprentice House was added in 1809 at the north end of the site and should be considered as part of the overall workforce reorganisation that was taking place at that time. The replacement of hand-powered heckling – undertaken by skilled male operatives – by heckling machines from 1809 increased the proportion of women and children in the workforce. The Apprentice House was distinguished from the working buildings of the mill by its narrower sash windows, the use of plain stone bands to outline the gable ends and a similar dentilated eaves cornice to those of the contemporary Flax Warehouse and Cross Building (Fig 4.12). It was internally divided into a Manager's or Superintendent's dwelling at the east end and accommodation for the children at the west end. Walled gardens with outbuildings adjoined the north and east sides of the house.

An important aspect of the development of the early mill was the construction of a gas plant at the north end of the site in 1811. This will be discussed in detail in Chapter 8, but its construction is an indication of Marshall's commitment to investment in Ditherington. The lighting allowed extended working hours and may be connected to the construction of the Apprentice House, which housed a compliant workforce on the site under managerial control.

By 1812 Ditherington Mill contained all the buildings – apart from a dedicated bleachworks – required in a flax mill specialising in the production of yarn and thread. Few new buildings were constructed at the mill after this date. Changes to the steam-power plant necessitated the construction of new Boiler Houses (*see* Chapter 6), but nothing of these buildings survives above ground. The main structural development after this time, which should be seen as part of the overall reorganisation of production in the middle decades of the century, concerned the Dyehouse and Stove House, and enabled Dither-

Fig 4.12
The Apprentice House, on the left, was added to the north end of the site in 1811. The Cross Building, on the right, was rebuilt in 1812 following a disastrous fire.
[DP163731]

ington Mill to finish the yarn and thread brought by rail from the Leeds mill, which entered the site on a private siding. The expanded Dyehouse, built in the early 1850s, was an efficient, well-lit building, open to its ornate iron roof, with pilastered brickwork and arcaded panels in the side walls contrasting strongly with the near absence of embellishment in the earlier buildings. Parts of the adjoining Stove House date from 1842–3 and illustrate the further development of structural ironwork in the mid-19th century, with I-section floor beams and two-piece cast-iron roof trusses.[38]

The limited building activity after 1812 reflected the fact that flax mills rarely moved towards full integration – in the sense of uniting the spinning and weaving stages of production – as the process of mechanisation continued. Where woollen and worsted mills, for example, commonly brought weaving into the factory, either as a hand-powered process or, later, using powerlooms, the linen industry remained mainly specialist, at least in England, with spin-

ning mills supplying weaving factories. A little weaving may have been undertaken by the firm (*see* Chapter 7), but the production of linen cloth was not a major aspect of its work. In most flax mills there was, therefore, no need to add substantial weaving sheds to early spinning factories. In 1812 Ditherington was a large enterprise by contemporary standards, much bigger than most mills in, for example, the woollen and worsted branches of the textile industry. Its size was doubtless due in part to the fact that Marshalls was a well-established and profitable company, boosted by the capital brought by the Benyon brothers. William Brown, the Scottish flax spinner, remarked in 1821 that most flax mills in Leeds were makeshift affairs made up of ramshackle buildings (*see* Chapter 2), but that a few firms at the apex of the local industry, specifically Marshalls and Benyons in Holbeck, operated on a large and impressive scale. Ditherington certainly ranks with these mills at the apex of the English flax-spinning industry.

5

Ditherington and the development of the iron-framed mill: innovation and experimentation

TOM SWAILES, PAUL MURRAY THOMPSON AND MIKE WILLIAMS

The overriding importance of Ditherington Mill lies in the fact that it houses a building which is considered to be the first multi-storeyed structure in the world to have an internal frame of iron. As discussed in Chapter 4, this building – the Spinning Mill – was almost certainly built in more than one stage, between 1796 and 1800. Other early buildings in the complex – the Flax Warehouse of *c* 1810 and the Cross Building of 1812 – are also iron-framed, but the differences which they show to the Spinning Mill demonstrate the rapid evolution of iron-framed construction in what was a period of experimentation in structural and civil engineering, especially in industrial buildings. The revolutionary engineering employed in the construction of Ditherington did not, however, emerge from nowhere. The mill of 1796–1800 had antecedents and was a stage in a process of development steered by a network of Midland industrialists and engineers. This chapter examines the structural and architectural evolution of textile mills in the late 18th century, to place the contribution which Ditherington made to this process within a broader chronological context. It then goes on to show how Ditherington and other mills developed the use of cast and wrought iron in the 19th century.

The development of the 'fireproof' mill 1790–1800

Traditionally built mills, with timber floors and roofs, were highly susceptible to fire: prior to the introduction of gas lighting (*see* Chapter 8) artificial light was provided by naked flames and the atmosphere in some textile mills, laden with dust and lint, was highly combustible. This was especially the case in the manufacture of plant-based textiles such as cotton and flax.

Incidents of destructive fires, with losses of life, property and production, were common and few large concerns escaped unscathed. In 1788 Thomas Evans and Sons' mill at Darley Abbey, near Derby, was destroyed by fire, and Marshall and the Benyons suffered the loss of one of their mills in Leeds in 1795. Large flour mills were vulnerable, too. Albion Mill near Blackfriars Bridge in London was the model industrial building of its day.[1] Designed by Samuel Wyatt, an architect of country houses, London town houses and model farms, it was built between 1783 and 1786 with Boulton and Watt rotative steam engines and millwork erected by John Rennie. In 1791 it, too, burned to the ground (Fig 5.1).

Limiting the destruction caused by fire was therefore a matter of intense concern to both industrialists and their insurers. From the 1780s there emerged a group of manufacturers and natural philosophers, some in close contact with each other, responsible for separate stages in the progress towards what may be termed full 'fireproofing', which is believed to have been achieved for the first time at Ditherington in 1797. In mill construction, attention focused on the elimination of timber in floors and replacement with iron beams and ceilings of brick or 'hollow pots'. Because the use of iron in a building frame was a largely untested structural method, the early innovators faced new problems, focusing in particular on the technology of casting iron components, the behaviour of cast iron under stress, and the methods of producing a frame that, while strong enough to support a heavy load, was not so rigid and inflexible that it could not allow some essential movement in the building's structure.

By the late 18th century mill builders could draw upon a considerable body of expertise in the use of iron, an expertise developed particu-

Fig 5.1
The dramatic loss of Albion Mill in London in 1791 highlighted the need for new types of fireproof construction in industrial buildings.
*[*Fire in London, *print by John Bluck after a drawing by Auguste Pugin, published 1808, © Museum of London]*

larly in Shropshire and concerning both the manufacture of the material and its application in civil engineering works of great importance. A few kilometres down the River Severn from Shrewsbury, at Coalbrookdale, Abraham Darby I (1678–1717) pioneered the development of better quality iron by using coke for smelting and by improving casting methods. His grandson Abraham Darby III (1750–89) provided the greatest advertisement for the qualities of the material for engineering purposes in the construction of the Iron Bridge across the Severn Gorge, opened to traffic on New Year's Day 1781. The elegant bridge was regarded as one of the wonders of the age, a daring experiment which applied new scientific thinking to practical purposes.[2]

Confidence in the use of iron grew with its successful application to further civil engineering works, in particular aqueducts, during the great period of canal construction in the late 18th and early 19th centuries. The name most closely associated with the early use of iron in canal bridges is that of Thomas Telford. His first cast-iron canal aqueduct took the Shrewsbury Canal over the River Tern at Longdon-on-Tern in Shropshire (Fig 5.2).[3] Completed in March 1796 (the same year that construction at Dither-

ington began), the aqueduct trough was formed by flanged cast-iron plates supported by vertical and inclined cruciform-section pillars and struts. Telford's larger Pontcysyllte Aqueduct, which carried the Llangollen Canal over the River Dee, was completed in 1805 and used a trough of similar cast-iron construction. It provided a conclusive demonstration of the qualities of iron in major works of civil engineering.[4]

Running parallel to the application of iron in the construction of bridges and aqueducts were experiments in its use in buildings. One pioneer in the use of iron in this way was David Hartley (1731–1813) who, as well as being a Member of Parliament, was a scientist interested in methods of securing buildings against fire. In 1774 he published his ideas, which involved the use of sheets of iron within the floor structure of buildings, preventing or inhibiting the spread of fire from one floor to another – so-called fire plates.[5] After the destruction of Albion Mill in 1791 Wyatt proposed to salvage something from the ruins of the building by retaining its basic form and cladding the timber elements with iron sheeting, in the manner of Hartley's fire plates as patented in 1773. These plans, however, came to nothing. Sheathing timber members in iron or tin was used widely:

Fig 5.2
The Longdon-on-Tern
aqueduct on Thomas
Telford's Shrewsbury Canal,
built in 1796 entirely of
cast iron.
[DP163814]

Matthew Murray used it in the office range in his Round Foundry in Holbeck, Leeds, and Benjamin Gott, the woollen manufacturer and merchant, employed it in his mills in Leeds – at Armley in 1805–7 and later at Bean Ing. When Thomas Evans & Sons rebuilt the Long Mill at Darley Abbey, some time prior to 1820, they too used tin sheathing.[6]

An alternative and more thoroughgoing method of fireproofing, involving the substitution of timber with other materials, was evolving in the last decades of the 18th century. A central figure in this development was William Strutt of Derby. Strutt was born in 1756 at Blackwell near Alfreton in Derbyshire. His father, Jedediah Strutt, had patented machinery to knit ribbed stockings in the late 1750s and established a successful business in Derby, into which William entered at the age of 14. Prior to that he had been well schooled at the dissenters' academy at Findern in such practically useful subjects as logic, mathematics and natural philosophy. In partnership with Richard Arkwright, Jedediah Strutt founded the Derbyshire cotton industry at Cromford in 1771. He established his first cotton mill at Belper in 1778, and around the same time he acquired iron forges and an iron slitting and rolling mill and set up workshops for the manufacture of textile machinery. William Strutt was to become

in effect the technical director of the family firm, but this was not at the expense of a broadening scientific education. Erasmus Darwin had established a philosophical society on arrival in Derby and just two years later he was conducting experiments concerned with adiabatic expansion to explain the formation of clouds, assisted by William Strutt. In 1802 William succeeded Darwin as President of the Derby Philosophical Society.[7]

Strutt's experiments in mill construction at first focused on the elimination of the timber joists and floorboards making up the floor surface. In planning his Derby cotton mill, built in 1792–3, Strutt used his network of contacts to gather together information on the latest building techniques.[8] Important developments were happening in France and John Walker, an architect who had just returned from post-revolution Paris, wrote to Strutt in October 1792 about the Theatre du Palais-Royal, which employed hollow brick arches in its floors. He reported that he had 'ordered one of each sort of the hollow bricks, of which the Arches are composed' and that the building 'seems to me to be about 24 feet wide, the iron bars supporting the arches are about four feet from each other'. The iron bars referred to were probably tie-bars, to resist the thrust of the arches. Walker added the further detail that 'the roof of the Palais Royale is of framed Iron, with the larger sort of hollow bricks to fill up the panes'.[9] Next, on 8 May 1793, Matthew Boulton wrote to say that he had seen floors formed of arches using 'hollow pots' in Paris and also 'at Mr George Saunders's in Oxford St., London, who is an eminent Architect, & who had practised that art with success'.[10]

Although the Derby Mill was demolished in 1860, nearly a century later Skempton and Johnson were able to establish the details of its construction, and they could also inspect the practically identical structural framing of the contemporary but smaller Milford Warehouse.[11] The documentary evidence cited by Skempton and Johnson included a Boulton and Watt part-plan prepared in 1792 in connection with the design and supply of a 'sun-and-planet' steam engine, and a plan and section prepared in 1806 by the same firm in connection with installation of gas lighting. The Derby cotton mill was six storeys high, with external walls of solid brick-work, 35m long and 9.4m wide overall, with an internal width at ground-floor level of 8.2m divided into three aisles of 2.7m. The floors were made up of brick arches springing from substantial timber beams. The unbalanced horizontal thrusts in the floor loading were restrained by wrought-iron tie-rods. Because the weight of the brick arches throughout the mill was much greater than that of traditional floor construction, intermediate supports to the timber floor beams were required. This support took the form of two rows of solid cruciform cast-iron columns.[12] The roof was of conventional timber queen-post truss construction, with hollow-pot arches between the tie-beams of the trusses forming a fireproof ceiling.

Over the next two years Strutt followed the same pattern of construction in a small warehouse at the mill complex at Milford, near Derby, and in the West Mill at Belper, neither of which has survived. In the Milford Warehouse of 1792–3 solid cruciform cast-iron columns supported timber beams of 2.7m span. The beams passed through a U-head arrangement that was either an integral part of the top of the column or a separate casting. The one-piece beams were 300mm square Baltic Fir (Scots Pine), supporting brickwork arches of 2.1m to 3.2m span topped with sand to form a level bed for clay floor tiles. The arches were sprung from 'skewbacks' (triangular-section timber or cast-iron flanges secured to the sides of the beams) and wrought-iron ties between the columns connected the frames longitudinally and prob-

ably had the function of holding the beams in place during the construction of the brick arches. Skempton and Johnson noted that the arches to the end bays were of hollow-pot rather than brick construction to reduce dead weight, thereby lessening the lateral thrust exerted by the arches on the end walls. Plaster on laths provided fire protection to the otherwise exposed beam soffits. When Strutt built the West Mill at Belper in 1793–5, he employed very similar framing details to the Derby cotton mill and the Milford Warehouse.[13]

In its day, the Derby cotton mill was recognised as a building that broke new ground. In 1802 Britton and Brayley wrote that 'it was the first fire-proof mill that was ever built. The second mill constructed on the same plan was erected by the same proprietors at Belper, but two others have since been built on a similar principle; the first a flax mill at Shrewsbury: and very lately, an extraordinary large cotton mill at Manchester.'[14] Even though Strutt had not eliminated timber from the floor frames (which therefore might not be regarded as fully fireproof), his work was nevertheless seen as a great advance in mill construction. Of the other buildings referred to by Britton and Brayley, the second fireproof Strutt mill was the West Mill at Belper, the Shrewsbury Mill was the Ditherington Flax Mill, and the Manchester building was Philips and Lee's seven-storey mill at Salford (built between 1799 and 1801).

The building of the Ditherington Spinning Mill 1796–7

Strutt's initiatives were important stages in the development of fireproof construction, but his mills employed timber floor beams and were therefore still susceptible to fire. The significance of Ditherington lies in the fact that here, in the Spinning Mill of 1796–1800, iron was substituted for timber in the transverse beams. Combined with brick arches to the ceilings, the floor frame of a building was, for the first time, entirely constructed of non-combustible materials. While timber was still present in the building, in the roof and within the brick walls, none was exposed in the working areas of the multi-storeyed mill.[15]

The credit for the achievement of full fireproofing rests with Charles Bage, whom John Marshall and the Benyon brothes had taken into partnership in 1796 (*see* Chapter 4), in all likelihood because he brought with him an interest and expertise in the structural uses of iron. His family background gave him some knowledge of iron working but his early professional career took him into other fields. By the 1790s, however, he was clearly deeply engaged in the development of the use of iron in industrial buildings although, unlike his acquaintance Thomas Telford, he did not leave behind reports or authorised publications that give insights into his engineering work and methods.[16] His correspondence with William Strutt (only the Bage side of which survives), however, is of great value in illustrating both the development of Bage's ideas on structural issues and the apparently collaborative atmosphere which prevailed in the circle of Midland industrialists otherwise working largely independently to solve the pressing problems of the age.[17] The earliest letter is undated, but (based on evidence assembled by the late Professor Skempton) was probably written in mid-1796, and so dates from precisely the period when the mill at Ditherington was being planned and built (Fig 5.3). The letter was not the first in the correspondence, as Bage thanks Strutt for advice on inverted arches (for foundations) and then addresses questions related to the design of the load-bearing external walls. Bage continued:

> I believe new brickwork settles independently of the foundations. That is, the height of the wall from the ground floor to the wall plate shortens, by evaporation of the moisture from the mortar or some other cause. It was respecting this compaction (if it may be so called) I wished to collect some facts. Since my letter to you however I have been induced to believe such compaction is small, much less than I then supposed it. The sinking of the earth under the foundations can not be subject to any general rule, but whilst every part sinks alike it is not very material.

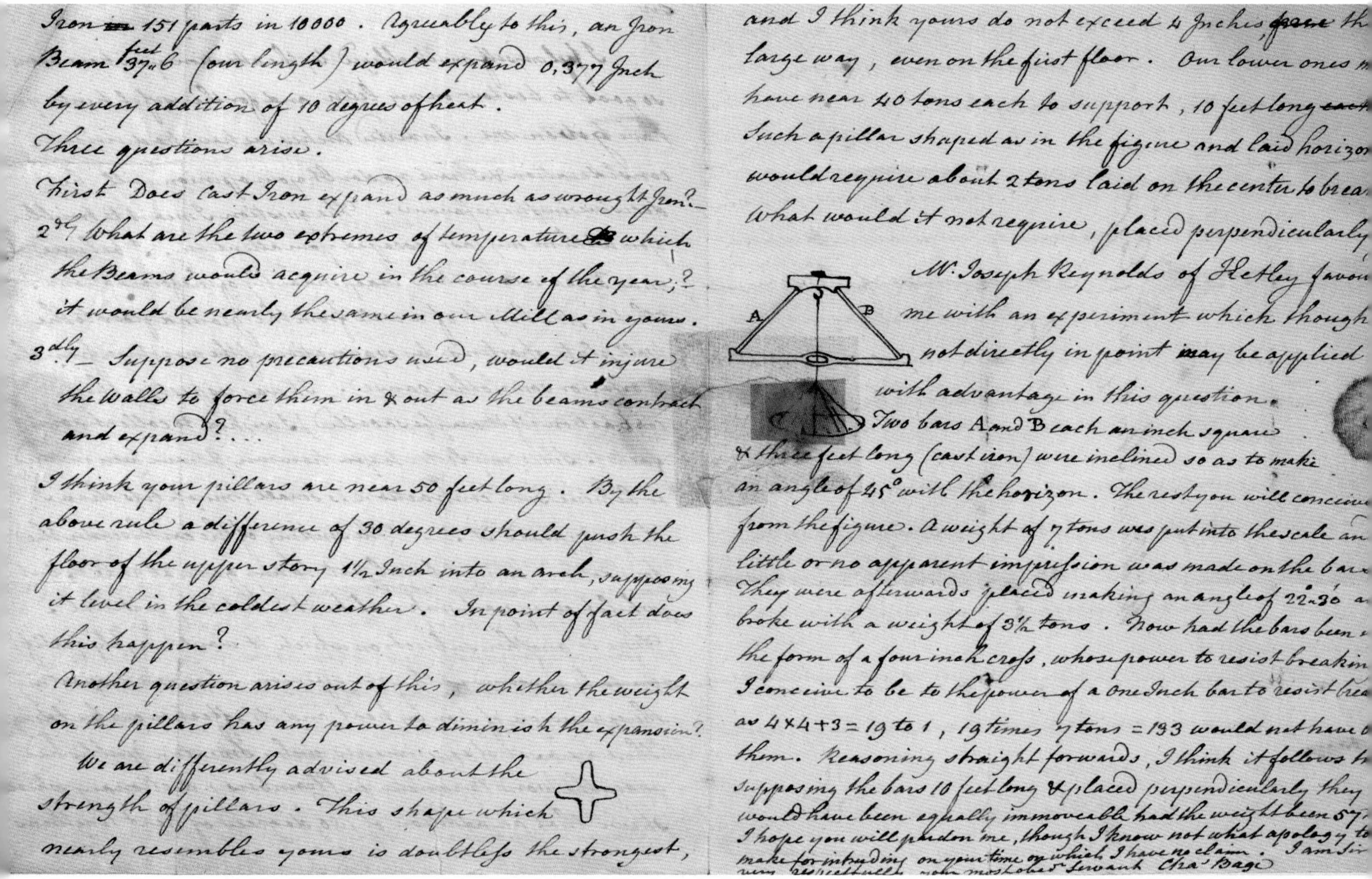
Iron 151 parts in 10000. Agreeably to this, an Iron Beam 37 feet 6 (our length) would expand 0,377 Inch by every addition of 10 degrees of heat.
Three questions arise.
First Does cast Iron expand as much as wrought Iron?_
2dly What are the two extremes of temperature which the Beams would acquire in the course of the year;? it would be nearly the same in our Mill as in yours.
3dly_ Suppose no precautions used, would it injure the Walls to force them in & out as the beams contract and expand?...
I think your pillars are near 50 feet long. By the above rule a difference of 30 degrees should push the floor of the upper story 1½ Inch into an arch, supposing it level in the coldest weather. In point of fact does this happen?
Another question arises out of this, whether the weight on the pillars has any power to diminish the expansion?
We are differently advised about the strength of pillars. This shape which nearly resembles yours is doubtless the strongest, and I think yours do not exceed 4 Inches the large way, even on the first floor. Our lower ones m have near 40 tons each to support, 10 feet long. Such a pillar shaped as in the figure and laid horizon would require about 2 tons laid on the center to brea What would it not require, placed perpendicularly?
Mr Joseph Reynolds of Ketley favou me with an experiment which though not directly in point may be applied with advantage in this question. Two bars A and B each an inch square & three feet long (cast iron) were inclined so as to make an angle of 45° with the horizon. The rest you will conceive from the figure. A weight of 7 tons was put into the scale an little or no apparent impression was made on the ba They were afterwards placed making an angle of 22.30 a broke with a weight of 3½ tons. Now had the bars been the form of a four inch cross, whose power to resist breakin I conceive to be to the power of a One Inch bar to resist brea as 4×4+3 = 19 to 1, 19 times 7 tons = 133 would not have them. Reasoning straight forwards, I think it follows t supposing the bars 10 feet long & placed perpendicularly they would have been equally immoveable had the weight been 57. I hope you will pardon me, though I know not what apology to make for intruding on your time on which I have no claim. I am Sir very respectfully your most obed Servant Chas Bage

Fig 5.3
The earliest of Charles Bage's surviving letters to William Strutt, written c 1796 when Ditherington Mill was being built, demonstrated that both men were actively involved in pioneering the structural application of cast iron. [Shropshire Archives 6001/2657/2 (DP163799)]

In the same letter Bage turns his attention to the internal frame of the building. It seems that the decision to use iron beams as well as pillars had already been made, but Bage was now seeking reassurance that the innovation would not bring with it unforeseen problems. On the effects of temperature change, Bage referred to published results of experiments made by Smeaton on the thermal expansion of iron, based on which he calculated that 'an iron beam 37' 6" in length (our length) would expand 0.377 inch by every addition of 10 degrees of heat'. Almost certainly Bage's concerns about the effects of temperature changes on an iron building frame stemmed from contemporary doubts about the design of the Longdon-on-Tern Aqueduct completed in March 1796. In 1797 Telford wrote that 'it was foretold by some, that the effects of the different degrees of heat and cold would be such as to cause expansion and contraction of the metal which ... would ... tear off the flanches which connect the plates lengthwise, and break the joints. Others said the expansion of freezing water would burst the sides'.[18] Applying the problem to mill buildings, Bage estimated that, when joined together, the iron pillars rising through Strutt's mill gave a height of 50ft (15.2m) and that a temperature rise of 30°F would lead to a lengthening of 1.5in, lifting the top floor by that amount, assuming it to be level in the coldest weather. Unfortunately we do not know Strutt's response to Bage's question: 'In point of fact does this happen?' The building at Ditherington provides us with the evidence that Bage was satisfied that such thermal effects were a problem in theory only.

Finally, Bage considered the strength of the cast-iron pillars under vertical load and sketched for Strutt an experimental arrangement used for testing the strength of cast-iron bars 1in (25mm) square and 3ft (914mm) long, with which, he wrote, 'Mr Joseph Reynolds of Ketley favoured me'. Joseph and William Reynolds were grandsons of Abraham Darby II of Coalbrookdale, and by 1796 were partners in the Ketley ironworks. It seems likely that the experiments had been made at Ketley in connection with the Longdon-on-Tern Aqueduct (see Fig 5.2).[19] There the supports to the aqueduct trough are in the form of vertical and inclined cruciform section cast-iron pillars and struts. A solid cruciform cross section had been used in the cast-iron columns in Strutt's mills at Derby and Belper, but structural design methods were not established. Bage wrote to Strutt:

We are differently advised about the strength of pillars. This shape which nearly resembles yours is doubtless the strongest, and I think yours do not exceed 4 inches, the large way, even on the first floor. Our lower ones might each have 40 tons each to support, 10 feet long. Such a pillar shaped as in the figure and laid horizontally would require about 2 tons laid on the centre to break it. What would it not require perpendicularly?

Bage then goes on to extrapolate from the Reynolds' experiment, and calculates that two bars of 10ft (3m) in the form of a 4in (102mm) cross would support a load of at least 57 tons (52 tonnes), or 28½ tons (26 tonnes) each. In the absence of detailed explanation by Bage, we can only attempt to understand the basis of his calculation by working back from his result to the experiment. The assumptions that Bage made appear to be that a column's cross-sectional strength is proportional to its thickness and that the failure load of the pillar or strut is proportional to its length. Account has also been taken of the 45-degree angle of the struts in the experiment. The two assumptions are incorrect in modern structural engineering terms, but Bage's method still provided a basis for design.

Construction of the Spinning Mill at Ditherington began in 1796 and the building was complete by 1800. Externally it had little to distinguish it from contemporary mills: it was not longer or higher than many cotton mills of the period, and its architecture was plain and functional. It was the internal structure of the mill which made the building so important. Here, for the first time, the floor frames were made entirely of non-combustible materials. It is important to understand in detail the structural forms employed so that the significance of the mill in the rapidly developing field of structural engineering can be assessed.

The Spinning Mill: the iron frame

The internal frame has three principal iron elements: cast-iron transverse beams which are joined at the centre span the width of the mill between each bay; three rows of cast-iron columns which support the beams; and wrought-iron tie-rods which run axially between the beams to tie the iron frame together (Fig 5.4). The whole frame structure was carefully designed for assembly on site, with joints for the beams, columns and tie-rods incorporated into the castings. The buildings at Ditherington are not fully framed, since the brick walls support part of the weight of the floors, but the columns are located vertically above each other to transmit the loads in the central parts of the floors directly to the foundations. In 1797 the problems of attaching cast-iron beams to brick walls, and of joining

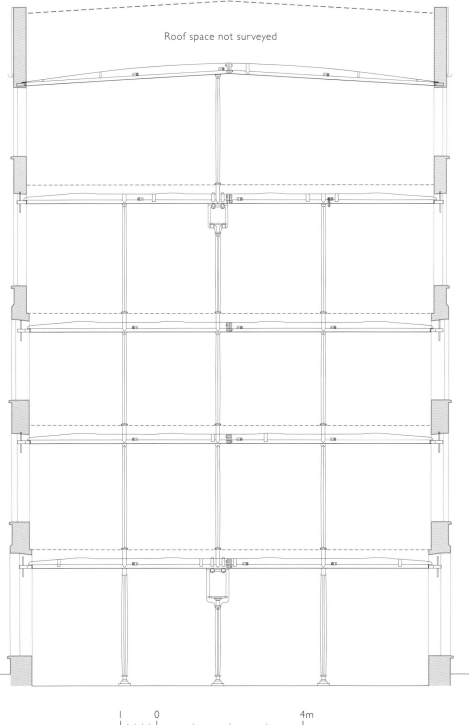

Fig 5.4
The Spinning Mill, cross section of the internal iron frame.

the beams and columns – something not previously tackled – significantly influenced the design of the frame.

The cast-iron transverse beams were the most important innovation at Ditherington. No documents have survived that relate specifically to Bage's design process. Given Bage's knowledge of Strutt's mills the beams are probably a direct development from the latter's fireproofed timber beams with iron skewbacks. In cross section, the beams have a solid triangular bottom flange or skewback and a slightly tapered web (Fig 5.5). They would have been cast upside down in open-sand moulds on the foundry floor, and the soffits show a distinctive concave meniscus with perforations and other defects caused by slag accumulating in the mould. In elevation, the webs have a level top edge with slightly arched higher sections located in the spans between the walls and the columns and between the columns themselves in the central area. An original feature of the beams is a series of projections, square in plan, running the full height of the web and containing a square bolt hole. The positions of the projections vary on each floor, and are assumed to relate to the transmission of power to machines (*see* Chapter 6).

The outer parts of the webs reduce in height to meet the 3in- (76mm-) thick flat end plates which are mounted in the walls and fixed in place by a single iron pin driven into timber pads built into the core of the wall. The beam ends are also supported by the brick of the inside wall face. Heavy timber was widely used in structural and mechanical engineering in the

Fig 5.5
The Spinning Mill, perspective reconstruction of the floor beams. At the time of survey (2014) most of the beams were still encased in concrete, so some details are conjectural.

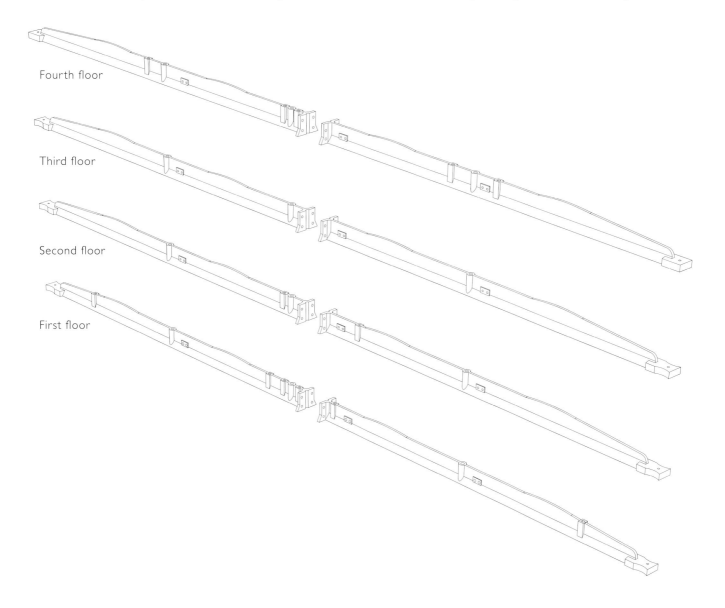

Fourth floor

Third floor

Second floor

First floor

Fig 5.6
The Spinning Mill, assembly
of the central columns and
the two-piece floor beams on
the ground floor.

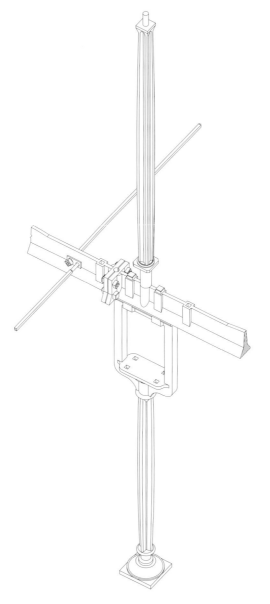

porates a half-inch- (12mm-) thick millboard packing but makes no other allowance for movement at the joint, for the bending forces in the floors or for any movement in the walls. The flanges include a vertical semi-circular groove, forming a hole 2in (51mm) in diameter when the flanges are bolted together, the purpose of which, it has been argued, may be connected with the power transmission system.[22]

The cast-iron columns, the second element in the iron frame, were joined to the beams to form a rigid frame (Fig 5.6). Housings cast into the beams were designed to take the tops and bases of the three rows of columns, which have spigots at their upper and lower ends fitting into the housings. Again, this form of construction fails to allow for movement between the beams and columns. The eastern beams are supported by a single row of columns at mid-span, and the western beams have two rows of columns, including one immediately adjacent to the central beam joint.

The columns are distinguished by their cruciform cross section which, along with a pronounced entasis, was thought in the mid-1790s to be the strongest shape for cast-iron columns (Fig 5.7).[23] The iron frame has previously been described as a purely functional design, but the mouldings on the columns are delicately formed. The columns in the ground floor have a more substantial cross section and have other aesthetic differences compared to those in the upper floors. They have a short cylindrical section at the capital, beneath which a simple projecting ring marks the top of the cruciform shaft. In the upper floors the columns have square top plates and small moulded capitals, which are shaped to connect with the cruciform shafts. The capitals comprise stepped and hollow-chamfered mouldings, but their precise form varies on each floor. Another variation concerns the alignment of the columns: on the ground floor, the cruciform section is set in line with the long axis, but on the upper floors the section is set at an angle of 45 degrees. The reasons for these variations are not understood.[24] It seems reasonable to conclude, however, that the differences in the columns indicate that they were made in more than one batch of casting at the foundry, but why this happened and what this might tell us about the building process and relationship between the foundry and the builders of the mill remain unclear. The mouldings on the columns are typical elements in later Georgian

1790s so its application here is not entirely surprising. Its use in the Spinning Mill might appear to undermine the claims that the building was completely fireproof, although the timber pads were not exposed to the working areas of the building.[20] This method of fixing the ends of the beams was structurally inadequate but suggests a concern for the lateral movement of the beam ends. Bage was aware that the length of the beams might be affected by changes in temperature, and by the mid-1790s it was considered that fixing the beam ends to the walls by pins would enable the beams to support higher loads.[21] The joint between the two beams making up the full span comprises a simple bolted flange which incor-

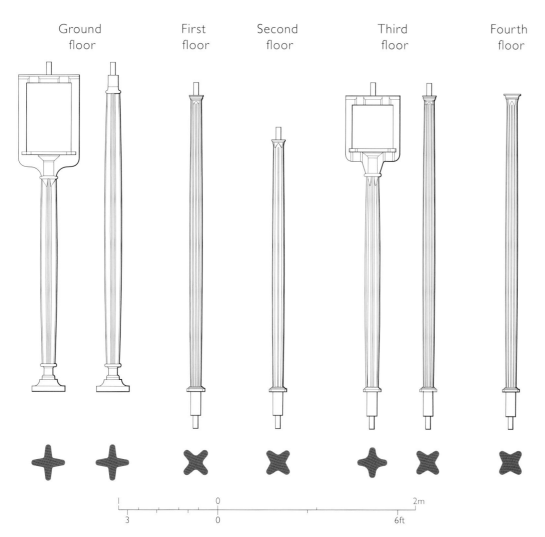

Ground floor   First floor   Second floor   Third floor   Fourth floor

3   0   2m   6ft

Fig 5.7
The Spinning Mill, elevation of cast-iron columns. The columns show significant differences in height, design, construction and embellishment. Profiles at scale x2 (see also Fig 5.18).

embellishment, indicating that the designer wanted to incorporate visually pleasing details in an otherwise functional structure.

The column bases also show considerable architectural detail, most of which was encased within the concrete floors installed in the 1890s on conversion of the site to a maltings. The ground-floor columns have square base plates mounted on substantial stone footings of tooled ashlar, above which is a hollow-chamfered moulding and, above this, a cylindrical section and projecting ring similar to those used in the column capitals (Fig 5.8). The columns in the upper floors have a thinner plate at the base of the cruciform shaft. These plates are embellished with a simple circular moulding; those in parts of the upper floors in the northern half of the building are octagonal in plan rather than square. Beneath the base plates, a short cylindrical section is connected to the same housings in the beams as the columns in the floor below.

Fig 5.8
The Spinning Mill, detail of the base of a central column (see also Fig 1.2).
[AA022777]

53

Fig 5.9
The Spinning Mill, detail of an original tie-rod with U-shaped connector (see also Fig 5.6).
[AA022790]

Strutt's Milford Warehouse and probably in his 1792–3 mill, as described above.[25] At Ditherington tie-rods were adapted for use with a cast-iron frame for the first time, and they remained a feature of fireproof mills for most of the 19th century. The handmade rods are 1in (25mm) square and assembled in separate lengths for each bay. They pass through a thickened section of the beam webs and are fixed in place with metal wedges. Several of the tie-rods in the upper floors incorporate forged loops or U-shaped connectors, possibly in an attempt to compensate for expansion of the iron (Fig 5.9). At the ends of the building the tie-rods pass through the end walls where they are threaded and bolted to external cruciform tie-plates made of wrought iron.

Over the top floor of the mill is a fireproof ceiling of brick vaults, springing from transverse beams of similar cross section to the floor beams on the lower floors, but with a simpler web which has a convex curve to its upper edge. The aim seems to have been to create a fireproof, spacious and well-lit top storey (Fig 5.10; *see also* Fig 5.4). The beams are supported by a single row of tall columns, located just off centre above the columns in the lower floors.

Integral with the original construction of the frame are three sets of longitudinal wrought-iron tie-rods, which are exposed beneath the ceiling vaults on each floor. They secured the structure during construction and also countered the horizontal thrust of the brick vaults. Wrought iron had been quite widely used previously for ties and straps, particularly in timber roofs. Similar iron tie-rods were used before Ditherington, in conjunction with timber beams and brick ceiling vaults, for example in a warehouse at Boars Head Mills in the early 1790s, in

Fig 5.10
The Spinning Mill has an unusual roof, of a type not seen in any other mill, with inclined brick vaults springing from cast-iron beams.
[AA022797]

The beams have a similar central joint and similar end plates to the floor beams of the lower storeys. The eastern ceiling beams include square projections near the centre line, similar to those in the floor beams, which suggests that the top floor had a single row of brackets for a line shaft or pulleys. Additional circular projections in the sides of the webs are reinforcement for the bolts used to fix the cast-iron valley gutters and the wooden roof structure.

What is especially remarkable about the structure is the way that the brick vaults and supporting beams slope down to the eaves, with a fall of just over 310mm from the centre to the side walls. No other building of the period, at Ditherington or elsewhere, is known to have this extraordinary structural form, which can only be explained in functional terms by the need to drain water from the roof. Externally, the series of transverse roof ridges, one to each bay, gives a distinctive sawtooth elevation to the side walls. Above the brick vaults, lightly built wooden A-frame trusses carry a slate covering. Why Bage adopted this unusual form of roof is not clear; it is possible that by 1800 he had not yet reached the stage of confidence which would have allowed him to experiment with a gabled roof supported by full-span cast-iron trusses. Just a few years later, in the Flax Warehouse and the rebuilt Cross Building, such trusses were employed in buildings of similar span.

The beams, columns and tie-rods provided the internal frame for the mill. The arches forming the support for the floors were formed by brick vaults springing from the triangular bottom flange of the beams. In this particular aspect of the building Ditherington may not have been innovatory, for brick arches had been used by Strutt in his earlier buildings at Derby, Milford and Belper. A single layer of bricks makes up each arch: in the outer parts of the arch the bricks were laid on edge, but in the central area, where the floor thickness was reduced, they were laid flat.

The mill of 1796–1800 at Ditherington represented a seminal change in structural engineering. It demanded a new approach to structural design and applied mathematical rationalisation to the performance of structural elements. It was the first to eliminate timber from the floor frames and the first to fully integrate the three components – beams, columns and tie-rods – into a complete framing system, one which also incorporated provision for a mill's power transmission system. As will become apparent in the following chapter, the iron frame did not simply support the floors, it also made provision for the transmission of power, which was itself partly determined by the layout of machines. The innovative nature of the building was recognised from its earliest years, for a description of 1803 stated that the iron frame components 'as well as supporting this extensive fabric, serve as principal instruments, thro' which the multiplicity of machinery in this vast undertaking performs.'[26] As to who may be credited with the leading role in the development of fireproof construction in these years, Bage himself was modest. Later, in 1811, he chose to play down his role in the close collaborative working which characterised this period. Instead he acknowledged Strutt's primacy by writing to him 'how much we are obliged to you for teaching us to make buildings fireproof'.[27]

The degree to which the structure of the mill of 1796–1800 was experimental as well as innovatory is evident in the fact that some of its features were not repeated in buildings erected only a very few years later. Ideas on iron framing and the structural integrity of fireproof buildings evolved rapidly in the period between 1796 and 1812 (the date of the rebuilt Cross Building at Ditherington), and the mill's methods of joining beams and columns, the profiles of the beams and its extraordinary roof structure were quickly superseded, both at Ditherington and elsewhere. Whether this was because the inherent flaws in the mill's structure were recognised or whether independent engineers came to different solutions cannot be judged on any evidence available today. After *c* 1800, cast-iron framed mills used more structurally sound methods of connecting floor beams around the column heads, and adopted types of joints which allowed for some movement in the beams.

The later development of iron-framed mills

Following the completion of the mill at Ditherington, the next stage in the development of the iron-framed mill appears, on the evidence of papers in the Boulton and Watt collection, to have been the extension to Salford Twist Mill constructed in 1800–1 (Fig 5.11).[28] Built for the cotton spinners Philips and Lee, although originally intended to spin flax, the mill was seven storeys high. It has not survived and some of its structural features are therefore unclear. However, it is known that the columns were of hollow cylindrical section and that steam heating was conducted through them, as also was the case in Houldsworth's Mill in Glasgow (built in 1804).[29] As at Ditherington, the mill had beams continuous over supporting pillars, but here the beams were of an inverted T-section. They were also of a rather greater span at 4.2m between the columns (but of lesser overall length). Surviving drawings indicate that the beam design was refined during the construction of this mill, and that an earlier design similar to that at Ditherington was rejected in

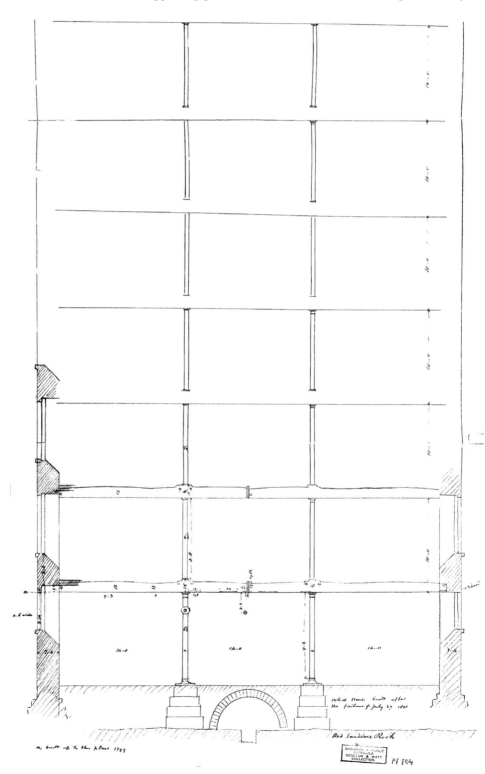

Fig 5.11
Cross section of an extension to Salford Twist Mill, as proposed in c 1800. This was the next iron-framed factory to be built after Ditherington. [Reproduced with the permission of the Library of Birmingham, Portfolio 804 (DP140544)]

favour of the inverted-T type. George Lee, one of the partners in the mill, was an industrialist with a strong interest in civil engineering, being in contact with William Strutt and other like-minded men, and it is likely that he was responsible for the framing design, with Boulton and Watt preparing drawings to his instructions. The inverted T-section was the beam form adopted in many of the iron-framed buildings of the following years. The change may indicate that superior casting techniques had been developed, which allowed the elimination of the triangular bottom flange used in the Ditherington Spinning Mill beams.

Charles Bage went on to design further fire-proof mills, not for Marshalls but for the Benyons who, along with Bage, were from 1802 negotiating to leave the partnership and set up on their own in both Leeds and Shrewsbury.[30] While still in partnership with John Marshall, Bage had continued with his experiments with the structural properties of cast iron. In a letter of 1801, he had provided Thomas Telford with details of tests on full-scale cast-iron beams, and from their dimensions it seems likely that these were prototypes for the Benyons' new mill in Meadow Lane, Leeds, completed in July 1803 (Fig 5.12).[31] Here the beams were of an inverted

T-section, simply supported over four bays of 9ft (2.7m) span, with a web of 11½in × 1in (292mm × 25mm) and a flange of 3in × 1½in (76mm × 38mm), supporting brickwork arches of 10ft (3m) span. Bage also recognised that the triangular 'skewback' flange used in the mill at Ditherington could be dispensed with. In August 1804 Simon Goodrich visited the Meadow Lane mill and sketched the beams from a description given to him by Matthew Murray's foreman. The connection of beams to columns provided lateral restraint but allowed a degree of rotation by means of wrought-iron 'shrink rings' fitted over lugs cast onto the sides of both beam ends. This connection arrangement, or something close to it, proved to be one of the most enduring in iron-framed mills over the next half century. One might speculate that it was a practical detail suggested by Matthew Murray, whose foundry was nearby and who supplied the steam engine for the mill and probably also the iron frame components. If this was the case, the modern practice of the structural designer sizing the steelwork elements and the contractor designing and detailing their connections can be seen to date back to the period of the first iron building frames. The sizing of the beams, however,

Fig 5.12
A wing of Benyon and Bage's mill in Holbeck, Leeds, prior to demolition in the 1950s. The cruciform section columns can be clearly seen. [Courtesy of Leeds Library and Information Service]

was certainly due to Bage, and his beam design method will be considered shortly.

On 5 January 1803, in reply to a letter from William Strutt, Bage confirmed his intention to call and see Strutt in a fortnight. If he did so (the correspondence does not reveal this), then the principal topic of their conversation was likely to have been a disastrous fire which occurred the following week:

About three o'clock this morning a most tremendous fire broke out in one of the large Cotton Mills belonging to Messrs. Strutt, at Belper, which raged with incredible fury, and in a few hours destroyed it, with all the valuable machinery, waterwheel etc. The cause of this dreadful accident is not yet known. The loss will be immense as no part of the property is insured.[32]

Strutt was naturally determined to rebuild in fireproof form, but to what design?

Perhaps recalling Strutt's use of timber beams in his earlier Derby mill, Bage wrote to him in May 1803 to offer that 'If on a balance of advantages & disadvantages you should at length prefer Iron beams, I should be glad to submit my reasoning on the strength and shape of them to your examination.'[33] At the end of August 1803 he duly sent to Strutt carefully prepared sheets on cast-iron beams and roof frames (Fig 5.13). He stated the basis of his method for determining the strength of beams thus:

The Strength of an Iron Beam in any section of it, may always be represented by the contents of some analogous solid; the principle of which is this, that the solid is composed of an infinite number of parallelograms, one side of which represents a horizontal line across the section, and the other side the perpendicular distance of that horizontal line from the top of the beam.

Fig 5.13
Charles Bage's methods for determining the strength of cast-iron beams, as described in a letter to William Strutt in 1803.
[Shropshire Archives 6001/26571/13 (DP163796)]

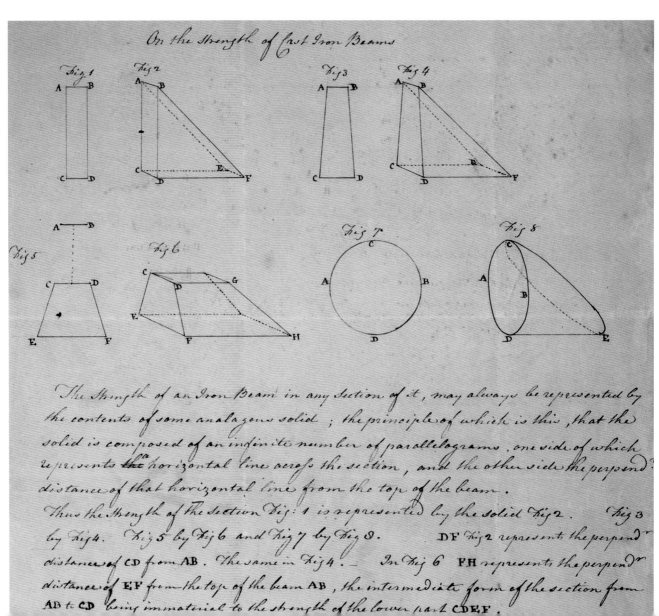

His analogous solid looks like the modern structural engineer's triangular stress block, and the parallelograms of which it is formed are similar to the stresses we consider to act on the longitudinal 'fibres' of a beam. In a covering letter Bage wrote:

My conscience has long upbraided me for having delayed to send you some theorems for ascertaining the strength of cast iron beams, but with the care of building two Mills, the ordinary business of the present Mill, and what has now become a matter of moment, attention to military marches and counter-marches, I really find but little leisure.[34]

The two mills to which Bage referred were both for the Benyons, the newly completed one at Meadow Lane in Leeds, and the other in Castlefields in Shrewsbury.

It is not possible to establish how influential Bage was in the design of Strutt's new mill at Belper, the North Mill of 1804. The precise structural relationship of this building to Bage's near contemporary work at Leeds and Shrewsbury is unclear, because only the Belper mill survives. What is known, however, is that the method of joining the beams by shrink rings at Belper differed from that adopted in the Meadow Lane Mill and that the cast-iron beams at North Mill had a triangular-section soffit, continuing the line of the brick arches down to a point.[35] These features, one might suppose, indicate that despite Bage's willingness to share ideas on designs for cast-iron beams, his recommendations were not all adopted and that Strutt was following an independent path. North Mill had the by now standard brick vaults supported by cruciform-section cast-iron columns.[36]

The development of cast-iron construction is also evident in the experimentation with mill roof trusses which characterised the first decade of the 19th century.[37] It is clear from Bage's work in the first years of the century that he was not satisfied with the roof form which he had devised for Ditherington Mill. Probably sometime during the protracted severance from Marshalls before 1804, he made and tested two alternative cast-iron roof frames at full-scale which, as has already been suggested, were in all likelihood prototypes for the Benyons' Meadow Lane Mill.[38] His first test was on a gabled roof frame made in two halves to span 38ft (11.6m) with supports at the centre and the ends. Writing in August 1803, he described

it as follows: 'The bottom beam or rail … 5¾in deep Section. All the other rails 4in deep Section. The side projection 1½in. Thickness of the pattern everywhere ¾ – the casting somewhat more.' Clearly the bottom beam was shaped with the support of brickwork arches in mind. Before loading the frame some careful adjustments were made to ensure that it was bearing evenly on all three supports. Then cast-iron pillar sections were balanced across the bottom and pigs of iron were laid on top of these. Probably the test was carried out at the foundry where the test frames had been made and where the materials used as weights were readily to hand. After a satisfactory test under a total distributed load of 501 hundredweight (about 25,000kg), Bage described what he did next: 'With a view to ascertain the effect of the center pillar sinking more than the walls, I lowered the support at B in a very gentle manner. On dropping ⅛ Inch the frames broke in pieces.'[39] Learning from this result, Bage conducted a second test with a half frame made to a different design of 19ft (5.8m) span, the intention being to test both the frame design and the method of support. No roofs are known to survive to this design, but the tests are indisputable evidence of Bage's awareness of the dangers of differential settlement for structures of brittle cast iron. Bage also sent a 'Plan of Iron Framing for a Roof where there are two pillars to support it'. Beneath the plan he put a hurried note to Strutt: 'Have you chosen your plan, & is it better?'[40]

The earliest known use of a cast-iron roof in a mill is that over William Strutt's North Mill at Belper, built in 1804.[41] The roof trusses can be described using terms familiar in timber carpentry. Principal rafters (curved at the foot to allow for greater headroom in the central floor area) are made up of two castings, bolted together, and rise only as far as a collar. The principal rafters are bolted to the tie-beams, and angled struts between the two are similarly bolted. The roof form appears to be something of a halfway house between timber construction and a more confident treatment of cast iron for structural purposes, and it does not correspond closely to Bage's description of his experiments with cast-iron trusses. Strutt appears, therefore, to have ignored the advice given by Bage on the design of the roof trusses.

The immediate successors of the North Mill roof departed from the legacy of timber construction and adopted a design based on that

Fig 5.14
*The roof of Barracks Mill,
Whitehaven, built in 1809,
has cast-iron principal
rafters, struts and purlins.
Its design is notably similar
to that of the roofs of the
Flax Warehouse and Cross
Building at Ditherington
(see also Fig 2.12).*
[BB98/16789]

tested by Bage in 1803. Houldsworth Mill in Glasgow, built in 1804, may have been the first to adopt this type of roof truss.[42] The next well-attested cast-iron roof of triangulated form is that over Barracks Mill, Whitehaven, built in 1809 for flax spinning by the mill owner Joseph Bell in partnership with John Bragg, a flax and hemp merchant (Fig 5.14).[43] The roof's design closely resembles Bage's description of his experimental roof trusses; it is not clear that he was responsible although his influence might be inferred from the similarity. In recent years a range of circumstantial evidence has come to light which suggests that Matthew Murray may have been responsible for the design (*see* below).

The culmination of the development of fireproof mills during this early period was probably Armley Mills in Leeds, now preserved as an industrial museum, which dates from a rebuilding of 1805–7 by Benjamin Gott. This building's cast-iron frame comprises a refined type of inverted T-section beams with cylindrical columns. These are probably the earliest surviving cylindrical columns in a textile mill. The beams incorporate cast-in fittings to support line shafting and are joined at the columns with side-mounted shrink rings. They may have been derived from the beams at Salford Twist Mill, and were clearly a development from the

beam and columns designs at North Mill, Belper. This floor structure was similar to that used at other fireproof mills well into the 1820s. The cylindrical columns were structurally more advanced than the cruciform columns used at Ditherington and other flax mills up to *c* 1820 and beyond.[44] The roof of Armley Mill is of conventional timber construction, although this may be a replacement of the 1820s.[45]

The Flax Warehouse and the Cross Building at Ditherington

Both the Flax Warehouse and the Cross Building at Ditherington are iron framed and it is therefore important to establish their dates in order to identify their place in the sequence of early iron-framed structures. There is no doubt about the Cross Building, documented as having been rebuilt in 1812. The date of the Flax Warehouse, however, is less clear. It has been suggested that it was built in 1805, making it the third earliest surviving iron-framed building in the world. The date is derived from insurance valuations, that for 1805 listing a 'Heckling Shop and Flax Warehouse', with the added detail that 'the lower Rooms [are] heated by Warm Air from a Stove underground'. It seems likely, however, that the building in question is the first, pre-fire, Cross Building, known to have been used in the early years for both heckling and storage (*see* Chapter 8). The sketch plan made in 1811 by Boulton and Watt in connection with the installation of a gas plant at the mill depicts the pre-fire Cross Building with a stove attached to its north side (*see* Fig 8.1). The conclusion must be that the description in the 1805 valuation relates to the first Cross Building and not to the Flax Warehouse which survives today. A later date of *c* 1810 for the construction of the Warehouse is suggested by accounts of 1811 which itemise £2,360 against the Flax Warehouse, a large sum which appears not to be a valuation of stock but instead expenditure on construction. If the revised date is accepted, the Warehouse takes its place rather lower down the hierarchy of iron-framed buildings.[46]

The iron frame of the Flax Warehouse illustrates the progress that had been made in the production and use of structural iron since the construction of the Spinning Mill in 1796–1800 (Figs 5.15 and 5.16). In the Warehouse, the details of the individual components, the method of assembly and the design of the roof all reflect a greater understanding of iron-

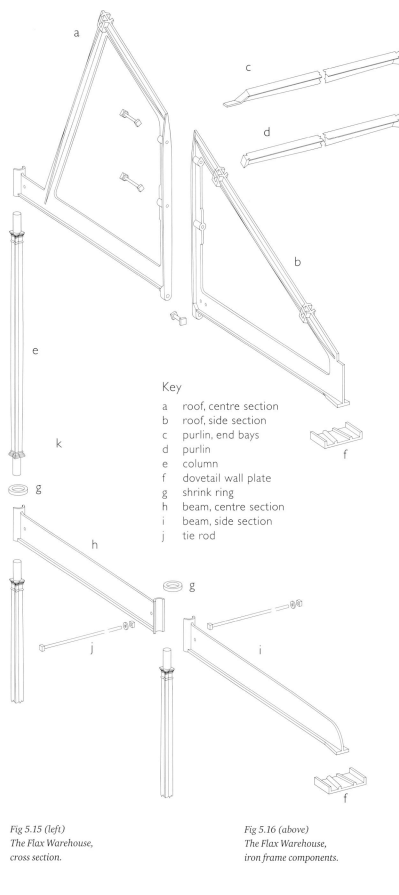

Key

a   roof, centre section
b   roof, side section
c   purlin, end bays
d   purlin
e   column
f   dovetail wall plate
g   shrink ring
h   beam, centre section
i   beam, side section
j   tie rod

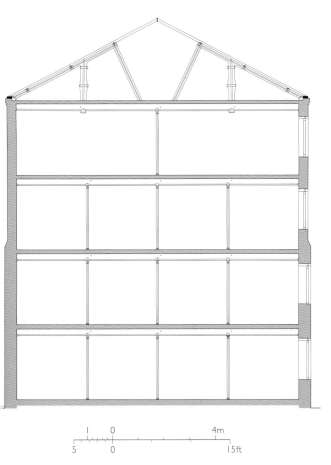

Fig 5.15 (left)
The Flax Warehouse,
cross section.

Fig 5.16 (above)
The Flax Warehouse,
iron frame components.

Fig 5.17 (right)
Similar columns and beams to the Flax Warehouse were used for the warehouse of the Benyon's Castlefield Factory, built c 1810 and later converted to housing. [DP163740]

case are of 1in- (25mm-) diameter circular section with threaded ends secured by nuts.

The columns in the Warehouse are of similar slender scantling to those in the Spinning Mill but have a thinner and more pointed cruciform cross section which is continued into the delicately moulded capitals and bases. The distinctive shape of the columns appears to have aesthetic rather than functional value and is also seen in columns in the Cross Building, in the surviving former warehouse (c 1810) of the Benyons' Castlefields Factory and in Barracks Mill, Whitehaven (1809) (Fig 5.17).[47] It contrasts with the simpler classical embellishment typical of the cylindrical columns being introduced at mills such as Armley Mills in this period.[48]

The Flax Warehouse has a gabled cast-iron roof structure integral with the rest of the iron frame, assembled from two pairs of castings forming queen-strut trusses supporting cast-iron purlins and wooden rafters. The intricate castings incorporate T-section tie-beams, of similar cross section to the floor beams, with joints that are bolted together to form cruciform-section outer struts. The upper edge of what is in effect the principal rafter includes dovetail housings for three ranks of cast-iron purlins, which are of T-section with a convex web. The use of dovetail joints in the roof and in the ends of the floor beams, which fit into housings in cast-iron plates in the walls, seems to be a relic from the traditions of timber building.

The Cross Building was rebuilt shortly after the fire of 1811 (Fig 5.18). Its iron frame and roof are notably similar to those of the Flax Warehouse, although its ground-floor columns bear more resemblance to the columns in the ground floor of the Spinning Mill, albeit with a different form of embellishment to the capitals (Fig 5.19). The building is about 1.8m narrower than the Warehouse, requiring just two rows of columns with three-piece floor beams and fewer roof castings. In the roof, the trusses comprise only a single casting on each side, contrasting with the Flax Warehouse, where two castings are used. In what appears to be an early modification, short T-section rafters have been slotted onto the middle rank of purlins. These are bolted at the apex and incorporate dovetail housings for an upper rank of purlins (Fig 5.20).[49] When considered in the context of the rapid development of iron construction, the similarities in the iron frames of the Flax Warehouse and Cross Building are further evidence that the buildings are probably close in date.

framed construction, and the ironwork itself is of far higher quality. Notable differences in the overall design of the frame were the use of four-piece floor beams, jointed at the heads of the three rows of columns, and the fully framed gabled roof structure.

The floor beams show several key improvements over those in the Spinning Mill. Better casting techniques enabled lighter beams to be made to more consistent dimensions. The beams in the Flax Warehouse are of inverted-T cross section, the form that came to be widely used until the mid-19th century, but with a narrower bottom flange than later examples and a web with a horizontal top edge. The exposed underside of the flange has a distinctly convex cross section, an early feature which was later abandoned, indicating that the beams were cast in closed moulds. At the joint with the columns the beam ends have a semi-circular yoke which clamps around the circular head and base of the columns. The yokes are held together by a single wrought-iron shrink ring, which presumably allowed some movement in the joint. At the outer ends of the beams the bottom flange widens into a dovetail which fits into a housing on a cast-iron wall plate, a great improvement to the use of timber pads in the Spinning Mill. Longitudinal wrought-iron tie-rods connect the beam webs to either side of the columns, but in this

Facing page

Fig 5.18 (top left)
Cross Building, cross section. Profiles at scale ×2.

Fig 5.19 (bottom left)
Flax warehouse and Cross Building, elevations of cast-iron columns (see also Figure 5.7).
A: Flax Warehouse ground floor
B: Flax Warehouse upper floors
C: Cross Building ground floor
D: Cross Building upper floors

Fig 5.20 (right)
Cross Building, iron frame components.

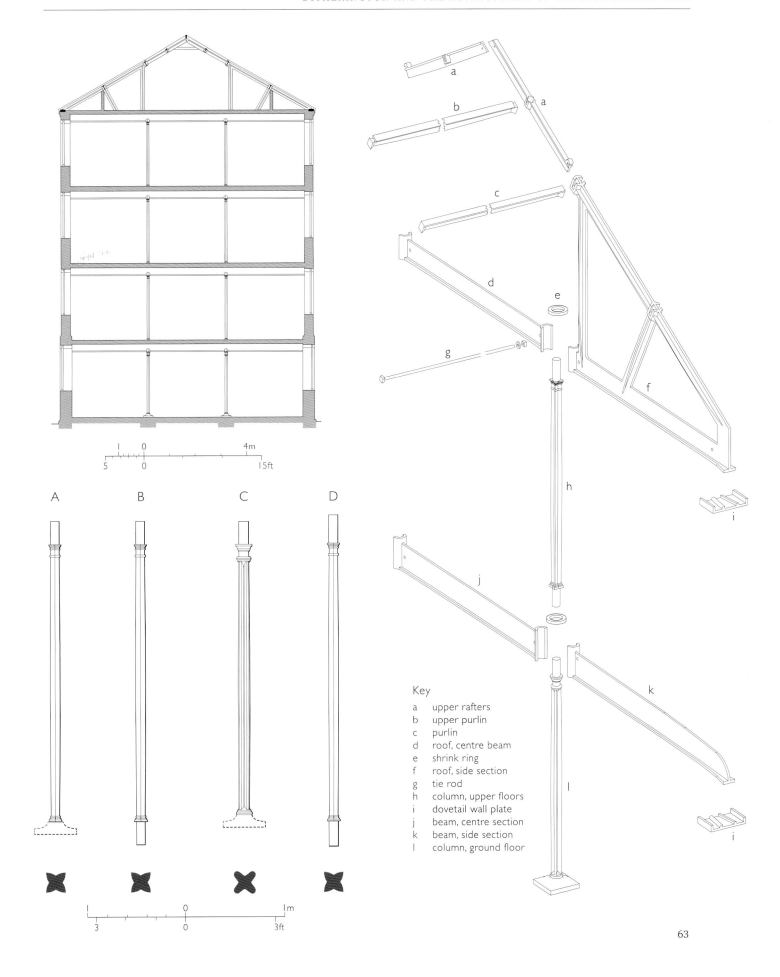

5 0 4m
0 15ft

A   B   C   D

3 0 1m
3 0 3ft

Key

a   upper rafters
b   upper purlin
c   purlin
d   roof, centre beam
e   shrink ring
f   roof, side section
g   tie rod
h   column, upper floors
i   dovetail wall plate
j   beam, centre section
k   beam, side section
l   column, ground floor

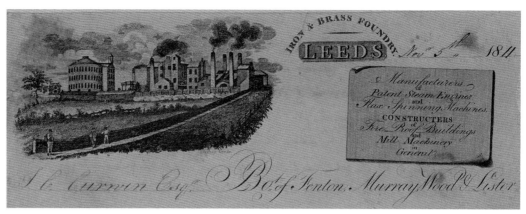

Fig 5.21 (above)
Matthew Murray of Leeds,
pioneering engineer and
former partner of John
Marshall, may have been
responsible for the iron
frames of the Flax
Warehouse and the
rebuilt Cross Building.
[W Smith, ed, 1882, Old
Yorkshire, 3 (London:
Longman, Green and Co),
facing page 261]

Fig 5.22 (above right)
Letter heading of Matthew
Murray's Round Foundry
in Leeds, "Constructers [sic]
of Fire proof Buildings",
dated 1811.
[Cumbria Archive Service,
Curwen Collection D/Cu2]

Builders of the first generation of fireproof mills

Study of the first generation of fireproof flax mills shows clear patterns and variations.[50] Common features are cruciform-section cast-iron columns and beams of similar form. Variations include the form of the roof trusses. However, the role of the key designers remains obscure and a matter for speculation. We have seen that just a few years after the first mill at Ditherington was built, George Lee and Boulton and Watt built an iron-framed mill at Salford, with significant differences in the design of its cast-iron components, and that William Strutt developed his ideas in his North Mill in 1804.

Bage clearly remained important after the construction of the Spinning Mill at Ditherington, and it is difficult to believe that his 1803 experiments with roof trusses did not influence later work. There is, however, circumstantial evidence that Bage's ideas might have been taken forward by Matthew Murray, John Marshall's former employee and at this time a leading iron founder, machine maker and engine maker (Fig 5.21). By 1803 Murray was already constructing fireproof buildings, such as a range at his Round Foundry, which was certainly present by that date and employed cast-iron beams, cylindrical columns and brick vaults (Fig 5.22). By 1811, and perhaps for some years before, the firm of Fenton, Murray and Wood was advertising itself as 'Constructers of Fire Proof Buildings'.[51] In Scotland it is documented that a Leeds firm, almost certainly Fenton, Murray and Wood, built the fireproof West Ward Mill in Dundee in 1807, for which they certainly supplied the engine and textile machinery for James Brown of Cononsyth who had travelled to Leeds to do the deal. The original mill at Broadford, Aberdeen, was

put up in 1808 for Scott and Brown, the latter in all probability the same James Brown. Again, Fenton, Murray and Wood supplied the engine and most of the machinery and are the best candidates for the supply of the iron framing and plans.[52] Some contemporary mill buildings in England are so similar in constructional detail that they too have been attributed to Fenton, Murray and Wood. They include Barracks Mill in Whitehaven (built in 1809), the 1814 Campion's Mill in Whitby, and, within the Marshalls mill in Leeds, a warehouse of 1806 and the 1815–16 Mill C. These buildings have in common cruciform column sections and inverted T-section beams with a narrow flange.[53] Furthermore, it is known that Fenton, Murray and Wood provided steam engines for the Whitehaven and Whitby mills.[54] Although documentary evidence is lacking to ascribe the buildings to a single hand, their structural similarities and Fenton, Murray and Wood's supply of engines and other machines make a strong case for Murray's responsibility for their design. Could Murray also have designed the Flax Warehouse and Cross Building at Ditherington? His long association with John Marshall and the use in the Ditherington buildings of identical structural forms are strong indications that this was the case.

Iron-frame construction after 1815

Charles Bage was the first to develop a fireproof cast-iron framed building, but following his death in 1822 he was largely a forgotten man outside Shrewsbury, and it was left to others to bring it to perfection. By the early 1820s iron frames for buildings had become a significant part of the work undertaken by Thomas Cheek

Hewes of Manchester, a leader in the millwrighting trade and employer of up to 150 men, who erected mills throughout Britain and fitted them out with machinery. Fairly quickly the hollow or solid circular section replaced the structurally less efficient solid cruciform as the preferred form of cast-iron column, but it was not until the 1830s that Hewes' former employee William Fairbairn used a significantly improved form of cast-iron beam in a mill building.[55] Fairbairn had first made tests on cast-iron beams in 1824 while working on a fireproof extension to Benjamin Gott's Armley Mill in Leeds. Afterwards, he enlisted the help of the Salford mathematician and physicist Eaton Hodgkinson to carry out an experimental investigation of cast-iron beam forms, and Hodgkinson published the results in the influential *Transactions of the Manchester Literary and Philosophical Society* in 1830.[56] While Bage and Strutt had corresponded privately on design matters and had thereby inadvertently limited the dissemination of knowledge, this publication placed the principles for the 'Hodgkinson Beam' immediately in the public domain, setting out a formula for the design of beams for different load and span conditions which could be used by any mill or railway engineer. Ten years later, with experimental research work again supported by Fairbairn, Hodgkinson published a design method for the cast-iron column, still of value in the structural assessment of buildings today, for which he was awarded the Gold Medal of the Royal Society.[57] Fairbairn himself was not aware of Charles Bage as the pioneer of the iron building frames that he was improving. Unwittingly Fairbairn helped draw a veil across Bage's role when, in his widely read book *On the Application of Cast and Wrought Iron to Building Purposes* he wrongly described George Lee's Salford Twist Mill as the first cast-iron framed building.[58]

The further development in the use of cast and wrought iron is illustrated at Ditherington in the Stove House and the Dyehouse. The surviving part of the Stove House, probably dating from the 1830s, includes an internally framed west wall of cast-iron columns and beams, and a roof with cast-iron trusses and purlins. The iron frame has cylindrical columns and I-section beams joined by short spigots clamped by shrink rings (Fig 5.23). The frame formerly supported the west ends of the floor beams which spanned the building. These beams have since been removed but were probably identical to the surviving attic floor beams, which are of I-section with a fish-bellied bottom flange. The cross-sectional form of the beams and the beam-to-column joints are typical of those which replaced the iron frames of the early 19th century. The roof trusses comprise two-piece queen-strut castings bolted at the centre and supporting a single rank of cast-iron purlins. This is a less complicated structure than the roofs of the Flax Warehouse and Cross Building but retains similarities in its method of assembly (Fig 5.24).

Fig 5.23
The framed internal wall of the Stove House, showing the use of I-section beams joined with shrink rings to cylindrical columns, typical construction of c 1840.
[DP163675]

Fig 5.24
The c 1840 cast-iron roof of the Stove House.
[DP163687]

Fig 5.25
The lightweight, wide-span roof of the rebuilt Dyehouse, dating from the early 1850s.
[DP163673]

The roof of the Dyehouse is of a much more sophisticated design, and represents some of the latest thinking in the construction of metal roofs in the 1840s and 1850s (Fig 5.25). It is a wide-span lightweight design which uses the different structural properties of cast and wrought iron. Roofs of this type had begun to be used for smaller textile mill buildings in the 1820s, but were also developed for other innovative structures, including railway stations.[59] The roof comprises slender, rectangular-section wrought-iron principals with ornate angled compression struts and a system of wrought-iron ties (Fig 5.26). The components are connected by a variety of bolted joints, contrasting with the dovetail housings used in earlier cast-iron roofs. The principals are bolted to cast-iron valley gutters mounted on tall cast-iron columns along the centre of the double-depth building. The aim was probably to create an unobstructed, well-lit interior, but the iron construction may also have been prompted by the hot and humid conditions in the Dyehouse. The slate roof covering is wired to iron laths that are located in slots in the upper edges of the principals, thus avoiding the use of wood completely.

By the 1840s a significant number of fireproof mills had been built with internal iron frames. In certain circumstances a small minority of these buildings proved to be dangerous. In October 1844 the collapse of a five-storey fireproof cotton mill at Oldham in Lancashire killed 20 people and prompted investigation by a Royal Commission reporting to Parliament.[60] The collapse was not the first of its kind, as in 1827 a similar event at a mill in Salford had resulted in 17 deaths. The progressive collapse mechanism in these two cases, and in most other cases since, involved the failure of one element, either a floor arch or a cast-iron beam, in an upper floor. This local failure caused part of one floor to fall onto another, and that in turn to fail, with the potential for the collapse to progress to ground level. William Fairbairn, one of the experts who investigated the 1844 Oldham mill collapse, maintained that such buildings would be safe provided they were properly designed and constructed. Fairbairn went on to design the cast-iron framed structure of Salt's Mill in Yorkshire, one of the largest and finest fireproof mills. Once fabricated wrought iron, with its ductile qualities, had become a practical and economically viable proposition, Fairbairn advocated its use in lieu of brittle cast iron in critical parts of the iron frame.[61]

By the mid-19th century opinion about the safety of fireproof construction was divided. One articulate critic was James Braidwood, chief of the London Fire Brigade.[62] Braidwood realised that the term 'fireproof' was a misnomer, and that when heated in prolonged exposure to a severe fire ironwork would lose its strength, and could be more dangerous than slow-burning heavy timbers. Braidwood also advocated compartmentalisation, that is, the subdivision of buildings into separate fireproof compartments to limit the spread of fire. Even for conditions of normal use, Braidwood favoured timber construction as it would deform visibly and thus provide warning of overload, and he argued that it required a lesser level of expertise for safe construction than an iron-framed fireproof building. In 1866 Charles Young published a detailed critique in which he likened the fireproof building to a blast furnace designed for the burning of its contents.[63] In many warehouses the amount and value of combustible contents was greater than that contained within a mill or factory, and fires were more likely to get completely out of control, even where the building itself was incombustible. Braidwood himself was killed in 1861 in the Tooley Street disaster, a fire that swept through many warehouses over a period of 15 days and was widely regarded as London's worst since the Great Fire of 1666.[64]

For some decades in the late 18th and early 19th centuries, textile mills were at the forefront of the development of new forms of construction, an evolution impelled by the need to limit the losses caused by destructive fires. The pivotal decades either side of 1800 can best be seen, perhaps, as a period of intense innovation and experimentation, with different forms of fireproofing and iron-framed construction developed in rapid succession by Midland and northern industrialists and engineers. Bage's Spinning Mill at Ditherington represents an

important stage in the development of the iron-framed mill, for it was the first building to achieve a floor frame of incombustible materials. Some of its features may, with hindsight, be seen as an engineering blind alley; its design was rapidly superseded, even in buildings constructed only a few years later within the same site, and over time its structural weaknesses became apparent.

In a long view, however, the mill can be seen as a vital step in the development of fully-framed multi-storeyed buildings of widely differing types, from industrial to commercial and residential structures. It is, perhaps, not too far-fetched to trace the ancestry of the modern skyscraper to Bage's design at Ditherington. The lessons learned from dealing with issues of fireproofing in early textile mills – essentially, how to achieve a structurally sound internal metal frame – informed later developments in building design and engineering to permit the construction of safe multi-storeyed buildings. A key part of these later developments was to extend the internal frame of the fireproof mills into a fully three-dimensional structure, in which the frame supported the walls as well as the floors. By the 1890s, the use of steel and concrete enabled the construction of more complex fully-framed buildings, reaching a much greater height than had previously been possible. Bage's mill at Ditherington constitutes an important step in the evolution of the structural techniques which today are applied across the globe and which have produced the landscape of our modern cities.

Fig 5.26
The Dyehouse roof represented some of the latest thinking in roof design, combining wrought-iron principals with ornamental cast-iron compression struts and wrought-iron tie-rods.
[DP163669]

6

Steam power at Ditherington Mill

RON FITZGERALD, PAUL MURRAY THOMPSON AND MIKE WILLIAMS

Ditherington Mill is one of the very earliest survivors of a new generation of steam-powered textile mills built during the 1790s at a time when water power was still the normal means of driving a factory. Steam freed millowners from the need to be located on a watercourse capable of providing sufficient power to work machinery, and permitted development away from rivers, which in some parts of the country had become highly valuable and congested industrial corridors. Lying away from any natural watercourse, the site at Ditherington offered no potential for the use of water power and investment here was a clear demonstration of confidence in steam as a means of driving a mill of substantial size. The power system, including both the engines and the transmission of power to working floors in the mill, was closely related to the quantity and arrangement of machinery and was, therefore, a fundamental influence on the design of the building. This chapter will trace the development of power in the mill from its first years, when a Boulton and Watt engine was purchased, through different stages of additions and replacements, culminating in the 1870s in the installation of new engines of a more modern design. The early part of the story is illuminated by correspondence between John Marshall, the Benyons and Bage and Boulton and Watt of Soho, Birmingham, the dominant supplier of steam engines before 1800, and by drawings held in the Boulton and Watt archive (Fig 6.1). The first decades of the mill's operation demonstrate vividly the limited power of the early engines, which imposed limitations on the size of the mill and were one of the main reasons for the construction of the complex in several phases (*see* Chapter 4). The early story also illustrates the developing competition in steam engine construction, with Fenton, Murray and Wood of Leeds challenging Boulton and Watt for supremacy by circumventing patent restrictions and building engines of superior construction.

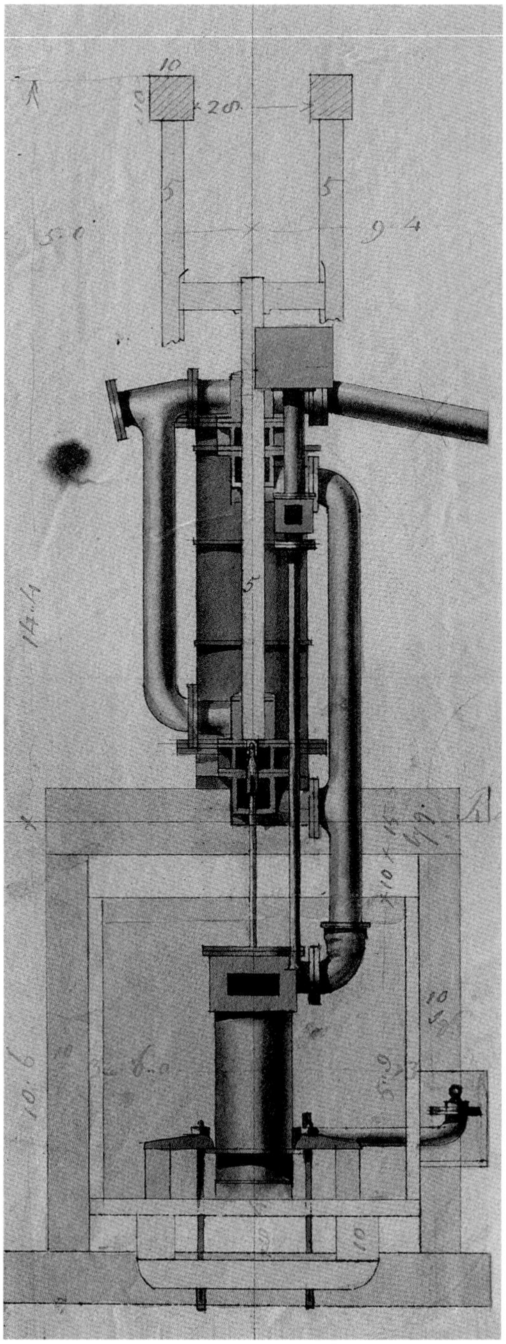

Fig 6.1
End view of the cylinder, steam pipes and condenser cistern installed with the 1797 engine at Ditherington Mill. [Reproduced with the permission of the Library of Birmingham, Portfolio 131–133 (DP163757)]

The early development of steam power

The forerunners of the exclusively steam-powered textile mill were a generation of factories that used simpler atmospheric engines to raise water for waterwheels, a combined form of power that was still common in the 1790s in mills in both rural and urban areas.[1] These factories were equipped with either Savery or Newcomen 'atmospheric' engines with low-pressure 'haystack' boilers (Fig 6.2). The atmospheric engines could not easily produce the rotative motion that was needed to drive mill shafting, but they did have a proven record, mainly in mines, for pumping water. By recycling water they could, therefore, permit longer continuous operation than was the case in mills which relied solely on water power, and the technique enabled more mills to work in locations where the water supply was limited (Fig 6.3). The combination of an atmospheric engine combined with a waterwheel was still being recommended by millwrights in the early 1790s, when John Marshall used this method at his flax mill in Holbeck, Leeds.[2]

Complete freedom from reliance on water power depended on the development of a reliable steam engine capable of providing the rotative motion essential for directly driving a power transmission system. A number of engineers, most notably James Watt and James Pickard, introduced a series of modifications that, by the 1780s, began to produce engines which, although initially unreliable, promised the desired result. Perhaps the best known of Watt's innovations was the separate condenser, first patented in 1769, by which steam was extracted from the cylinder and condensed in a separate iron vessel.[3] The condenser enabled Watt's engine to use steam more efficiently and

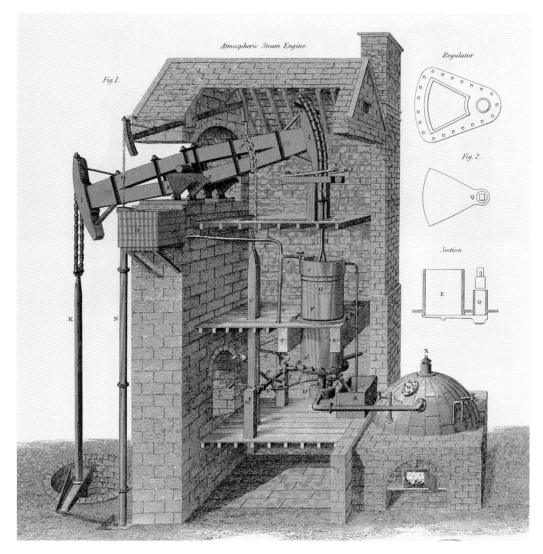

Fig 6.2
A Newcomen pumping engine of the type commonly used in mills and mines before the development of the rotary beam engine. Note how a chain connects the pump rod to the working beam.
[From Rees 1819–20 (DP163824)]

Fig 6.3
This illustration of Bedworth Worsted Mill, Warwickshire, c 1791, includes a rare depiction of a Savery engine with a haystack boiler used to pump water to an internal waterwheel. [Warwickshire County Record Office, CR136/V66 (DP137768)]

to produce a stronger vacuum in the cylinder, increasing the power of the engine while reducing its consumption of coal. Rotative motion was achieved by two rival methods: the crank, patented by James Pickard in 1780, and the sun-and-planet, patented by Watt in 1782.

Engines of this type were still atmospheric, since the weight of the atmosphere was the agency by which the piston descended. A further improvement by Watt allowed steam to enter the top and bottom sides of the piston alternately, giving two power strokes – up and down – worked by steam. This 'double acting' principle was one of the key features of Watt's patents, improving both the power output and the regular motion of the engine. A patent granted to Watt in 1784 introduced the 'parallel motion', which converted the vertical move-

ment of the piston rod to the curved motion of the beam end. This was essential in a double-acting engine in which the upstroke of the piston transmitted drive to the beam.[4] Patents protecting both Pickard's and Watt's developments began to lapse in the mid-1790s, but the final – and crucial – one, which protected the separate condenser, expired in 1800.

The partnership between Matthew Boulton, the Birmingham metal goods manufacturer, and James Watt was formed in 1775. By the mid-1780s condensing steam engines built by the firm were being installed in textile mills either as the sole source of power or providing direct drive in tandem with a water-powered installation. The earliest known example of a direct-acting condensing steam engine was provided in 1785 by Boulton and Watt for a

Papplewick (Nottinghamshire) cotton mill, where it worked alongside a waterwheel, but proved temperamental.[5] In the same year, or possibly the following, a more successful direct-acting engine – with a tiny output of only 4 horsepower – was installed in another Nottinghamshire mill, and in *c* 1789 an engine of 8 horsepower was provided to drive Peter Drinkwater's cotton mill in Manchester.[6] Despite continuing improvements, there were only 15 Boulton and Watt engines working in textile mills in 1790 and most of these had proved troublesome.[7] After 1790, however, further improvements in performance led to more widespread adoption of the reciprocating steam engine: by 1800, over 100 Boulton and Watt engines had been installed in textile mills.[8] When in 1796 John Marshall came to add a mill to his Holbeck factory, and when in the same

year the mill at Ditherington was being built, he turned exclusively to steam power.

Textile mill engines of the type originally installed at Ditherington differed markedly from the larger, more complex and much more powerful engines developed later in the 19th century (Fig 6.4). The Watt engines were usually located in internal engine houses, and their working beams, structural framing and even parts of the foundations were of heavy timber. The working beam was either supported by a timber frame or pivoted on a cross wall, referred to as a 'Lever Wall' in the drawings prepared by Boulton and Watt for their customers. The latter was similar to the method of supporting the working beams of mine pumping engines. After *c* 1800 the method of supporting the working beam changed, the lever wall being replaced by a heavy cast-iron beam, often styled in the form

Fig 6.4a
Reconstruction of a rotary condensing beam engine, mid-1790s, of the type developed by James Watt and installed at Ditherington.
[Based on drawings in Reproduced with the permission of the Library of Birmingham, Portfolio 44–45]

Fig 6.4b
Detail of Fig 6.4a showing parallel motion valve gear.

Fig 6.4c
Detail of Fig 6.4a showing parallel motion.

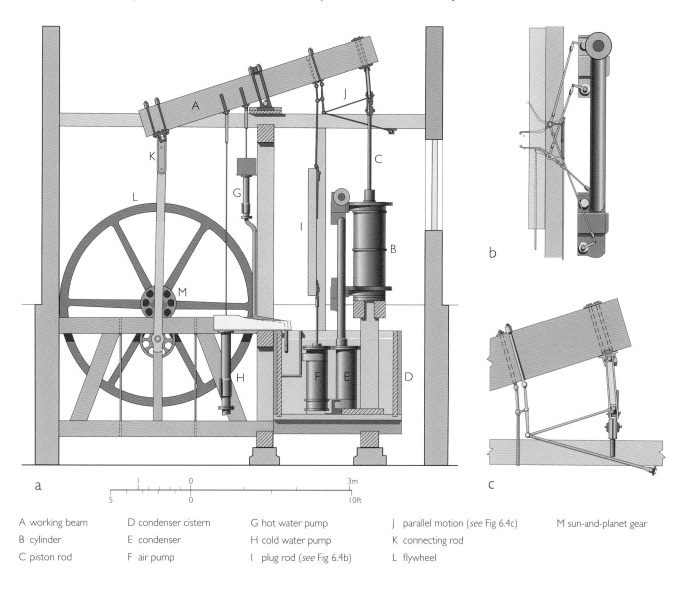

a

A working beam	D condenser cistern	G hot water pump	J parallel motion (*see* Fig 6.4c)	M sun-and-planet gear
B cylinder	E condenser	H cold water pump	K connecting rod
C piston rod	F air pump	I plug rod (*see* Fig 6.4b)	L flywheel

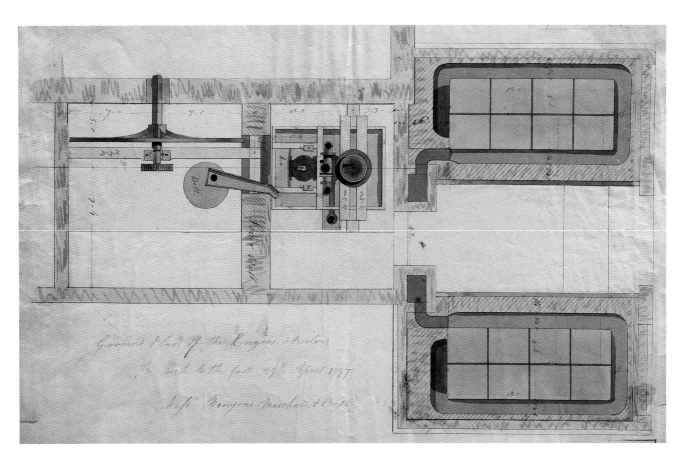

Fig 6.5
Plan of the proposed engine and boiler installation at the south end of Ditherington Mill, 1797.
[Reproduced with the permission of the Library of Birmingham, Portfolio 131–133 (DP163756)]

of an entablature and supported by two or more cylindrical columns. The piston in the upright main cylinder worked one end of the working beam directly and was connected to it by a parallel motion. The valves were set up to allow the steam to expand in the cylinder after the inlet valve was closed, and this 'expansive working' extracted more energy from the steam and was hence more economical.[9] The valves were activated in sequence by pegs on a rod suspended from the working beam, a technique that was copied from the earlier atmospheric engines.

The boilers of early steam-powered mills also differed considerably from the more familiar later types, being smaller, of different design and construction, and producing steam at a much lower pressure. The circular haystack boilers associated with early atmospheric engines were at first used by Boulton and Watt, but by the early 1790s the firm was specifying rectangular 'wagon' boilers for their mill engines. Up to the early 19th century the boilers were often located, somewhat precariously, in the basement of a mill, but at larger mills such as Ditherington they were usually sited in external boiler houses, close to a supply of water; in the case of Ditherington, this was the

newly constructed canal alongside the site (Fig 6.5). The boiler houses incorporated brick flues connecting each boiler to the chimney, which in this period was usually built into the main structure of the mill, with the top section extending above the roof. The early boilers were neither reliable nor long-lasting, and were often replaced within 10 years.[10]

The procedure for the manufacture and installation of the early engines reflected the fragmented nature of the engineering industry in the late 18th century, but the order for the first engine for Ditherington coincided with a significant reorganisation of engine production by Boulton and Watt. Prior to 1796 the facilities and skills needed to manufacture the parts of an engine were widely dispersed, and the firm itself only manufactured the more complex items such as the valves, mostly at its Soho Manufactory, first located in Handsworth, Birmingham.[11] Some of the major parts, notably the cylinders and piston rods, were contracted out to specialist firms: the cylinders were made in John Wilkinson's ironworks at Bersham, near Wrexham, using a patented boring machine, and the piston rods in either Cumbria or London.[12] Other components, including work by carpenters, millwrights, smiths and foundries, were contracted to businesses in the area where the engine was assembled. The assembly and commissioning of the engine at the mill were supervised by a trusted engineer employed by Boulton and Watt. From 1796 onwards engine production became more centralised, as the firm moved from Handsworth to establish one of the first integrated engineering works at their new Soho Foundry in Smethwick. Thereafter, more of the engine parts were made in the foundry, and after the firm acquired their own boring machine it was also able to make its own cylinders.[13] Significantly, Fenton, Murray and Wood, one of Boulton and Watt's main rivals, established another pioneering works at the same time. Their Round Foundry, built from 1796 adjacent to John Marshall's flax factory in Leeds, became Marshalls' main supplier of engines and machinery after the patent restrictions on Watt's engines ceased in 1800.[14]

In addition to the engine and boilers, the third part of a textile mill's power system was the means of transmitting power from the engine to the machinery on the different floors of the building. In early mills this was achieved by using horizontal and upright main shafts and lighter shafts, pulleys and belts, the last taking drive to individual machines. Evidence of early power transmission systems is generally sparse, with few surviving documents and with physical remains often removed or obscured in later alterations. The methods used, however, seem to have been more diverse than in later mills, reflecting the experimental nature of millwrights' work in this formative period and the more varied approach to early machinery layouts (see Chapter 7). Cast iron was used for the main shafts in some mills by the mid-1780s, but heavy timber shafts continued to be the more widely used option up to the mid-1790s.[15] A general indication of the types of shafting used at Ditherington is provided by evidence of John Marshall's first mill at Holbeck, which in 1795 contained a variety of powered shafting (presumed to be horizontal line shafts) including cast-iron 'tumbling shafts' in the roving room, 'drum shafts' for the spinning machines and a combination of 'Shafts, wheels, drums and belts' for the cylinder frames.[16] In some cases machinery in early mills was powered by pulleys from an overhead shaft, in others from an underfloor shaft with either belts or light vertical shafts passing through the floor.

The 1797 power system at Ditherington Mill

The initial requirement for power at Ditherington was for an engine to drive machinery in the first stage of the Spinning Mill completed in 1797. The story of the purchase and erection of the original 20-horsepower engine, to be installed at the south end of the Spinning Mill, is well documented in correspondence between Marshalls and Boulton and Watt. In May 1796, even before the land in Shrewsbury had been bought, the company wrote to Boulton and Watt stating that an engine would be required for their new mill:

> You will oblige us by advising the price of a 20 horsepower Engine & what would be deducted from the price for each item as under being furnished by ourselves viz – Boiler, Fly Wheel, Rotative-Shaft, Connecting Link, Sun & Planet Wheels. We expect we shall want the engine about 1st Feby next, but shall be obliged to you to send us plans for the Engine House soon as you can as we shall begin of the building immediately.[17]

A contract appears to have already been prepared as an agreement survives dated 1 May 1796. The contract reveals the Soho company's desire to protect their patents and reduce the likelihood of industrial piracy. It stipulates that Messrs Boulton and Watt would contract for their concurrence and assistance

> towards the said Thomas Benyon, Benjamin Benyon, John Marshall and Charles Bage setting up, erecting completing and finishing at their own cost and charge at Shrewsbury aforesaid a steam engine of the improved construction according to his, the said James Watt's invention [and] … according to the plans, directions and materials to be furnished by the said James Watt and Matthew Boulton … the said Thomas Benyon, Benjamin Benyon, John Marshall and Charles Bage shall and will truly pay … at the expiration of three months after the day on which the materials hereinafter mentioned … be delivered … the sum of Seven Hundred, forty and two pounds lawful money … that the said engine shall not previously to the twenty fourth day of June in the year One Thousand Eight Hundred be removed out of the kingdom of Great Britain to any place

beyond the seas nor to any place more than ten miles distant from the said place of erection without the consent of the said James Watt and Matthew Boulton ... the said engine when finished and in good and proper order shall be able to work the said machinery with a power or force equal to that which twenty horses acting together do commonly exert ... James Watt and Matthew Boulton [will] furnish and provide an experienced workman to direct and assist in the erection of the said engine.[18]

From the schedule of parts to be supplied by Boulton and Watt it is clear that the building of the engine was to be carried out in the same way as that adopted for the engine supplied in the previous years to Marshalls for their Leeds mill (Fig 6.6). The connecting rod with bolts and pin, the sun-and-planet motion, connect-

Fig 6.6
Extract from the original contract and specification for the 1797 engine at Ditherington, dated 1 May 1796.
[Reproduced with the permission of the Library of Birmingham, MS3147/2/10/109]

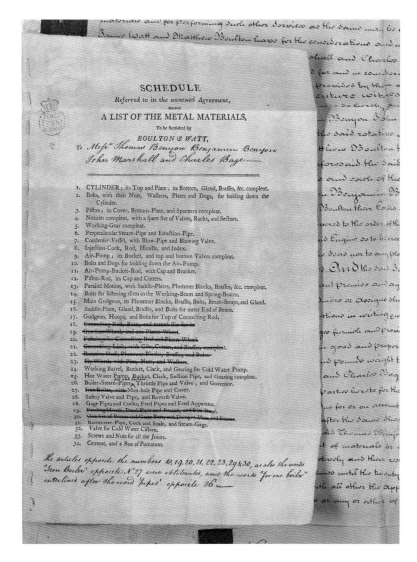

ing links with gibs, cottars and brasses, the rotative shaft with plummer blocks and the flywheel were all to be provided by Marshalls. They were also to be responsible for the boiler and its fittings.[19] It is not known to whom Marshalls intended to resort for these materials. The iron for the mill itself was to come from Hazledine's foundry (although whether from his newly established Longden Coleham site is not clear), and it is therefore possible that Hazledine also provided the parts for the engine. However, at just this time Fenton, Murray and Wood were in the process of building their new works. They advertised on 11 July 1796 that they were in a position to cast items of the above description, although whether their machining capacity was available is not stated.[20]

A week later Marshalls accepted the Boulton and Watt price of £742 but asked for a rebate of £10 to £12 on account of the connecting rod, which they were also to supply. The delivery date was revised to 1 March 1797. They added that as the plans supplied for the Leeds engines had been returned to Boulton and Watt, new drawings were required. The location of the Engine House was to be decided by Marshalls but they requested that Boulton and Watt supply details of the openings in the walls and the heights above engine datum of such openings.[21]

The final conveyance of the mill site was not completed until February 1797, but a letter to Boulton and Watt dated the 16th of that month indicates that the building was nearly finished by that time.[22] The partners urged delivery of the engine. The contract delivery date had been passed when the following letter was sent to Soho:

Shrewsbury. March 22nd 1797.
We are favoured with yours of the 16th Inst. inclosing sundry drawings of parts for the engine. As it is intended that the boiler should be in place by the time the engine arrives we wish for such instructions as will enable us to put it up ... Inclosed is a drawing of the engine house chimney and intended Boiler House.[23]

The parts for the engine were despatched in the last days of June and first days of July. They were carried by canal from Birmingham to Stourport, then by the River Severn to Shrewsbury, arriving on site during early July.[24] Boulton and Watt sent Joseph Varley as their site erector and the engine was commissioned by 11 September 1797.[25] Two wagon-type boilers were installed in an external Boiler House, adjoining the internal Engine House at the south end of the Spinning Mill, and were probably in place before the engine arrived.[26] The completion of Shrewsbury's new fireproof flax mill was reported in the local newspapers, and, although they do not specifically state when it started working, the mill and the engine were certainly in use by November 1797.[27]

The superb drawings prepared by Boulton and Watt for Ditherington, together with the correspondence between them and Marshalls, give a good indication of the form of the engine. The drawings were produced to guide its assembly, however, and do not provide a record of what was actually built, although the plans of the Engine House itself indicate that the dimensions of the extant building are very similar to those of the original design.[28] Most of the smaller engine details are not shown, including the valve gear, parallel motion and governor,

although the likely form of these components can be deduced from contemporary drawings of similar Boulton and Watt engines. The Engine House itself appears to be a slightly conservative design for 1797. Its cross wall to support the working beam was more commonly seen in earlier atmospheric engines, and by the mid-1790s Boulton and Watt engines often used a heavy timber frame to support the beam.[29]

The main cylinder, located in the cylinder chamber at the east end of the Engine House, had a bore of 23¾in (600mm) and was mounted directly above the condenser cistern to the east of the cross-wall, close to the boilers and the water supply from the nearby canal (Fig 6.7 and *see also* Fig 6.1). The working beam, pivoting on the cross-wall, was of timber, 10ft (3m) long, 16in (400mm) wide and 22½in (570mm) deep, and drove the main shaft in the ground floor of the mill via a sun-and-planet gear. In the larger western chamber of the Engine House, a cast-iron flywheel of 14ft (4.2m) diameter

Fig 6.7
Proposed elevation of the 1797 engine and section of the Boiler House at Ditherington. Note the lever wall supporting the working beam and separating the cylinder chamber (left) from the flywheel chamber. [Reproduced with the permission of the Library of Birmingham, Portfolio 136–137 (DP163755)]

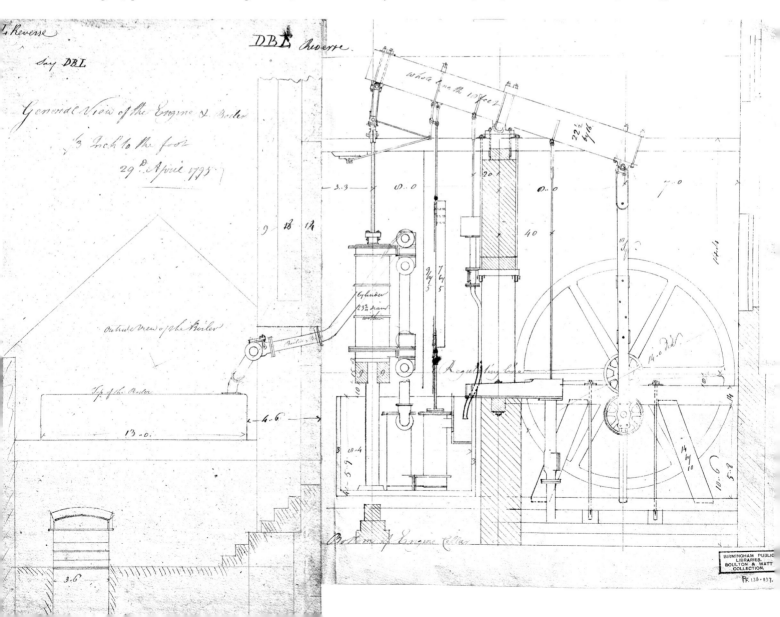

occupied the full length of the room and was mounted on the main shaft, close to the north wall. The flywheel was supported on a substantial timber trestle.

The drawings indicate that the external Boiler House was attached to the east side of the mill in the space next to the canal. It had internal dimensions of 8.5m north–south by 5.6m wide and contained two 3.9m-long boilers stoked from the east end, which was probably open. A central walkway between the boilers gave access to a door into the Engine House. The brick flues from the boilers converged above the door into a single chimney attached to the mill wall (Fig 6.8 and *see also* Fig 6.5).

The Ditherington engine was notably similar to the Boulton and Watt engine erected a year earlier at Marshalls' mill in Leeds, suggesting that the Leeds mill provided a model for the Ditherington installation. The Leeds engine

was slightly larger, at 28 horsepower, but also had a 14ft (4.2m) flywheel, a similar-sized condenser cistern and a cross-wall dividing the Engine House into two chambers. The main difference between the two engines was in the position of the Boiler House.[30]

The 1797 engine was replaced in *c* 1810, so no mechanical parts or timber structural supports remain today. The Engine House has, however, survived and its features demonstrate a close correspondence to the Boulton and Watt drawings. It was attached to the south end of the mill in a bay which also contained the internal staircase, and still retains the room layout shown in the original drawings, with the smaller cylinder chamber to the east and the larger flywheel chamber to the west (Fig 6.9). An opening approximately 1m square (now blocked) in the wall dividing the Engine House from the mill ground floor indicates the position of the

Fig 6.8
Cross section of the 1797 boiler installation, facing the east elevation of the Spinning Mill.
[Reproduced with the permission of the Library of Birmingham, Portfolio 131–133 (DP163759)]

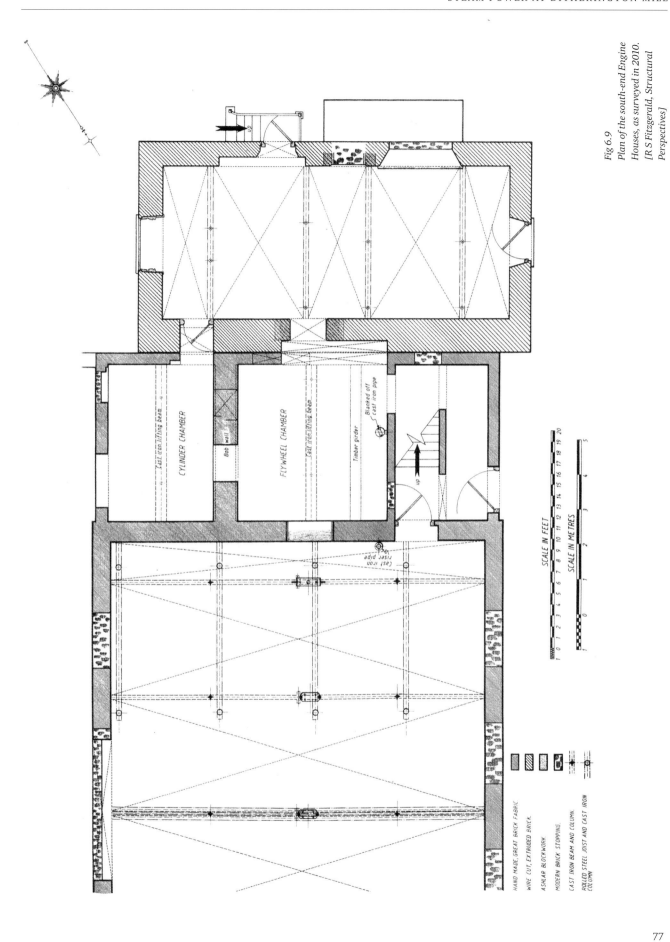

Fig 6.9
Plan of the south-end Engine
Houses, as surveyed in 2010.
[R S Fitzgerald, Structural
Perspectives]

CYLINDER CHAMBER

Cast iron lifting beam

Bob wall

FLYWHEEL CHAMBER

Cast iron lifting beam

Timber girder

Blanked off
Cast iron pipe

up

Cast iron
riser pipe

SCALE IN FEET

0 1 2 3 4 5 6 7 8 9 10 11 12 13 14 15 16 17 18 19 20

SCALE IN METRES

0 1 2 3 4 5

HAND MADE, GREAT BRICK FABRIC

WIRE CUT, EXTRUDED BRICK.

ASHLAR BLOCKWORK

MODERN BRICK STOPPING.

CAST IRON BEAM AND COLUMN.

ROLLED STEEL JOIST AND CAST IRON
COLUMN

Fig 6.10a (right)
Interior of the 1797 Engine
House, facing north with
the blocked opening of the
flywheel shaft on the left.
The wall to the right is the
lever wall of the original
Engine House.
[DP163665]

Fig 6.10a (right)
Interior of the 1797 Engine
House, facing north with
the blocked opening of the
flywheel shaft on the left.
The wall to the right is the
lever wall of the original
Engine House.
[DP163665]

Fig 6.10b (far right)
Interior of the 1797 Engine
House, facing south. The
ceiling was inserted
sometime after the beam
engine was removed. The
arch probably dates from
the addition of the 1810
Engine House, which can
be seen through the door.
[DP163666]

former flywheel bearing. The absence of evidence for a spur wheel or gearing suggests that the engine was installed well above ground level, with the flywheel centred on the main shaft supported by the columns in the ground floor of the mill (Figs 6.10a, 6.10b).

Power transmission in 1797

Most early 19th-century mills used a main upright shaft to transmit power to line shafts on each floor, but at Ditherington there is no clear evidence either in the Engine House or at the south end of the main rooms in the mill that such a system was employed.[31] Instead, in 1797 the 20-horsepower engine may have provided direct drive only to a horizontal shaft on the ground floor. The ground-floor columns on the centre line of the mill, in line with the opening to the Engine House, incorporate rectangular housings for what was probably a shaft of unusually weighty construction (*see* Figs 1.2, 5.4 and 5.7). It seems probable, therefore, that this, rather than an upright shaft, was the primary means of transmitting drive in the mill in its first phase.

Within each floor, the mill's iron frame provides indications of the importance of the power transmission system to the mill's designer. Throughout the building the castings of both the floor beams and the columns have features to support the power transmission

system. Like the central columns on the ground floor, those on the third floor incorporate distinctive rectangular housings for the support of a second main horizontal drive shaft. The lack of similar evidence on the other levels suggests that power was transmitted to them from the two main horizontal drive shafts through the intervening brick-arched ceilings. It has been suggested that machinery could have been powered from vertical shafts located in circular recesses within the main beam joints, but in the ground floor these are partially covered by the column heads.[32] Other evidence suggests that belts passing through the brick vaults may have been the original means of taking drive from one floor to another. The vaults have numerous slots in the brickwork (now filled in) through which belts might have passed, although the slots seem to have been less well defined than in some other textile mills.[33] James Marshall's notebooks of the late 1820s mention the presence of 'belt holes', some of which were blocked when machines were relocated, presumably referring to holes in the ceilings and floors (*see* Fig 6.13).[34]

The floor beams also have clear evidence, recently exposed during building work, of the original distribution of power around the mill. The beam castings include a series of distinctive projections, square in plan, which appear to have been bolt housings, probably related to the original machinery layout (*see* Fig 5.5). The projections contain a vertical square hole running through the full height of the beam, which suggests they were intended for bolting some kind of bracket to the underside of the beams. In the ground and third floors, pairs of identical projections still contain the bolts that secure the central columns to the beams. At the time of writing, more of these projections are being exposed as the concrete floors are removed, but it is clear that they were arranged in a different pattern in each storey. Those in the outer parts of the floors may have supported light shafts or belt pulleys transmitting power from the central shafts to the outer rows of machines, a form of power transmission that was probably used in Leeds flax mills in *c* 1820.[35] The differences in the castings of beams on the various floors raise very interesting questions about the planning and building of the mill: one might conclude that beams were cast for each floor with specific machine layouts in mind and that the beams were seen not simply as elements of the floor frame but also as integral parts of the power transmission system, designed with a preconceived and fixed layout of machinery in mind. If so, the construction of the mill can be seen as a fully integrated process from the planning stage through to completion. This may have been appropriate for the first years of the mill's operation, but later changes in the numbers, layout and types of machines are likely to have made the first arrangement redundant within a short time. Later mills adopted more flexible and less intricate means of supporting drive shafts within their working floors.

Marshalls, Boulton and Watt, and Fenton, Murray and Wood 1797–1801: subterfuge and evasions and the installation of the north-end engine

The commissioning of the Boulton and Watt engine in 1797 was followed immediately by the planning of a second engine to power the Spinning Mill, ultimately installed in 1800. The question for Marshalls was: should they go back to Boulton and Watt for a second engine; or should they look for alternatives? These years coincided with the progressive lapsing of Boulton and Watt's restrictive patents, and therefore the cessation of their punitive premiums, and with the arrival on the scene of strong rivals in the field of engine making.[36]

The company defended itself vigorously in expensive litigation against a number of new competitors, some of whom were beginning to produce engines of superior construction. John Marshall's long acquaintance with Matthew Murray (a relationship cemented by early financial backing for Murray) gave him the option of using the local Leeds man for his new engines, for Murray was emerging at this time as Boulton and Watt's first successful adversary in steam-engine building.[37] The purchase of new engines for Marshalls' mills in Holbeck and Shrewsbury illustrates the commercial battles being fought out in many different areas in these years. Marshalls may have genuinely left open the possibility of turning once again to the Birmingham company, but the firm may also always have had Murray in mind for the supply of the new engines. The story of these years is on the one hand that of fierce protection of legal rights, and on the other procrastination and opportunism.

The correspondence between Boulton and Watt and Marshalls in the months following the installation of the 1797 engine concerns payment for that first engine, but the issue of drawings prepared by Boulton and Watt and retained by Marshalls also arises. Three letters, written within days of each other in November 1797, press for the return of the drawings. The last is revealing:

> Our drawings having in some instances fallen into the hands of persons who have endeavoured to employ them to our detriment we have found ourselves under the necessity of requesting them in all cases to be returned. Under these circumstances we are confident you will excuse us for not departing from a regulation essential to our interest & especially as its deviation is not of material moment to yourselves.[38]

Marshalls continued to prevaricate and not until 16 December 1797 did they write assuring Boulton and Watt that: 'The drawings you may be assured have never been out of our possession nor copied. In a day or two you will receive them by coach.'[39]

That the drawings had not been copied is almost certainly untrue. Two months previously James Lawson, the area agent and engine erector employed by Boulton and Watt, who was often in Leeds, had written to Matthew Robinson Boulton, Matthew Boulton's son:

Liverpool 7th Oct 1797

At Shrewsbury I waited on Mr Bage & found Mr Benyon also, they were very civil to us & promised to remit in a day or two which I suppose they have done before this time. The drawings Mr Bage will not give up without you insist on it, by letter, which I should not think of much consequence as I have no doubt they are already copied – and I have seen some drawings of Murray's – which were copies of the Leeds Engine.[40]

Matthew Murray's part in these proceedings was already clear to Boulton and Watt. There can be no doubt but that Murray was intent upon embarking on steam engine building at least from the beginning of his new factory in Water Lane. His first years in Leeds as engineer responsible for the development of the textile machinery and ensuring the smooth operation of Marshalls' mills had probably excluded much consideration of wider engineering possibilities. Despite this, it is reasonable to suppose that he had been involved with other aspects of the development of the mills, including the steam engines and millwork. The short period at the commencement of his career spent at his first independent workshops, at Wortley, in south Leeds, was probably still dominated by Marshalls' machine demands, particularly as Murray and Wood were called on to replace the machinery destroyed in the 'B' Mill fire at the Holbeck site. The move to a new purpose-built works in Water Lane, however, marked a change in the scale and extent of operation.[41] The central parts of the new factory were to be two foundries, not usually associated with the manufacture of specialised textile machinery until much later. The ground for the factory that was later to become the Round Foundry was purchased in February 1796 and almost immediately Murray, with his partner Wood, was advertising for greensand moulders. In July, the foundry was complete and a further advertisement informed the public that it was capable of casting parts for steam engines among a list of other products.[42]

There then ensued a protracted dispute between Murray and Boulton and Watt, which centred on Murray's alleged piracy and evasion of patent restrictions. Boulton and Watt's first indication of steam engine activity came in a letter from George Hawks of Newcastle dated 31 July 1795. Having been disappointed in a lead time quoted by Boulton and Watt, Hawks had visited the Low Moor Iron Works near Bradford and found the company busy making a cylinder and air pump on Watt's principle for Messrs Murray and Wood in the belief that the work had been sanctioned by Boulton and Watt.[43] The dispute escalated in connection with engines that Murray was proposing to provide for Fischer and Nixon's woollen mill in Holbeck and for a mill in Hull. In November 1797 John Rennie, the great civil engineer, wrote to Soho from London to inform Matthew Robinson Boulton that '[t]here is a Mr Murray, an Engine Maker at Leeds, who is now erecting a 40 horse & sixteen horse steam Engines – this man makes very free with your patents – would it not be well to look sharply after him.'[44] Boulton concluded from Rennie's letter that he was referring specifically to the expired parallel motion and sun-and-planet wheel patents but was equally aware of the danger that might arise from Murray adopting the central patent of the separate condenser, due to expire in 1800. He wrote to James Lawson in Leeds instructing him to pursue discreet enquiries, while acknowledging that should Murray be building engines with a view to adding the separate condenser after the patent had expired there was little that they could do.[45] In this, Boulton correctly perceived Murray's intention but he was prepared to resist this eventuality for the remaining period of the patent's term. As far as Murray himself was concerned, Lawson was to avoid a direct confrontation but if engaged in conversation to extract as much information as possible. At the same time Lawson was to

> tell him that his Engines will not be licensed, that his proceedings will be watched & the slightest encroachment upon our property inexorably punished. This delivered with becoming gravity, will at least render the fellow cautious & perhaps make Marshall more so – God willing, that Presbyterian Knave shall smart for this one day or other![46]

The threat posed at this time by Murray to Boulton and Watt's hitherto unchallengeable supremacy was clearly apparent to the Soho firm. Watt's patent for the double-acting cycle and the sun-and-planet gear expired in March 1796. Pickard's patent for the crank also ceased two years earlier. Watt's parallel motion patent expired in August 1798. The Boulton and Watt master patent for the separate condenser remained in force, protected by a 25-year extension, but it was due to expire imminently, in April 1800. By a policy of prevarication, Murray and his most important client, John Marshall, hoped to weather the interval with engines in service awaiting the time when Boulton and Watt's monopoly no longer existed. Writing to Matthew Robinson Boulton in June 1798, James Watt Jnr conceded that

> Murray is pushing himself everywhere into employment for Mill Work & Engines & he must succeed by dint of impudence, if not by ability as I see no way of opposing him but by countenancing the establishment of a small foundry here in opposition to him as his local advantages must otherwise deprive us of all chance of competition. The fellow reports that he has still orders for several Engines, but I believe they are all in buckram as no names are mentioned except Marshalls for whom he says he is to erect one here and one at Shrewsbury.[47]

It was against this background that the next generation of engines built for Marshalls began to take shape. James Watt Jnr's letter makes it clear that Marshalls were planning to extend the Shrewsbury mill power plant, a plan that would result in c 1800 in the installation of an engine of 40 horsepower. The run-up to installation, however, was not smooth and has, fortunately for later historians, left a substantial paper trail that vividly illustrates the tensions and febrile atmosphere which characterised the last years of Boulton and Watt's hegemony.

The first shot in the protracted campaign was fired by Marshalls. Perhaps as a stratagem or to determine a competitive price for a new engine for their Shrewsbury mill, the company wrote to Boulton and Watt on 26 March 1798 (Fig 6.11):

> We expect in 9 or 10 months to want a 30 horsepower Engine & we request you will inform us what your terms would be for an Engine at that time. As it will not work much more than a year under the patent you will of course make a difference on that account. We doubt not that you will see the matter in its proper light & will agree with us in thinking that the purchasers of your Engines should not be placed in a worse situation than those who erect common engines now with an intention of adding your improve-

ments at the expiration of your patent. We shall certainly prefer an Engine of yours if we can have it without making too great a sacrifice of our own interest.[48]

Boulton and Watt quoted a price of £1,261 and allowed no concessions in regard to the imminent lapse of their patent rights.[49] A second enquiry followed from Marshalls in June when they asked for prices of engines in the range of 24 to 35 horsepower and delivery times for a 20- or 30-horsepower engine.[50] Boulton and Watt replied with estimates for 24- and 30-horsepower machines, stating that they did not find it worthwhile to build intermediate sizes.[51] The metal parts as usually furnished by them, with one boiler, for a 24-horsepower engine, were priced at £1,132. and for a 30-horsepower engine at £1,261. Delivery time was six weeks to two months for a 30-horsepower

Fig 6.11
Letter from Marshall, the Benyons and Bage to Boulton and Watt, 26 March 1798, stating their interest in purchasing a second engine for Ditherington Mill. [Reproduced with the permission of the Library of Birmingham, MS3147/3/416/23]

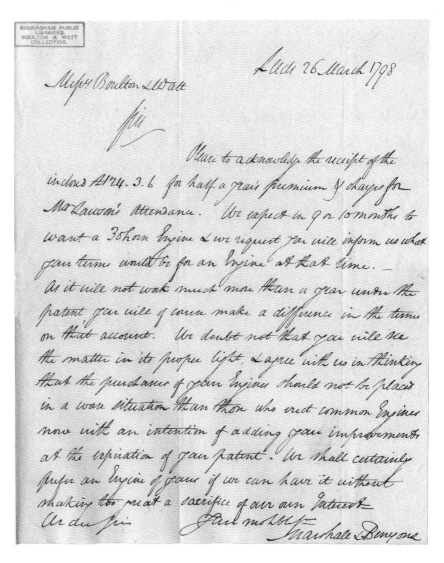

engine and slightly longer for the other. As far as the largest engine produced by Boulton and Watt was concerned, a later internal Soho note gives a breakdown of the price:

Our total price of a 40 horse is

	1,720	1.	00.

The estimated cost of the materials

	927	18.	00.
" " " " " steam case	23	16.	00.
" " " " " boiler	195	00.	00.
	1,147	14.	00.

Difference between

1,720	1.	00.
1,147	14.	00.
572	7.	00. premium

but the estimated cost of the materials generally exceeds their real cost & comprehends besides a manufacturing profit. You may compute 20% profit upon this item in addition to the former percentage say £185 which together with £572.7 = £757.7.[52]

Murray's prices were already known to Boulton and Watt through Lawson's endeavours in November 1797:

10 Horse Engine Cylinder 18 ins Dia 4 feet stroke
27½ strokes per minute   £300

20 Horse Dº 24 In Cylr 5 ft stroke
23 strokes per minute   £470

40 Horse Dº 33 In Diam 7 ft stroke
16 strokes per minute   £834

The price of the 20-horsepower engine was subsequently reduced to £378.[53] These prices included everything except the brickwork, giving Murray's engines a very substantial price advantage over Boulton and Watt's, especially as the premium payable on use of the Watt patent was not applicable to the Leeds-built engines. The 40-horsepower engine was available from Murray at less than half of the price of the equivalent Boulton and Watt engine. Nor was there any doubt about the quality of the Murray engines. Writing to James Watt Jnr in June 1798 Matthew Robinson Boulton said: 'We are fully aware that Murray from his superior workmanship is likely to become a more formidable rival than any of his predecessors in the piratical list & whatever doubts may be entertained in regard to the policy of licensing Fischer's Engine [for the mill in Holbeck] none

exist upon the necessity of using every exertion to perfect & improve our work.'[54]

Murray's position was steadily strengthening, a fact of which he was undoubtedly aware. Boulton and Watt, however, remained obdurate in their protection of the intellectual and manufacturing rights to their engine and in their resistance to any licensing overtures from rival manufacturers. Marshalls had 'written some artful letters to solicit our consent to Murray's applying our principles to a 40 Horse Engine for them, and do not seem disposed to take a refusal, which however they must digest, or go to Law with all speed.'[55]

In late February 1799 Boulton and Watt wrote formally rejecting Marshalls' proposal that the new Shrewsbury engine be built under license:

By you favour forwarded to us from Soho we [observe] that Messrs Murray & Wood of Leeds in consequence of the [ ] connection [ ] which we hitherto considered unfounded rumour [ ] are about to erect for you a 40 Horse Engine so constructed as not to [ ] with our patent and yet be convertable in [ ] [ ] Engine at pleasure in answer to the above & to your subsequent request, we shall only remark that having as you know at a great expense made preparations for supplying the public with Engines constructed to our Principles We see no reason why Messrs Murray & Wood should be made partners to our Parliamentary Privilege.[56]

There was, however, little that they could do to prevent the engine being constructed in such a way that the separate condenser could be added immediately after the patent's expiry, as the dispute about the Fischer's Holbeck mill engine had demonstrated.

Marshalls appears to have persisted in trying to secure a licence for Murray and a further letter followed from Boulton and Watt:

Soho 1st April 1799
We intended our letter of the 22nd Feb to be a full and final answer to your letter referred to in it and considering it in that point of view, we did not conceive any further reply necessary to the repetitions in Yours of the 25th of the same month.

To your late favour of the 23rd Ult we also think we cannot reply better than by referring you to our first letter upon the subject, in which we have intended clearly to express our dissent from your proposal. We have neither leisure at present, nor do we feel ourselves at all called upon to [explain] further the motives of our refusal. Whenever we see occasion ample cause shall be assigned.

Your reasons for preferring Mr Murray's services to ours are no doubt satisfactory to yourselves, however ill founded they may appear to us. We however deem any investigations of that subject here to be quite superfluous.

As the Expiration of the Term of our exclusive privileges, has (like everything else about it) been made the subject of ungenerous Cavil, we shall refer you to the prolonging Act of Parliament itself, which you will find printed in the statutes at large. It received the Royal Assent in June 1775.[57]

It must be construed from the last paragraph of this letter that Marshalls had asked Boulton and Watt a direct question concerning the separate condenser patent expiry date. In this he was almost certainly being disingenuous and the lofty reply seems to acknowledge this. Marshalls apparently repeated their question in September to which Gregory Watt tendered an identical response.[58]

Writing from Manchester to Soho two months later in November 1799, Lawson was able to offer further information:

I was with Mr Gott at M Murray's shops (about some mill work he is doing for them) and found they were at work on Air Pump, Buckets – of diff' sizes – and they report at Leeds that Mr Marshall means to put one to his new Engine at Leeds immediately. It is also said the materials are sent to alter the Engine at Shrewsbury – and also to Hull. Gavin will, I have no doubt, keep a good look out at Leeds & will inform you.[59]

Lawson's reference to Marshalls' Leeds engine related to a 30-horsepower engine added to the Holbeck factory's 'B' Mill by the end of 1799 and driving 500 more spindles by that time. The letter also shows that the engine built by Murray for the Shrewsbury mill had been delivered and that the condensing equipment had been sent. It would also seem that the Hull engine which had been the subject of earlier correspondence was about to receive its condenser.

Thus, as the 18th century drew to its close, Boulton and Watt were forced to concede that their monopoly had ended. There is no further correspondence in the company's archive concerning the Leeds or Shrewsbury engines and thereafter both firms challenged the other's patents, action which resulted in the 1803 withdrawal of Murray's 1801 patent for engine improvements. In 1802 the Soho firm took Murray seriously enough to attempt to plant a spy in his works in a reversal of the roles of poacher and gamekeeper. A year later they bought land adjacent to the Round Foundry in an attempt to prevent any future expansion of the site.[60]

Construction of the north-end power system

The correspondence between Marshalls and Boulton and Watt demonstrates that a second engine was planned for the Shrewsbury mill as early as March 1798, only a few months after the Soho firm's 20-horsepower installation had begun working. The question arises why a new engine might have been required. The most likely explanation is that the engine at the south end of the Spinning Mill was only capable of powering the first stage in the phased construction of the building. Fabric evidence in the completed mill points strongly to the conclusion that the Spinning Mill was built in two rapidly successive stages, almost certainly planned from the outset (*see* Chapter 4). Completion of the first stage (the south end of the building, comprising six full bays and two short bays, together with the attached power plant) allowed production to begin at the earliest opportunity, while construction of the second stage (the north end, comprising 10 full bays) continued. The large increase in the mill's productive capacity represented by the extension required at least a commensurate supplement to the power plant. The addition of a new engine of 40 horsepower – double that of the first engine – answered this need.

The available evidence suggests that the new engine was by Fenton, Murray and Wood of Leeds and that Murray intended to add a condenser as soon as Watt's patent expired.[61] The absence of any reference to the engine as a Soho product in the Boulton and Watt archive confirms that it was not of their manufacture. Reference in the Soho company correspondence (*see* above) to the fact that Murray had sent materials to Shrewsbury seems certain to relate to the supply of a new engine rather than to repair or adaptation of an existing engine. Marshalls' decision to buy engines from other suppliers after 1800 suggests that Boulton and Watt struggled to be competitive on price after their patent restrictions were removed, although it is known that the company continued to be major engine manufacturers. The choice of Fenton, Murray and Wood must also have been influenced by John Marshall's earlier collaboration with Murray and the continuing association between the two firms, a relationship which endured until both Murray and Wood had died.

Both the early Ditherington engines – that is, the Boulton and Watt engine of 1797 and the Murray engine of *c* 1800 – were mentioned in an 1803 description of the mill, and the north-end Engine House is shown on the 1811 site plan (*see* Fig 8.1). The latter also shows a Boiler House containing two boilers and a square chimney attached to the north side. The north engine is variously referred to as being of 40 or 45 horsepower up to 1820, when it was replaced by one of 56 horsepower.[62] This replacement involved the partial or total rebuilding of the Engine House, destroying evidence for the details of the earlier engine. The proportions of the north-end Engine House on the 1811 plan suggest, however, that it contained a beam engine, and the absence of indications for a cross wall or lever wall in the mill fabric indi-

cates that the working beam was supported by an entablature or a timber frame, either of which represented a development from the type of engine house at the south end of the mill. Other features of the *c* 1800 Engine House, such as the means of supporting the main cylinder or the flywheel shaft, were removed in the alterations of *c* 1820.

North-end power transmission

The north-end engine was probably always connected to an upright shaft in the end bay of the Spinning Mill. The ceiling vaults in the end bay include a large blocked trap for an upright shaft. The sides of this trap are formed by cast-iron beams of similar design to those in the rest of the mill, specifically having a cast-in skew-back, suggesting that the trap is original to this second phase of the building.[63] An upright shaft was present in this position in the 1830s, when the notebook of James Marshall, son of John, included a sketch plan of the power system in the north end of the third storey (Fig 6.12).[64] The sketch shows an upright shaft operating at 32rpm, driving side shafts attached to the end wall, which in turn were geared to line shafts running along both side walls. The system was to be set up to turn the line shafts at 250rpm, to drive newly installed wet-spinning machines. The presence in the top storey of heavy cast-iron brackets probably of mid- to late-19th century date, designed to support the top of an upright shaft and a pair of side shafts, suggests that the transmission system described by James Marshall remained in this position throughout the later working life of the flax mill.

The physical and documentary evidence thus suggests that the power transmission system was planned from the outset for a mill of phased construction. It seems likely that the smaller south-end engine drove the ground-floor main shaft (ultimately along the full length of the completed mill), supported by columns with purpose-built castings to carry it, while the north-end engine was used to power the main horizontal shaft on the third floor, supported by columns with similar castings, this second horizontal shaft being driven by an upright shaft located in the mill's north-end bay. It is likely that drive was taken from both horizontal shafts to the intermediate and top floors of the mill by belts running through the floor.

Fig 6.12
Sketch plan of the upright shaft and adjoining line shafts in the north end of the Spinning Mill, from the notebook of James Marshall, 1830. The note to 'fill up all the belt holes' suggests that the new line shafts would replace belt drive through holes in the mill floors. [Leeds University Library Special Collections MS200/37, 22–23 (DP163774)]

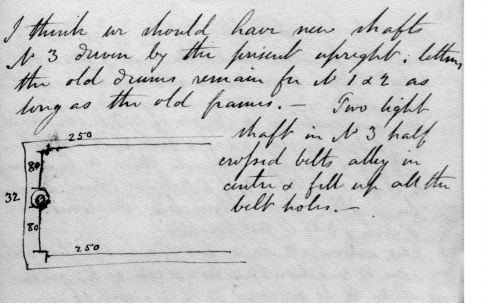

The *c* 1810 south-end engine

The two engines powering the mill by *c* 1800 had only a short life. The early type of Boulton and Watt engine was, with its extensive use of timber, built of a material that was inherently unstable. In engines of this type the timber frame – with its numerous joints – warped and became distressed and the timber connecting rods twisted, causing catastrophic misalignment of the sun-and-planet gear. The main beam was also a frequent source of problems. For this reason, and also because the power of steam engines increased radically in the first years of the 19th century, few 18th-century Boulton and Watt-type rotative engines survived for any great length of time. In mills in all branches of the textile industry the continuing mechanisation of processes created demand for increased power. At Ditherington, the mechanisation of a number of processes – heckling from *c* 1809, roving a little later and wet spinning from the late 1820s – necessitated changes to the power installations of 1797 and *c* 1800.

First to be replaced was the Boulton and Watt engine at the south end of the mill. The addition of a new 60-horsepower beam engine here, part of the reorganisation and expansion of the site from *c* 1810 to *c* 1812, is recorded in an account book in the Marshall archive, with an entry dated 7 January 1811 including £3,940 for the 'Bottom end engine and house'.[65] This was a substantial amount, exceeding that paid for either the purchase of the Hanwood estate, where the bleachworks was built, or the construction of the Flax Warehouse, indicating both the engine's size and its importance to the business. The new Engine House was attached to the south of the 1797 Engine House (Fig 6.13). The newly constructed building and the new Boiler House attached to the east are shown in outline on the 1811 site plan (*see* Fig 8.1).

The maker of the new south-end engine is not known, although it was certainly not supplied by Boulton and Watt. Its timing alongside the rebuilding of the Cross Building and the Warehouse, which are potentially attributed to Fenton, Murray and Wood (*see* Chapter 5), and the fact that by this time all Marshalls' engine purchases at Leeds were by Fenton, Murray and Wood, make a strong case that both the house and engine were provided by the Round Foundry. No drawings or descriptions of it have been found, but physical evidence indicates that the engine was 'house built' (that is, built

into the structure of the Engine House rather than being free-standing on timber or iron supports), substantially larger and of slightly different configuration to the earlier engines. The new Engine House had a single chamber (Fig 6.14), originally lit by two tall windows in the south wall. The lever wall employed in early engine houses was here substituted by an entablature beam, doubtless of cast iron, carried on heavy ashlar blocks, which are still visible in the south wall. The main cylinder was at the east end of the Engine House, adjacent to the Boiler House, for which two new boilers were purchased in 1811.[66] The engine had separate crank and flywheel shafts, contrasting with the single-shaft design of the 1797 engine: ashlar blocks for the support of the crankshaft are set into the south wall. The relative positions of crankshaft and flywheel indicate that a pair of gear wheels connected the two, a type of layout

Fig 6.13
The south elevation of the c 1810 Engine House retains the stone mountings for the engine's entablature beam at mid-height. During the maltings conversion the Engine House was raised by a storey and six rectangular windows were inserted. Attached to the wall on the ground floor is the added housing for the push rod connected to the bore hole which supplied water for the boilers.
[DP026469]

Fig 6.14
Interior of the c 1810 Engine House. The brick-vaulted ceiling was inserted for the installation of a new Hick Hargreaves engine in the 1870s. Prior to this the Engine House had been open through the equivalent of four storeys in the mill.
[DP163663]

course with a more powerful prime mover. It is possible that the *c* 1800 engine had timber components, for Murray appears not to have made the transition to all-iron construction by this date.[68] By 1820, however, all-iron construction had become the standard, and the output of mill engines had increased considerably. Either because more power was required due to the increase in mechanically driven machines, or because the *c* 1800 engine was showing signs of wear, a decision was taken in 1819–20 to install a new, more powerful engine at the north end of the Spinning Mill.[69] On the basis that Murray had supplied Marshalls with the engine of *c* 1800 at Ditherington and two later engines at Leeds, as well as providing two engines for the Benyons at their Leeds mill, it is highly unlikely that any new engines for Ditherington would be anything other than Murray machines.[70]

It is likely that the surviving Engine House at the north end of the mill was built to accommodate the new engine rather than the installation of *c* 1800. It has the same overall footprint as the earlier Engine House, shown on the plan of 1811 as projecting from the mill's east wall, but some of its features are incompatible with a date of 1800 yet consistent with one of 1820: it is largely constructed of standard-size brick rather than the great bricks of the site's early buildings, and in its fireproof roof it employs the developed form of cast-iron beam, with an inverted T-section and without a skewback, in contrast to the beam forms in the mill itself. The Engine House originally rose through the equivalent of three floors in the adjacent Spinning Mill, and its cast-iron roof beams have holes for lifting rings positioned to facilitate maintenance of a beam engine. The fabric evidence suggests that the Engine House was rebuilt to the same overall plan and design as its predecessor to accommodate the new engine (Figs 6.15 and 6.16).

Little is known of the engine itself. It was of 56 horsepower, only a modest increase on the earlier installation – perhaps an indication of the latter's unreliability or obsolescence. What is clear from the form of the Engine House is that it accommodated a beam engine, and it is likely that this included the improvements developed in steam-engine construction in the early 19th century, specifically in being house built into the structure of the Engine House with the working beam supported not on a timber trestle or lever wall but instead on a cast-iron entablature beam, spanning from wall

commonly employed in early 19th-century beam engines to enable the flywheel to run at higher speed.

How the new engine connected with the existing power transmission system is not known in detail. The alignment of the flywheel shaft suggests that it was coupled to the existing main drive shaft in the mill's ground floor but, given the large size of the engine, it seems likely that an upright main shaft may have also have been used to power the upper floors from the south end of the mill. Any evidence for such a transmission system has, however, been obscured or removed by later alterations, in particular the insertion of maltings equipment in the 1890s.[67]

The 1820 north-end engine

Like the first Boulton and Watt engine at the south end of the Spinning Mill, Murray's engine of *c* 1800 at the north end was replaced in due

to wall; the ashlar support for such a beam remains in place, together with the plaster skirting of a former floor at the same level. The projection of the Engine House from the east wall of the mill indicates that it was designed to place the flywheel in line with the main drive shaft, on the centre line of the mill. The engine cylinder, therefore, was located at the east end of the Engine House, as shown on the 1855 site plan, and was lit by a tall arched window. Like its predecessor, the 1820 engine appears to have driven the main upright shaft at the north end of the Spinning Mill, and there is fabric and documentary evidence that at some point drive was also transmitted to the Cross Building. This building retains evidence of bearing boxes that supported line shafting, and Henry Marshall's notebooks of the 1830s contain sketches showing the position of drive shafts (see Fig 7.5).[71]

Mid-19th-century alterations to the power system

The amount of machinery working in the mill declined in the second half of the 19th century and there was, therefore, no need for new, more powerful engines. From the 1830s, however, changes to the spinning stage of

Fig 6.15
The north-end Engine House, sandwiched between the Spinning Mill and the Malt Kiln. Largely rebuilt in c 1820 to house a new beam engine, it was formerly lit by a characteristic tall arched window in the east elevation, now blocked.
[DP163700]

Fig 6.16
Interior of the north-end Engine House, with the large ashlar supports for the flywheel shaft in the north-end wall of the Spinning Mill. The ceiling dates from the later installation of a Hick Hargreaves engine in the 1870s.
[DP163659]

production created a need for a significantly expanded steam plant. The new wet-spinning machines introduced from the late 1820s used a trough of hot water to briefly soak the yarn prior to drafting, and steam piping was installed in the spinning rooms to heat the water (*see* Chapter 7). James Marshall's notebook indi-cates that heating steam was supplied from the north-end Boiler House to most floors in the Spinning Mill and Cross Building, via an upright pipe in the adjacent staircase. Steam pipes were used in some rooms for heating and in other rooms steam was released from valves to pro-vide both heating and humidification.[72]

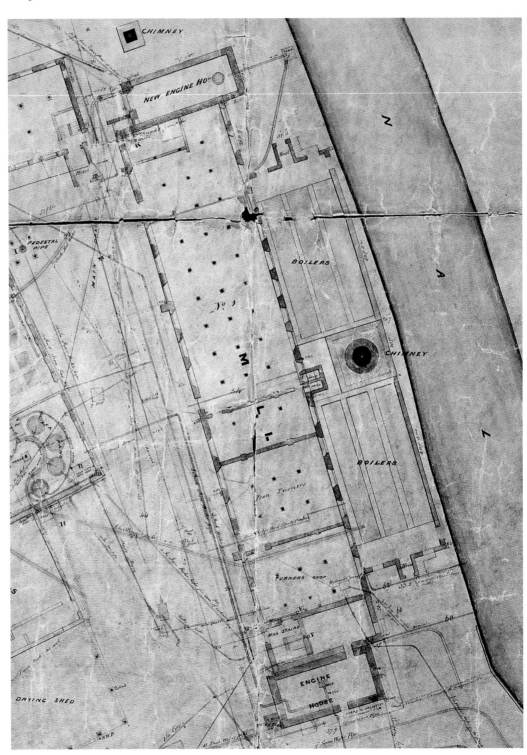

Fig 6.17
As shown on this 1855 plan of the site, a pair of much larger Boiler Houses were attached to the east side of the Spinning Mill in the mid-19th century, supplying steam for both engines and the processes in the Spinning Mill and the Dyehouse. [Shropshire Archives 6000/19533 (BB016001)]

The evolution of the power system meant that by the mid-19th century the site had two Boiler Houses, for south and north engines. Each had been replaced at least once since the mill began operating. In the 1840s a larger Boiler House was built adjoining the east side of the mill. Its construction was probably necessitated by the building of a larger Dyehouse able to process an increasing flow of yarn from Leeds.[73] The Boiler House is shown half-built on the 1849 plan, with a chimney positioned midway along the Spinning Mill's east side, and shown completed on the 1855 plan (Fig 6.17). It was a symmetrical design, extending along the full length of the mill's east elevation, containing two sets of three long boilers flanking a central chimney. The large footprint of the chimney suggests it would have been a conspicuous local feature extending above the roof of the mill. Neither the chimney nor the Boiler Houses have survived, although a modified east-side extension, with a lean-to roof, is shown in early 20th-century photographs of the complex after the maltings conversion.

A related development in the 1830s was the installation of a bore hole or well in the yard to the west of the south Engine House, probably to supply groundwater for dyeing and other processes.[74] Bore holes were sometimes added to textile mills when canal or river water became too polluted for use in a steam plant or for processing.[75] At Ditherington, the bore hole was 60ft (18m) deep, and its wider upper section contained plunger pumps that were driven by an underground push rod from the south Engine House (Fig 6.18; *see also* Fig 6.14).[76] The rectangular brick structure which contained the mechanism driving the push rod remains attached to the south side of the Engine House.

Steam power in the last decade of linen production

In the late 19th century the size and complexity of textile mill engines increased in parallel with the size of mill buildings, but changes to the function of the mill at Ditherington meant that large engines were no longer needed. There were two key drivers of the reduced need for power. First, tow production and mechanised heckling ceased in the 1850s as the reorganisation of the business saw an increasing concentration on line spinning and thread

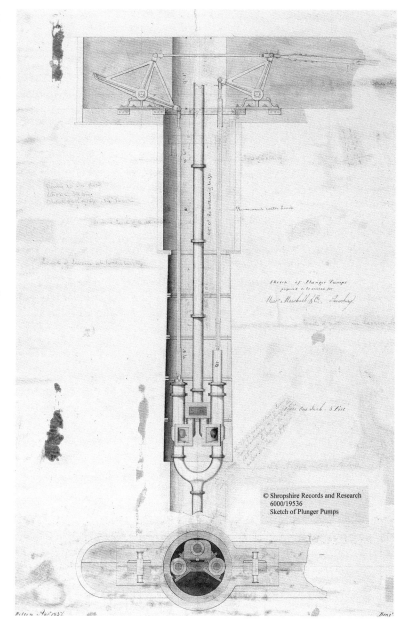

© Shropshire Records and Research
6000/19536
Sketch of Plunger Pumps

twisting, a change intended to complement rather than duplicate the operations of the Leeds site. Second, demand for linen goods fell in the following decades, and capacity was roughly halved in an attempt to align production with this decline.[77] Despite this reduction, the two beam engines of *c* 1810 and 1820 were, after long service and many modifications, scrapped and replaced with two much smaller modern engines with high-pressure boilers. The new engines were installed in the north and south Engine Houses in *c* 1874. They were both apparently of the same type: 30-horsepower, single-crank Corliss engines with 24in (610mm) cylinders, manufactured by

Fig 6.18
From the 1830s, water for boilers and processes was obtained from a bore hole in the yard using a pump driven by a push rod from the c 1810 Engine House. [Shropshire Archives 6000/19536 (BB016004)]

Hicks and Sons of Bolton.[78] These were compact, modern engines of the sort used in smaller industrial premises at that time, far less powerful than those being installed in new textile mills. Their use at Ditherington is indicative of the reduced need for power in the mill from the 1870s. After the installation of the new engines, the old boilers were listed in the stock books as 'broken up'.[79] Boilers for the new engines – Howard high-pressure boilers with economisers – were listed from the following year.[80]

The size of the new engines meant that they could be comfortably fitted into the existing Engine Houses, which were reduced in height by the insertion of new brick-vaulted ceilings supported by wrought-iron or steel beams. The stone beds of the new engines survive beneath the later concrete floors of both Engine Houses. The space available for the south engine suggests that it was arranged with its cylinder to the west of the main shaft box and that the engine drove a main shaft supported by the ground-floor columns, as had been the case since the Spinning Mill had started working in 1797. The north engine's cylinder would have been to the east of the main shaft; its flywheel was accommodated in a rectangular trap built into the new ceiling and a vertical slot in the west-end wall (*see* Fig 6.16). This engine appears to have driven the full-height upright shaft in the north-end bay of the mill. The surviving cast-iron brackets that supported this shaft in the upper storeys probably date from the installation of the 1874 engine, and indicate that, despite the reduction in processing in the Spinning Mill, mechanically powered operations continued on the two upper floors in this period.

Ditherington Mill was built during a seminal period in the development of steam power. It is an exceptionally early survival from the first generation of textile mills that were conceived and built to be powered by the double-acting condensing engines developed by James Watt. Early expansion of the mill's power plant, just a very few years after Watt's engine was put to work, illustrates wider trends in the history of steam power, when rivalries between the pioneering engine makers were being fought out in an atmosphere of fierce competition. The fundamental importance of the power system to a textile mill is reflected in its continuous development throughout Ditherington's working life, with the chronology of steam power being closely related to changes in processes, products and machinery. Unusually, the later alterations did not cause the wholesale replacement of the early features: the first Engine House, of 1797, survives intact (although of course without its engine), and the mill still displays numerous features related to both the original power transmission system and later modifications. Later in the 19th century specialised mill architects would place great emphasis on the influence of power systems when explaining their approach to textile mill design. At Ditherington the surviving evidence of both the power system and the iron structure, particularly the incorporation into the cast-iron frame of fixtures for power transmission, indicates that, already in the mid-1790s, Charles Bage envisaged the design of a mill not just as an exercise in engineering but also as the creation of an efficient working building in which structure, power and process were fully integrated.[81]

7

Ditherington Mill at work

MIKE WILLIAMS AND BARRIE TRINDER

The Industrial Revolution can be seen as a period during which the development of a consumer society, the advent of mass production of affordable goods and the exploitation of new markets and technological innovation acted together to drive rapid change. Also playing a significant part was the organisation of production – renewal of machinery and plant, the management of a workforce, the relationship between the stages of manufacturing and the development of new products – frequently on a scale not previously witnessed outside the nation's naval yards.[1] In the textile industry the Revolution focused manufacturing increasingly in highly capitalised mills so that an identifiable 'factory system' emerged, ultimately to replace dispersed working by independent artisans.

The Marshalls flax mills at Ditherington and Leeds should be considered alongside Arkwright's cotton mills as representing the forefront of the factory system in the 1790s, and the design of the first buildings at Ditherington, including that of the iron frame and the steam power plant, were determined by an awareness of the machines they were intended to house. Later, in the 19th century, successive generations of owners and managers continued this concern for the efficient deployment of processes and the workforce – a concern that was reflected in alterations throughout the site. This chapter will study the evolving management of the mill over the course of 90 years – a story illuminated by the survival of detailed annual inventories, the earliest of 1806, and by other documents in the Marshall company archive. Throughout the account it must be remembered that Ditherington was part of a larger concern, and its management and organisation were always linked to the company's other mills. From the mid-19th century, Marshalls operated as an extensive integrated business, in which the machinery and processes at Ditherington were planned to complement and support the output of the Leeds mills.

The Marshall family and Ditherington Mill: partnerships and management

The early history of the partnerships entered into by John Marshall has been recounted in detail in Chapter 4 and, as we have seen, Ditherington Mill was built while Marshall was in partnership with the Benyon brothers and Charles Bage. The Ditherington concern was not instantly prosperous, for which John Marshall blamed the ineffective management of Benjamin, the younger of the two Benyon brothers, who had moved from Leeds back to Shrewsbury to run the business. On 29 June 1802, less than five years after production commenced, the Benyons and Bage agreed to sell their shares to Marshall on the first Monday in July 1804. Marshall reflected that he would have allowed his partners to have the mill at Ditherington and confined himself to operations in Leeds if they had offered fair value for the former, 'but as they would not do that, I was determined to show how it would answer with good management'.[2] The partnership had served its purpose for both sides: Marshall had benefited from an injection of capital, badly needed in the mid-1790s, and the Benyons had learned the business of flax spinning. During their protracted separation from Marshall the Benyons and Bage created a parallel business, working from iron-framed mills designed by Bage at Castlefields in Shrewsbury and off Meadow Lane, Holbeck, in Leeds, the latter the first fireproof mill in Yorkshire, built in 1802–3.[3]

In 1804 the company was restructured, with Marshall taking on John Hives and William Hutton as junior partners. After 1810 John Atkinson joined as another junior partner. All three had worked for Marshall in Leeds and brought expertise rather than capital to the enterprise. William Hutton, described by

Marshall as 'an excellent manager of the manufacturing part of the concern' was sent to Shrewsbury to run the mill. When Hutton retired in 1815 his role was taken by Atkinson.[4] This did not prove a satisfactory arrangement, however, and soon Marshall became 'desirous of separating from Atkinson, because the Salop concern, under his management had become less profitable than before, or than it ought to have been'.[5] Taking Hives with him, Atkinson relinquished his partnership with Marshall in 1823 to set up independently in Leeds.[6] Thereafter the firm was run until closure solely by members of the Marshall family. John Marshall II (1798–1836) became a partner in 1820, James Garth Marshall (1802–73) joined in 1825, and Henry (1808–84) and Arthur (1814–98) were taken on in 1830.[7]

Like the partnership, the management of the mill in Shrewsbury was changed after Atkinson's departure. He was succeeded at Ditherington by William Whitwell, who handled the mill's accounts, and Peter Horsman, who was responsible for production. Whitwell had begun work for John Marshall as a bookkeeper in 1806, while Horsman was in a senior position at the mill by 1813. Horsman remained at Ditherington until his death in 1848 and Whitwell until 1850, after which their joint responsibilities were taken on in 1851 by Edward Parry, who had entered Marshall's service in Yorkshire in 1846. He remained in charge until the factory closed.[8] However, for 30 years after 1825 the running of the mill was overseen by James Marshall. It is his detailed record of the day-to-day operations that provides unique evidence for investment in new machines and for working practices in the factory.

It was the third generation of the Marshall family that struggled in changing economic conditions in the last decades of operation and oversaw the closure of the business in 1886. Those who were particularly concerned with the running of the company in that period were James Marshall II (1844–73), son of James, who became a partner in 1871 but was killed two years later while climbing Mont Blanc, and Henry's sons John Marshall III (1840–94) and Stephen Marshall (1843–1904), who became partners in 1867 and 1871 respectively. In his history of Marshalls of Leeds, W G Rimmer judged this generation harshly, pointing to their 'defective management' and the lure of a quiet life of retirement in the Lake District, living off the profits of their considerable investments.[9]

Ditherington Mill: the first years of production

Specialised flax-spinning mills were the norm in the late 18th century. Although a limited amount of weaving was undertaken at Ditherington in the early 19th century, the mill was primarily built to produce yarn and thread. The production of thread was a significant shift in company policy and appears to have been the initiative of the Benyon brothers, for up to this point it had not been produced at Marshalls' Leeds mill. There was, therefore, some complementarity between the two sites. In contrast with Marshalls' Leeds mill, Ditherington does not appear to have sent large amounts of yarn to weavers in the surrounding area. Instead, the coarser yarns produced from tow found an outlet in the carpet industry in the nearby towns of Kidderminster and Bridgnorth.[10]

Early flax factories shared similar approaches to internal organisation: they comprised both hand-powered processes, including heckling, and machine-driven stages of production – line and tow machinery was located in separate areas, and a large number of powered spinning frames needed to be accommodated. The clearest evidence for the internal layout of flax mills in the 1790s, before Ditherington was fully operational, comes from inventories of Marshalls' mills in Leeds, which produced both yarn and cloth. Here, hand-powered flax dressing was located in a separate workshop and in the warehouse, and hand-powered winding frames were sited in workshops and in the upper floors of the main mill. Mechanically powered processes were concentrated in the main mill building: spinning frames were located in its two middle floors, with one floor for line spinning and one for tow, each served by an adjoining floor containing dedicated preparation machines.[11] Weaving of both coarse and fine linen cloth was mainly undertaken on an outworking basis: in 1798 over 150 weavers carried out work for the firm in Leeds.[12] Another feature of early mill sites were facilities for the construction and maintenance of machinery and powered shafting, including engineers' and carpenters' workshops and stores for iron and timber; a smith's shop was built for the Leeds mill in 1796.[13]

Ditherington Mill was operational from September 1797 and from the start was equipped with the full range of processes for spinning yarn and thread from raw flax, with machinery arranged into separate departments for flax dressing, preparation, yarn spinning and thread twisting. At first, however, while the factory was being developed most processes may have been carried out in the Spinning Mill, possibly even before the building had attained its completed form. Before the addition of the Cross Building, which was certainly in operation by 1803, heckling and related processes may have been located in the Spinning Mill; since these were still manual processes they could presumably be sited temporarily in any convenient room. Warehousing was also added later, accommodated within the Cross Building and the Packing Warehouse, added by 1801, but it may also have originally taken up space in the Spinning Mill. Workshops, including a 'Turners shop' were located on the ground floor of the Spinning Mill and are shown on the plan of Ditherington produced in 1811 in connection with the installation of gas lighting (*see* Fig 8.1). They were probably present in 1806, for the inventory of stock of that year itemises £119 worth of mechanics' tools and over £400 worth of stocks of wood and iron.[14]

Ditherington machinery and processes 1806–20

The years up to 1812 saw a gradual expansion and reorganisation of the Shrewsbury section of John Marshall's business. Additions and alterations to both buildings and machinery represent a determination to make the factory more profitable under the new management put in place after the departure of the Benyons and Bage. Investment in Ditherington may have been undertaken partly because during the Napoleonic Wars supplies of flax from Ireland to Shrewsbury were less subject to interruption than those of Baltic flax to Leeds. Costs at Ditherington appear to have been higher than those at Leeds, but this can be explained in part by a more diverse product range. Most of the output of the Leeds plant was yarn that was sold to weaving companies in Barnsley, but two thirds of the yarn spun at Shrewsbury was twisted into thread, which required sophisticated marketing. The remaining third was either used for a limited amount of weaving by the company or sold for rug weft, as yarn for carpets and for weaving by small-scale linen manufacturers in the town.[15]

Under the new management regime, Ditherington Mill speedily proved successful. A profit of £6,520 was realised in 1806, and one of £15,963 two years later was, Marshall noted with evident satisfaction, more than he had paid to the Benyons and Bage for their share of the capital in 1804.[16] By 1812 all the principal buildings had been constructed and a bleachworks had been established at Hanwood, 8km to the south west, to finish the products made at the mill. Even at its fullest extent, however, the mill was never to occupy more than half of the land that had been purchased for the original development in 1796.

Within the mill, investment was focused on machines. The Benyons had taken away some machinery when they left the partnership in 1804, and there was probably unused space for several years afterwards.[17] Nevertheless, the annual inventories of machinery, which survive from 1806 and provide the first detailed evidence for the types and numbers of machines used in each department, demonstrate a consistent policy of renewal and re-equipping from the earliest years.[18] Already in 1806 the original machinery of 1796–7 was being altered and progressively replaced. In that year, there were 4 old tow spinning frames and 6 new ones; 18 old line spinning frames against 26 new ones; and 7 old twisting frames and 19 new ones. Tow-spinning frames were further subdivided into those used for 'long' and 'short' yarns, referring to their use of different grades of heckled flax. The number of line-spinning frames, over fourfold that for tow spinning, and the higher proportion of these which were listed as 'new', suggests that the business was focusing more on higher-value products. A similar proportion of line spinning to tow spinning was found at the Leeds mill. The spinning rooms at Ditherington were probably far from full in 1806, however, for by 1812 the number of line-spinning frames in them had grown to 62. Between 1806 and 1812 the emphasis on thread production seems to have increased: the number of thread-twisting frames doubled and there were corresponding increases in machinery and buildings used for thread winding, dyeing, drying and finishing. Dyeing (and possibly bleaching) was already located at the site: 'dye wares' were itemised separately from 1806, and the original Dyehouse had been built by 1804.[19]

Once the main structures had been completed at Ditherington, most processes remained in their original rooms within the different buildings until the 1820s (Fig 7.1). Despite frequent programmes of modernisation, some processes continued in the same areas throughout the working life of the mill.[20] The disposition of departments was similar to the practice established at Marshalls' Leeds mill. The Cross Building was at first used for heckling and storage.[21] Spinning and preparation took place mainly in the Spinning Mill. The storeys within the Spinning Mill were identified in early inventories as rooms one to five, numbered from the ground up. The mill combined the segregation of line and tow processes with a 'top down' arrangement, with the earliest stages in the upper rooms. Rooms five (the top floor) and four were used respectively for line and tow preparation. Room three was used for tow spinning at the south end and for line spinning to the north. Room two, the first floor of the mill, contained most of the line-spinning department, with thread twisting at the north end. Room one, the ground floor, appears in the first years of its operation to have been used largely for mechanics' workshops and storage, probably associated with the installation and

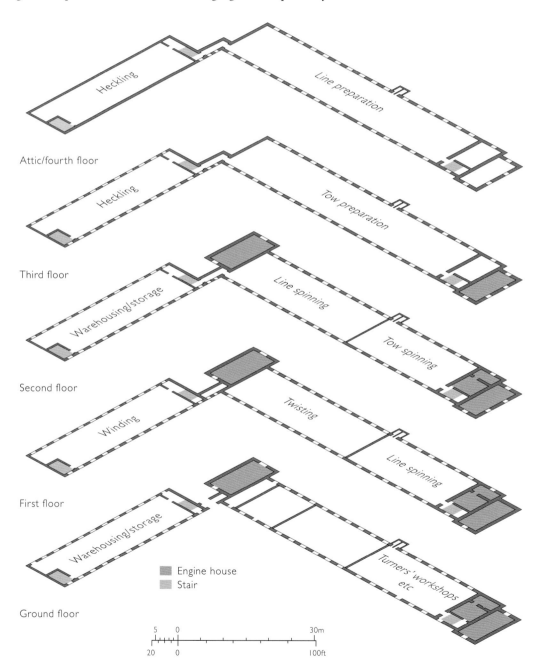

Fig 7.1
The probable arrangement of the main processes at Ditherington Mill up to around 1809. The main departments remained in the same areas throughout the working life of the flax mill, although warehousing was transferred to the Flax Warehouse after it was built in 1810.

Attic/fourth floor

Third floor

Second floor

First floor

Ground floor

Engine house
Stair

5   0   30m

20   0   100ft

maintenance of machinery. The cross-wall in the lower three storeys helped to further segregate processes, with, for example, line spinning on one side and thread twisting on the other. The cross wall may have been the north-end wall of the 1797 mill, utilised later to separate the different departments. It was removed on conversion to a maltings in the 1890s.

Along with increasing emphasis on line spinning and thread twisting, a major change to the range of processes began in 1809 with the introduction of mechanical heckling to both the Ditherington and Leeds mills (Fig 7.2; *see also* Fig 2.4). This marked the start of a revision of machinery and processes throughout the mill that continued well into the 1820s. Mechanical heckling was faster, extracted a higher proportion of line and was more economical, since the new machines were attended by women and children who were paid significantly less than the men who had carried out the manual heckling.[22] Eleven heckling machines were listed on 1 January 1810 and the number increased steadily to 26 by 1820. They were probably initially located in room five, the top storey of the Spinning Mill, where their layout was described in the late 1820s.[23] The improvements in heckling were reflected in the continued expansion of line spinning and twisting and correspondingly less growth in tow production. The addition of the new machinery was also related to the replacement of the original south-end engine with one of about three times the power, in a new external Engine House, in *c* 1810.

After its rebuilding in 1812 as a four-storey structure, with room numbering following on from that in the Spinning Mill, the Cross Building continued to house heckling, located in the top two floors (rooms eight and nine). The Cross Building also accommodated yarn winding, located on the first floor (room seven). This gave a close functional and physical relationship between the floors in the Cross Building and those in the Spinning Mill, with the heckling department and yarn winding in the former connecting easily via the shared staircase bay with the preparation rooms and spinning and thread twisting floors in the latter. The addition of the new Flax Warehouse in *c* 1810 liberated space in the rebuilt Cross Building and increased the mill's storage capacity. Through astute stock management, Ditherington was able to continue to work to capacity in a period when the availability and cost of flax was uncertain.[24]

The increase in the mill's productive capacity during its first 15 years of operation is indicated by the inventory of 1812, which listed the machines under headings for each of the main departments for the first time (Fig 7.3).[25] The mill then contained 62 line-spinning frames and 17 'reels' for yarn winding, and there were 52 thread twisting machines and 21 thread reels. Except for a gradual increase in the proportion of 'new' spinning frames, a few more preparation machines and the continued increase in mechanical heckling, the overall numbers of machines showed little change

Fig 7.2
Heckling machinery
and operatives in John
Marshall's Leeds mill,
c 1840.
[Courtesy of Leeds Library
and Information Service]

thereafter until 1819. The new spinning frames may have been made of iron, although the mill still contained 48 wooden frames in the late 1820s.[26] The clear emphasis on thread production was unusual in the early 19th century, when most flax mills in the north of England still concentrated on yarn that was put out to handloom weavers, and may explain the relatively large scale of the power systems in Marshalls' Ditherington and Leeds factories. An informed estimate of the power requirements in relation to the number of spindles at Leeds flax mills in *c* 1820 suggests that the Marshalls mill had roughly twice the power needed for a typical yarn mill;[27] at Ditherington the quantity of twisting and finishing machines, used for converting yarn into thread, was nearly equal to the number of spinning frames, a clear indication that more power was needed than in mills which only produced yarn.

Between 1813 and the early 1820s the Ditherington business included a limited amount of weaving, an experiment that has been associated with the management of the mill by Robert Atkinson. The products were mainly heavy canvas and candlewick fabrics but latterly included some fine linens. Twenty-six weavers were employed in 1816, a figure which rose to 51 in 1820.[28] Handlooms were probably used from 1813 to 1816, but from then until the early

1820s the Weaving Accounts suggest that most of the firm's weaving was done with powerlooms.[29] The absence of these looms from inventories before 1825 suggests that weaving may not have been undertaken within the mill at Ditherington. Instead, the intriguing possibility arises that Marshalls came to an arrangement with their former associate Charles Bage, who in 1815 had set up a mill at Kingsland, Shrewsbury, specifically to experiment with powerloom weaving. Bage died in 1822, and the 'eight old powerlooms' listed in the Ditherington inventories from 1825 to the mid-1830s may have been transferred to Marshalls' mill on the running down of Bage's business.[30] John Marshall's erstwhile partners, the Benyon brothers, appear initially to have been more interested in the vertical integration of their business after setting up on their own account. Soon after building their mill at Meadow Lane, Holbeck, they built a range of handloom shops, completed in 1804–5, and in Shrewsbury they set up loom shops in Barker Street and at Coleham, some distance from their Spinning Mill, and were seeking to take on weavers in 1806.[31]

John Marshall was always keen to remain independent of other firms in the flax industry. Bleaching was frequently undertaken by specialist concerns which could exercise some control over production. From an early date, however, Marshall built his own bleaching facilities. In 1796 he built a bleachworks at Wortley as a satellite of his Leeds mill, and in *c* 1809–10 he bought a former woollen mill at Hanwood, a few miles from Ditherington, and converted it to a bleachworks.[32] Surviving notebooks record Marshall's attempts to apply new techniques to the finishing of flax yarn, thread and cloth.[33] Faster chemical bleaching processes were successfully developed in the cotton industry in the late 18th century, and Marshall liaised with several cotton firms, including obtaining samples of bleaching liquor, in his attempts to apply the new methods to flax. Chemical bleaching of flax was only partially successful in this period, however, failing to produce the pure white finish of traditional bleaching. The accounts for Hanwood Bleachworks indicate that by the 1820s and 1830s Marshall had adopted a combination of traditional and modern methods, consuming large quantities of potash and vitriol purchased from a variety of sources.

Ditherington machinery and processes 1820–50

The decade of gradual improvements to flax preparation and spinning permitted by the introduction of mechanical heckling from 1809 was followed by a more extensive reorganisation and re-equipping of the mill in the 1820s and 1830s. Apart from successive additions to the Dyehouse, no major new buildings were constructed. The focus was firmly on the replacement of old machines with updated versions as the company sought to profit from buoyant markets for finer yarns and thread. The most significant changes included the introduction of gill machines for preparation; the installation of new types of wet-spinning machinery; adapting tow production so that it too could be used for making thread; and ending weaving at both Ditherington and Leeds. The thorough reorganisation of processes that all this required was overseen by James Marshall, whose notes and sketches from the late 1820s survive as a uniquely detailed record of the workings of an early 19th-century flax factory.[34] Despite the radical overhaul of the Shrewsbury mill, most of the main departments remained in their former locations and no extensions were needed to the main buildings. The site was working to capacity in this period, the mill employing 498 hands in 1821, of which the largest number, 198, were in the spinning department.[35] By the early 1840s, the number of employees at the mill had risen to 800.[36]

The changes at Ditherington were modest indeed in comparison with the huge investments that Marshalls made in Leeds in the same period, but they did return the mill to financial health. After a dip in profits between 1816 and 1821, profits averaged nearly £16,000 per annum between 1833 and 1850, with peaks of £22,977 in 1837, £26,088 in 1838 and £20,341 in 1850. This success was based in part on the mill's concentration on thread production, and Ditherington probably also benefited from being a small part of a large industrial empire rather than an independent concern.[37] Accounts in the early 1840s suggest that Marshalls had established a substantial export trade in thread with the United States, with sales to customers in New York, Boston and Philadelphia, although thread was also sold on a modest scale to retailers in Shrewsbury, Ludlow and Oswestry. The ironic consequence of the success of thread production in the Shrewsbury mill was that twisting to make thread was added to the firm's Holbeck site from the late 1830s. The modernisation of the Leeds mill, and the construction of the Egyptian-style Temple Mill in particular, meant that the Ditherington section of the business produced less than half of the firm's thread by the mid-1840s.[38]

Gill drawing frames were first introduced by other firms but appear in the Ditherington inventories from 1820, following a similar pattern as before, with older machines being gradually replaced with new over several years. By 1828 line preparation involved three successive stages using different variants of the new drawing frames. The layout of the preparation rooms in the top two storeys of the Spinning Mill was sketched in detail in the early 1830s.[39] Line preparation was still in room five, the top floor of the mill, and tow preparation in room four below. Both contained well-spaced groups of gill drawing machines arranged in four longitudinal rows, contrasting with the densely packed and transversely located spinning machines in rooms two and three. The preparation rooms were powered by four line shafts, one above each group of machines; an earlier system of driving machines by belts through holes in the floors was apparently superseded by overhead line shafting.[40]

Perhaps the most significant change to the mill was the introduction of wet spinning. This complemented the improvements in heckling and preparation and marked the culmination of the wide-ranging improvements to machinery and processes that had taken place throughout the early 19th century. Spinning capacity had increased by the 1820s to the point where the number of yarn spindles reached 3,408 in 1827, while the number of thread-twisting spindles reached 2,821 by 1832.[41] Marshalls had begun to introduce wet spinning in Leeds in 1827 and two years later decided to use the new process at Shrewsbury. In 1829 James Marshall began to plan how he could fit the new machines into the mill, noting that he 'examined the frames to see which should be broken up to make room for wet-spinning … I have no doubt that the wet sping would make the tow threads as good as our present line'.[42] He also identified where the new machines might be located, writing 'I think the best place for the wet spinng will be No 3. – there are the greatest number of wooden frames: it will be convenient for either line or tow & there will be room for a good number together'.[43] The change proceeded slowly but by 1836 there were 3,740 wet spindles, some 77 per cent of the spindles in the mill.[44] The wet spinning machines were metal-framed and their introduction was accompanied by the installation of a system of steam piping to heat the water through which the rovings were passed. Steam was supplied from the Boiler House at the north end of the mill and may also have been used to heat some of the rooms.[45] In the new system, tow could now be used to make 18-lea yarn; before 1812 it could typically only make 6-lea yarn.[46]

The annotated sketches of machinery layouts in James Marshall's notebooks indicate that up to the late 1820s the spinning frames had been installed transversely, running from side to side across the mill between the columns marking out each bay, in rooms two and three (Fig 7.4).[47] Given that a similar number of machines were in use after the reorganisation of the 1830s it seems likely that the transverse layout was retained thereafter. The bays are described as 'alleys' in the notebooks, possibly a reference to their use as walkways between the machines. This suggests that the spinning frames were positioned back to back with the rows of spindles on the fronts of the machines facing the walkway in the middle of each bay. The heaviest parts of the machines would therefore be above the floor beams, and the walkways would be in line with the windows. This arrangement may explain how such a large number of machines could be located in the limited number of bays in rooms two and three of the Spinning Mill.

The changes to preparation and spinning led to corresponding adaptation of other departments. By the early 1830s James Marshall was particularly concerned with the reorganisation of the old flax dressing and heckling department in the Cross Building so as to keep pace with the increased spinning capacity of the mill, noting in 1831 that '[w]e must provide more space for line and tow preparing as we proceed with our wet spinning. One plan is to raise the mill and cross building each a story'.[48] In 1831–2 an attic room was created in the Cross Building, which involved constructing a new floor, new stairs and roof skylights. The new room was used for sorting line flax before it was taken into the line preparation room in the top floor of the Spinning Mill;[49] sorting had

Fig 7.4

The locations of the line and tow spinning machines and their transverse orientation across the Spinning Mill are indicated in this entry in James Marshall's notebook for 1829.

[Leeds University Library Special Collections MS200/37, p.6 (DP163771)]

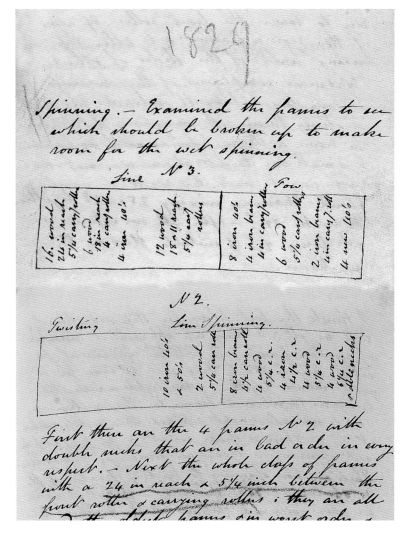

previously taken place in the Flax Warehouse. The changes included reorganising the heckling and related machines in the second and third floors of the Cross Building, powered by a pair of inserted line shafts that were driven from the Spinning Mill (Fig 7.5). Further heckling machines remained in the line preparation room in the top floor of the Spinning Mill.[50] Plans to add a storey to the Spinning Mill to provide additional space were not implemented and in fact no extensive rebuilding or new construction proved necessary.[51] An important rationalisation of the business in this period is evident in the cessation of weaving, confirming the concentration of effort on thread produc-

tion. The valuation of the weaving stock was reduced abruptly between 1824 and 1826, was no more than notional in 1836 and had disappeared completely from the accounts a decade later.[52]

Marshalls' increasing focus on the production of dyed thread and Ditherington's emerging role as the finishing mill for yarn and thread brought from Leeds made the Dyehouse of central importance at the Shrewsbury mill. No detailed descriptions survive of dyeing processes at the site, although Stock Books and other documents give a general indication of how the buildings were used. These indicate that in the late 1820s a wide variety of natural

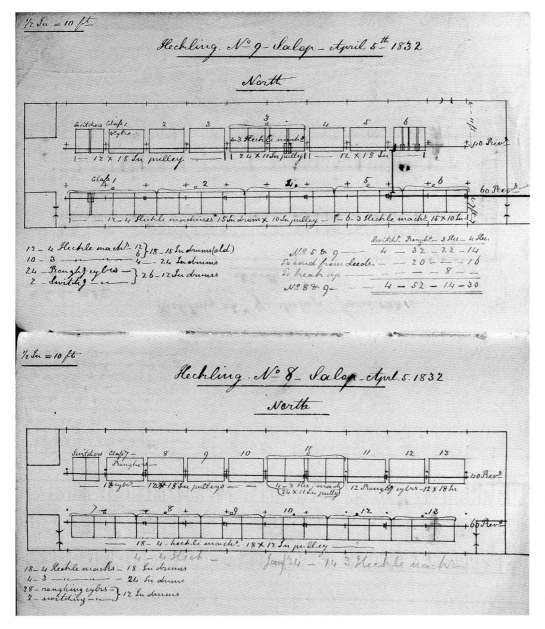

Fig 7.5
A plan of the heckling machines and line shafting in the Cross Building in 1832. [Leeds University Library Special Collections, MS200/34, notebook of H Marshall, 1832 (DP163782)]

99

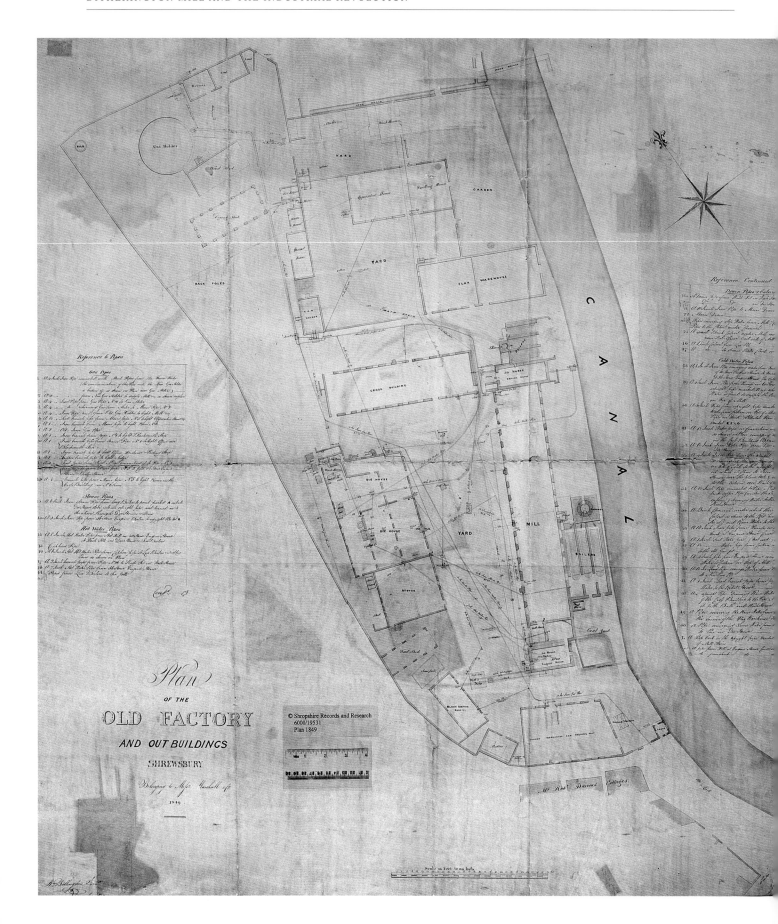

Plan

OF THE

OLD FACTORY

AND OUT BUILDINGS

SHREWSBURY

dyes were held in stock for producing blues, reds, yellows and other colours, together with a range of vegetable and mineral compounds that were suitable for the related processes.[53] The increased emphasis on dyeing at Ditherington necessitated the progressive enlargement of the Dyehouse (Fig 7.6). By the late 1840s it had been extended along both sides and at the north end, forming an interior divided into six main rooms. The Stove House had also been enlarged with an extension along its east side.[54] Stock Books from the late 1820s refer to a variety of natural dyestuffs, including Indigo, Peach Wood, Logwood and Shumac, along with vats for boiling the liquor and separate tubs for each type of dye.[55] Other vats, equipment and fittings were used for washing and wringing the dyed thread. To supplement the Stove House, a steam-heated drying chamber may have been installed in an end bay of the Cross Building in 1830.[56] Open-air drying was still the preferred method in the early 1830s, however, with the north-western part of the site containing 31 racks and over 400 thread poles in this period. The increased capacity of the Dyehouse was probably an important factor in the addition of a new Boiler House and free-standing chimney, located to the east side of the Spinning Mill; steam was piped into the Dyehouse from the new Boiler House, and hot water supplied via the north-end Engine House.[57]

The separate bleachworks at Hanwood was making a small profit by the 1820s. Its main products were a wide range of yarns, thread, heavy canvas and fine linens, most of which were available half-bleached, quarter-bleached or fully bleached.[58] The list of materials, fittings and utensils indicate the use of potash and vitriol as the main bleaching materials, and the Stock Book indicates that the top floor of the works was used as a drying room.[59] It seems likely that a sloping hillside adjacent to the site was used as a 'tenter' drying area.[60]

Between 1812 and the late 1830s Ditherington Mill witnessed a complete overhaul of processes which affected machinery in all the main departments, and ensured that one of the first flax factories could remain up to date and competitive. By the 1850s the same quantity of raw flax could be spun into five times as much yarn as had been possible in the 1820s, and the finer yarns and threads were much more valuable products.[61] Along with Marshalls' mill at Leeds, Ditherington was one of the pioneers of mechanical heckling and had responded to major changes in the markets for linen products by installing the latest machinery and enlarging the steam power system whenever necessary. The various improvements all contributed to the development of a specific role within the Marshalls flax empire, that of a specialised thread mill. The contribution of Ditherington to the overall business was significant in these years, with the Shrewsbury mill returning profits consistently for the whole period between 1812 and 1850, often outperforming Marshalls' Leeds mill.[62] None of these profits were required to be diverted to the construction of new buildings, for the existing structures proved sufficiently adaptable to accommodate most of the changes in machinery and products, with their large size and heavy floor construction providing an adequate amount of flexible and usable floor space. In the mid- and late 19th century, however, textile mill design, construction and organisation all advanced considerably; and Ditherington's narrow plan began to hinder the further updating of processes.

The declining fortunes of Ditherington Mill from the mid-19th century

Within a few years of the death of John Marshall in 1845 the company began to face severe problems. The dramatic expansion of the mills in Leeds and Shrewsbury had depended largely on Marshall's astute understanding of the flax trade and the regular updating of machinery and processes. Under the management of his sons after 1850, however, changing markets for linen goods and increasing competition from other manufacturers, particularly in Ireland and Scotland, and from the cotton industry, which mass-produced cheaper goods, threatened the company's pre-eminence. In 1853 James Marshall, who had managed Ditherington Mill but had entered politics in 1847, resigned his seat in Parliament in order to devote more time to the business. His relations with his younger brother Henry were, however, strained, Henry remarking of James in 1853 what 'a strange notion must have been in his mind of what the general management consists in'. The disagreement festered, and James withdrew from active involvement in the company in the late 1850s. It seemed progressively clear that, perhaps partly due to disagreements

Fig 7.6 (facing page) Ditherington Mill in 1849, showing the Dyehouse before it was rebuilt in the 1850s. [Shropshire Archives 6000/19531 (BB016002)]

within the family about roles and responsibilities, the company was ill-equipped to face the challenges which lay ahead.[63] Dissension also characterised the third generation's management of the mill in its last years of operation: John III and Stephen, both sons of Henry, had different ideas about the future of the firm after they took over responsibility in 1884 following their father's death.[64]

Ultimate failure was not, however, due to lack of either management effort or new invest-

ment. After 1850 the mills in Leeds and Shrewsbury were operated as a more efficient integrated business, replacing some of the earlier duplication in production. Ditherington Mill and Hanwood Bleachworks were increasingly used to finish yarns and thread that were spun at Leeds, a relationship made possible after railways were built close to both sites in the 1850s and by the rebuilding on a larger scale of the Dyehouse (Fig 7.7). Smooth working was facilitated later by the construction of a

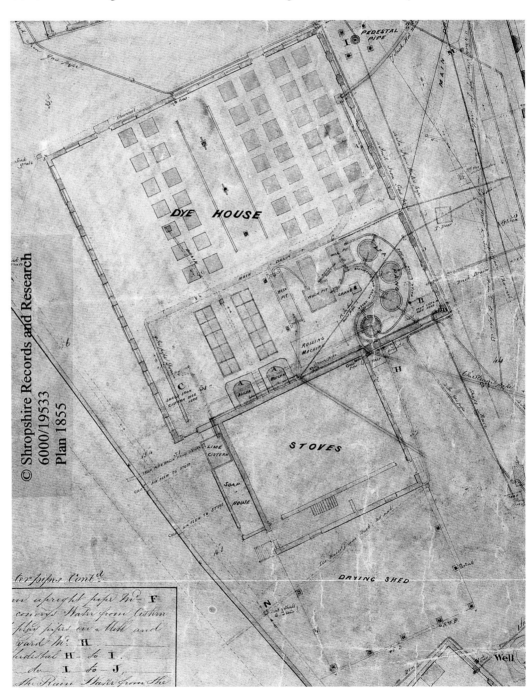

Fig 7.7
The newly rebuilt Dyehouse in 1855, showing the location of dye vats and steam piping.
[Shropshire Archives 6000/19533 (BB015995)]

© Shropshire Records and Research 6000/19533 Plan 1855

private railway spur from the main line into the mill premises. The new emphasis at Ditherington meant that heckling and all tow processes were halted by the late 1850s and preparation machinery in the Spinning Mill and the Cross Building was replaced by additional thread finishing machines. Line spinning and thread twisting were retained, however, the latter partly using yarn spun at Leeds.[65] One significant change at the mill resulted from the new methods of marketing thread that were introduced in the late 1850s. Previously it had been despatched from the factory in packets weighing 1lb (450g), but a woodworking shop was established in the Spinning Mill to make reels from Canadian and Scandinavian timber, and three printing machines and two embossing presses were installed to produce distinctive labels in a variety of fonts. 'Marshall's Shrewsbury Threads' became a recognisable brand, and it is difficult to associate such sophisticated and successful marketing with a company that was in terminal decline (Fig 7.8).[66]

The changes in production at Ditherington meant a gradual reduction in the types of machinery that had been so carefully developed at the mill over the previous six decades. In the final years of operations the machinery still partially reflected the original layout of processes, albeit without a heckling department and with only three floors of the Spinning Mill dedicated to yarn and thread production. Heckled flax was presumably brought to the site by railway from the Leeds mill, along with yarn and thread for dyeing.[67] The ground floor of the Spinning Mill was now used for thread polishing and the first floor entirely used for thread twisting.[68] The second floor contained drawing and roving frames for line preparation, together with line spinning. Reflecting the increased emphasis on thread finishing, the number of spinning spindles had been reduced from about 4,000 in 1850 to less than 2,000 in the late 1870s, while the number of twisting spindles fell from 4,000 to 2,500.[69] The Cross Building contained related processes on corresponding levels to the Spinning Mill, with yarn winding in the first floor and facilities for packing thread in the ground floor. Thus the top-down arrangement in the Spinning Mill and the horizontal connection with the Cross Building were partially retained in the final years of operation. Other processes, including twine balling, printing and repair of leather drive belts, were added to the site as part of the

reorganisation of the company's production but parts of the Shrewsbury mill are likely to have been empty or disused by the 1880s. Away from the mill itself, Hanwood Bleachworks was maintained as an important part of the business in the late 19th century. When it was offered for sale in the 1880s its vats and machines had been updated and the buildings extended to provide a bleaching facility for the whole Marshalls business, in spite of the reductions in machinery at Ditherington.[70]

The management changes of the last years – better integration and marketing, together with a limited amount of new investment – failed to turn around the company's fortunes. The last years of manufacturing operations saw a dwindling workforce at Ditherington, from something in the order of 600–700 after 1850 to 300 by the late 1870s.[71] Due to the firm's accounting method, it is difficult to assess the profitability of the Ditherington plant, for losses from the Leeds mill were accounted for in the Ditherington returns.[72] Even making allowance for this, however, it is clear that the factory was losing money steadily for more than a quarter of a century. After a substantial profit of £20,341 in 1850, losses followed in every year until 1862, when the accounts showed a modest profit of £962. Losses continued for the rest of the decade.[73] There was a period of modest prosperity in the mid-1870s, but the highest profit, in 1875, was no more than £4,384. The replacement in c 1874 of the earlier steam engines by two new horizontal compound Corliss engines indicates a strong commitment to making the mill profitable once more, but losses were continuous after 1876, reaching a peak of £23,660 in 1881. In the last year of operation, the mill lost £18,661. While the income of the Marshall family was obviously constrained by the losses, they continued throughout this period to receive the rents due on the buildings, steam engines and transmission systems in the mill, and this clearly had an effect on the factory's balance sheet.

Ditherington's rocky circumstances in its last years of operation may not have been apparent to outsiders. An account of Marshalls' operations published in 1883 described a busy operation, for the Shrewsbury factory was said to be responsible for dyeing and polishing thread, some of which was made from yarn spun at Leeds, and spinning was also stated to be carried on at the mill.[74] But rumours that the business was to be transferred to New Jersey

Fig 7.8
End labels for thread bobbins, as sold by Marshalls in the 1880s. [Leeds University Library, pages from The Shoe and Leather Trades Chronicle, *15 August 1882 (DP163788, DP163789)]*

became public early in 1886. Stephen Marshall, son of Henry and perhaps the most active of the third generation of the Marshall family, had investigated the possibility of moving the operation to the United States from 1884, but eventually rejected the idea.[75] Nevertheless, the company's former American agents established mills on the Passaic River in Newark which began to work on 4 October 1886.[76] The company used Marshalls' trademarks but encountered production difficulties and so staff from the Leeds factory, including the former superintendent, J Smiley Coe, were enticed to cross the Atlantic to contribute their expertise.[77] Some former employees of the mill at Ditherington probably went to New Jersey, but there was no mass migration, and the business was certainly not transferred to the United States.

Desperation at the future prospects for thread production led to the Marshall family's decision to wind up the company. Closure of both mills was announced in October 1885, and on 27 October 1885 Stephen Marshall visited Shrewsbury to discuss how this should be managed.[78] Another year passed before the factory doors were shut, at noon on Saturday 23 October 1886, during which time about 100 employees had left, leaving about 200 to be paid off.[79] Flax spinning as well as thread manufacture probably continued at Ditherington Mill until its closure.

The decision to close the business and the rumours that it was being transferred to America attracted political criticism. In July 1886 the socialist journal *Commonweal* contrasted the fortunes of the Marshall family with the poverty that confronted those who had worked for them, describing the conditions that mill-workers had suffered, particularly in the dusty heckling shops, and calling upon Stephen Marshall to follow his capital to the United States.[80] Shrewsbury's Conservative MP, H D Greene, claimed in 1904 that Marshalls started to manufacture thread with Yankee labour because they had been excluded from the American market by tariff duties, but 'One who knows' asserted that thread-making was not moved to the United States and that the reasons for closure were 'purely of a family nature'.[81]

The decline of Marshalls as a family business is one familiar in the history of British industry in the late 19th and early 20th centuries as successive generations developed different values and interests. The fortune made by the family, much of it derived from speculation and investment, was increasingly invested outside the business, a substantial amount being spent on estates in the Lake District. Time spent there and in continental travel may have held more allure for John Marshall's sons and grandsons than dealing with cantankerous employees in Holbeck or developing new markets for thread made at Ditherington.[82] Despite this, the business had not been allowed to run down, although this may have owed more to conscientious managers than to the partners. It was possible in 1882 for a sober trade journal to describe Marshalls' factories at Leeds and Shrewsbury as 'the largest and finest thread mills in the world'.[83] The record of investment at Ditherington in the 1860s and 1870s, and the success with which the brand image for 'Marshall's Shrewsbury Thread' was established do not suggest that the company was ailing or that its management was entirely without energy. Nevertheless, the winding up of the Marshalls business took place in the context of a general contraction of the flax and linen trade in Yorkshire. Exports from the United Kingdom of linen fabrics, thread and yarn declined in the late 1870s but thereafter remained steady, probably largely due to the success of Irish producers.[84] The Marshall grandsons may well have decided, in a pessimistic business climate, to give up the cares of business for the joys of life around Ullswater, but differently motivated, differently educated managers in a different business culture might well have developed new products and exploited new markets, as did their Irish and Flemish contemporaries.

8

The gasworks and gas lighting at Ditherington Mill

IAN WEST

The textile mills of Britain played a crucial role in one of the early 19th century's most important technological developments: the introduction of gas lighting. John Marshall and his partners were at the forefront of this, as they were with other significant technologies. Until the final quarter of the 18th century, work – like most other human activity – was almost entirely confined to the hours of daylight. While this may have been due in part to superstition and custom, there were also powerful practical factors which prevented working at night. The available sources of artificial lighting – candles and oil lamps – were very expensive and were ineffective for illuminating large spaces or for intricate work. Many early cotton-spinning mills such as Arkwright's Cromford Mill worked around the clock by the feeble light of candles and simple oil lamps, both to maximise the return on their investment and to make full use of their often limited water power (*see* Fig 4.4).[1]

The growth of factory-scale manufacture in the late 18th century provided an incentive for the development of artificial lighting. The first significant improvement came with the invention of the Argand oil lamp, patented by the Frenchman Ami Argand in 1784. This used a hollow cylindrical wick and a glass chimney to give a light equivalent to up to 10 candles.[2] Argand lamps, produced by numerous unlicensed manufacturers, were widely adopted in British textile mills but they, like candles, were expensive to use; in 1806, Marshall spent over £800 on lamps, oil and candles for his Shrewsbury and Leeds mills.[3] Moreover, oil lamps and candles needed constant attention to keep them burning satisfactorily and, in buildings littered with debris from textile processes, they posed a major fire risk. In the mid-1790s losses due to fires reached such a level that the major insurers withdrew or severely restricted fire cover for textile mills.[4]

It is unsurprising, therefore, that textile manufacturers were among the first to recognise the importance of early experiments in lighting by coal gas. Early trials included those being conducted around 1800 by William Murdoch, an engineer employed by Boulton and Watt. In these experiments, coal was heated in a closed vessel known as a retort and the gas given off – a mixture mainly of hydrogen, methane and carbon monoxide – burned with a luminous flame. The first practical application of gas lighting and the world's first proper gasworks were both commissioned in December 1805 for textile mills. One, at Salford Twist Mill, was supplied by Boulton and Watt and the other, at a cotton mill in Sowerby Bridge, Yorkshire, was built by Samuel Clegg, who had been Murdoch's assistant.[5] The success at Salford Twist Mill, where the gasworks provided safe and effective light to the factory at around 50 per cent of the cost of oil lamps and 30 per cent that of candles, attracted much attention and was instrumental in overcoming political and public opposition to the building of public gasworks. In 1812 the Gas Light and Coke Company obtained a Royal Charter which granted it powers to supply gas within central London, and gas lighting in streets, public buildings and the houses of the more affluent quickly spread through Britain and the rest of the industrialising world.[6]

Night working in most textile mills had virtually ceased by the 1820s due to practical and economic factors and legislation regulating child labour.[7] Nevertheless, the typical factory working day remained in excess of 13 hours, which meant that artificial lighting was required for a period in the mornings and evenings for up to six months of the year. Gas lighting offered clear advantages over oil and candles in illuminating large spaces economically, not just in terms of direct costs but also by

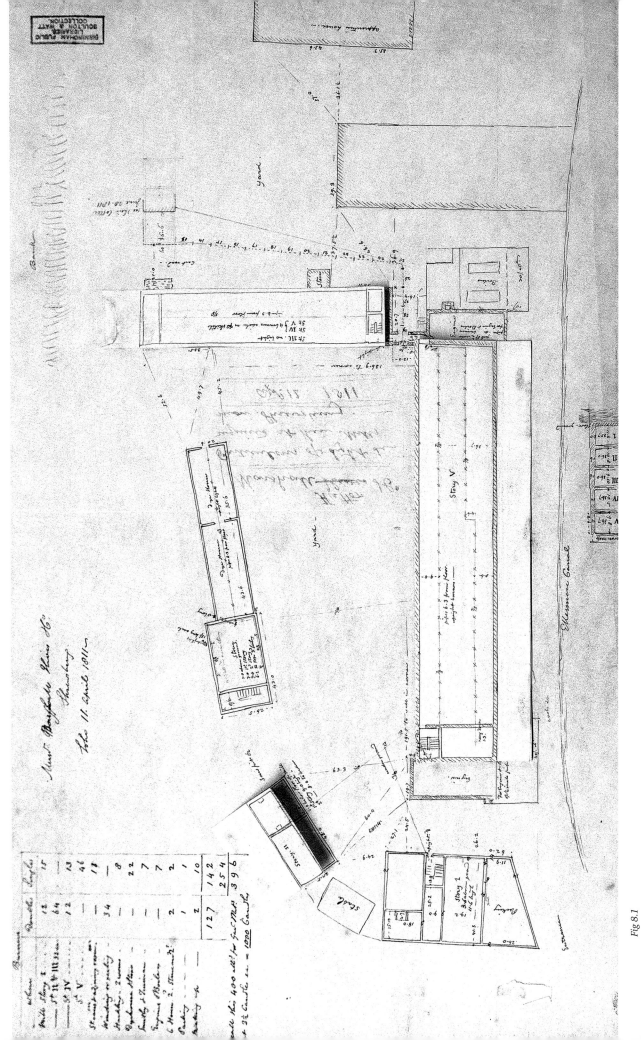

Fig 8.1

The 1811 plan of the gas installation by Boulton and Watt is also the earliest plan of Ditherington Mill. The upper floors were drawn on flaps pasted onto the plan. [Reproduced with the permission of the Library of Birmingham, Portfolio 810 (DP140532)] saving the labour previously required to trim wicks and fill lamps; improved fire safety was also reflected in reduced insurance premiums.[8] Consequently, by 1834, around 65 per cent of factories in Britain had adopted this form of lighting.[9] A significant proportion of these factories made their own gas, rather than taking gas from the public supply. In some cases this was because their remote location put them beyond the reach of gas mains, but even where this was not the case some factory owners chose to have the security of their own gasworks.[10] Both Boulton and Watt and Samuel Clegg ceased supplying gasworks equipment by 1816 but the technology of gas manufacture was relatively simple and numerous other local foundries and engineers, including Boulton and Watt's great adversary, Matthew Murray, moved into this expanding market in their wake.[11]

During 1806 and 1807 James Watt Jnr visited many of Boulton and Watt's existing steam-engine customers throughout Britain to interest them in this new form of lighting, but it is not clear whether he included Ditherington in his itinerary.[12] However, five years later both of Marshalls' mills were lit by gas. A Boulton and Watt gas plant was ordered for the Leeds mill in 1809 and in 1811 the first gasworks was built at Ditherington (Fig 8.1). The company accounts for that year show a sum of £1,866 for 'gas house and apparatus'; of this total, £1,150 was for the gas-manufacturing equipment, pipework and light fittings supplied by Boulton and Watt.[13] In 1808 Charles Bage, by then a partner in the nearby Castlefields Mill, visited a cotton mill in Longsight, Manchester, to inspect the gas lighting installed by Samuel Clegg, and in 1811 the Benyon Brothers and Bage also installed a Boulton and Watt gas plant at their mill.[14]

A Boulton and Watt foundry order and drawing show that the first Ditherington gas plant included three retorts, two cylindrical vessels for removing tar and other impurities from the gas, and a 6m × 3m × 3m rectangular gas holder.[15] The cast-iron retorts, approximately 1.3m long and D-shaped in section were housed in a brick furnace (Fig 8.2). These retorts were of a new design, with the gas outlet pipe descending

Fig 8.2
Boulton and Watt's 1811 drawing of the gas retorts for Ditherington Mill. [Reproduced with the permission of the Library of Birmingham, Portfolio 811 (DP140530)]

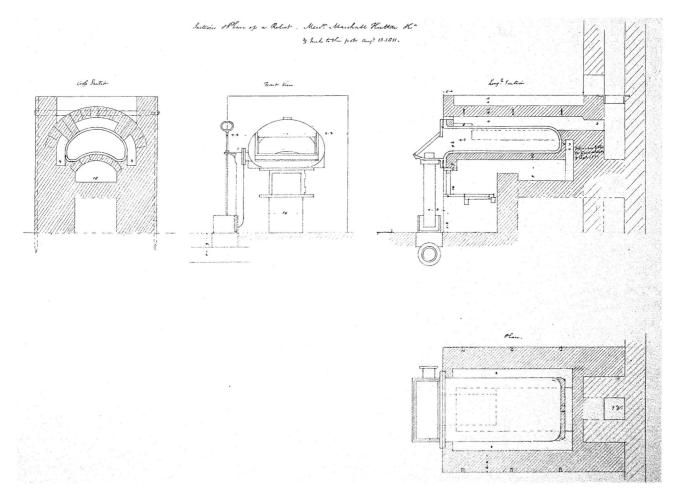

downwards from the mouth, which does not seem to have been widely used elsewhere. The gas holder consisted of a rectangular wrought-iron bell suspended in a brick water tank by means of chains, pulleys and counterbalance weights. No drawing of the layout of this plant survives but it is likely that it was very similar to the one designed in 1809 for Marshalls' Leeds mill, which also had three retorts and the same size of gas holder housed in a two-part rectangular building. The larger portion of this, approximately 7.3m × 5.5m internally, contained the gas holder and washer while the smaller part housed the retorts and tar separator.[16]

The 1849 plan of Ditherington shows a rectangular building, labelled 'Gas Holder', measuring approximately 7.3m × 4.8m internally to the north of the cross wing (Fig 8.3: see also Fig 7.6). This is almost certainly where the original gas holder was located.[17] The small square extension in the centre of the north-west wall accommodated the counterbalance weights for the gas holder. The retorts and tar separator were probably housed in a building which occupied the space to the north, between the gas holder building and the thread room.[18] On an 1855 version of the factory plan, the Gas Holder House is shown as a carpenters' shop and the space to the north, the site of the retorts, as a saw pit. Marshalls' accounts include an entry of £44 in 1853 for converting the Gas Holder House into a joiners' shop.[19]

The Boulton and Watt plan of 1811 provides details of the proposed arrangement of internal pipework and light fittings for each floor of the main buildings at Ditherington (see Fig 8.1). Although there is no evidence to confirm that

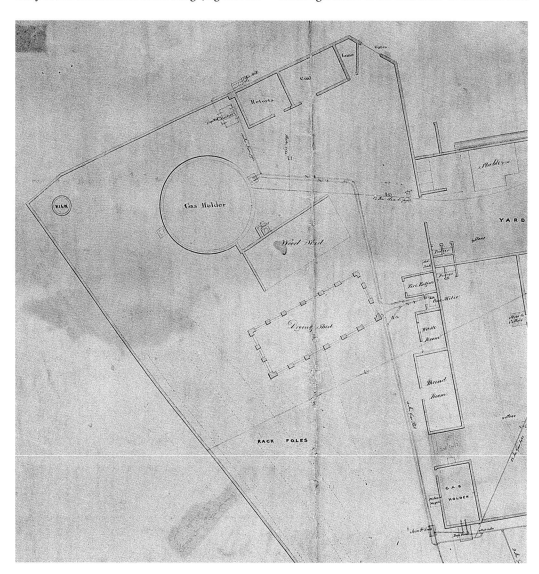

Fig 8.3
The Ditherington Mill gasworks in 1849.
[Shropshire Archives 6000/19531 (BB016002)]

the actual installation followed this plan, many aspects of these proposals were common to all the early gas lighting installations and continued to be followed for many decades.[20] In total, the design shows the whole mill complex as having 142 single burner and 127 double burner lights; each burner was roughly equivalent to 2½ candles in light output (Fig 8.4). By around 1820 most new gas lighting installations were using improved burner designs known as the 'fishtail' and 'batswing'.

Following the pattern adopted by most textile mills, a higher standard of lighting was provided for the areas devoted to the more intricate manufacturing processes. In the Spinning Mill the first and second floors, which were used for spinning, had 32 double burners on each floor, supplied by two horizontal pipes running the length of the room, suspended just below the ceiling. The burner pipes descended vertically from these, placing the lights approximately 1.5m above floor level. A similar arrangement was applied in the fourth floor of the Spinning Mill – known to have been used for line preparation – which had 46 single burner lights in two rows. The third floor, used for tow preparation, had 12 double burners in two rows at the southern end and 13 single burners at the northern end. The first floor of the Cross Building, used for winding, had 34 double burner lights arranged in two rows along the room. In contrast, the third floor of the Cross Building, used for heckling, had only four single burners. The ground and second floors of the Cross Building had no lights at all and were therefore probably used for warehousing. Other areas and other buildings designated for preparation, storage or other purposes generally had single burner lights fixed to the walls, except the Dyehouse, where the lights were arranged down the centre of the room.

Many factories which installed Boulton and Watt gas plants quickly found that they became inadequate for their needs and expensive to maintain. They were often, therefore, replaced with new and more sophisticated gasworks or abandoned in favour of gas from the public supply.[21] A detailed journal entry for Ditherington for 1834 suggests that in 1826 they had closed their private gasworks in favour of gas from the Shrewsbury Gas Light Company, founded in 1820. The entry goes on to describe in some detail the problems the mill was then experiencing as a result of there being an inadequately sized gas main from the gasworks.

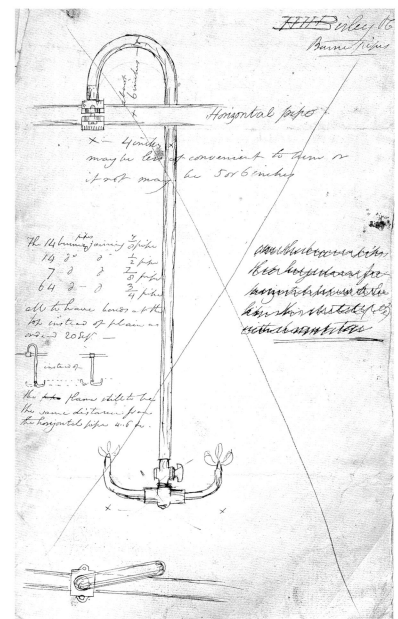

This meant that the gas holder provided insufficient pressure for the mill's lights to operate satisfactorily.[22] The journal describes how additional weights had to be added to the gas holder counterbalance system because the pressure from the public supply was not sufficient to fill the holder. The 2in (51mm) mains pipe from the public gasworks supplied both Marshall's mill and Benyon and Bage's Castlefields Mill. Together the two consumed around 850,000 cubic feet (24,000m³) of gas a year – almost 10 per cent of the Shrewsbury town gasworks' output.

Although the gasworks at Ditherington had ceased operating by this time, the journal refers to the mill still having a 'gas holder of 3,800

Fig 8.4
Sketch of a double 'cockspur' gas burner similar to those which would have been installed in Ditherington Mill in 1811.
[Reproduced with the permission of the Library of Birmingham, 3147/4/115 p286 (DP163769)]

cubic feet (108m³)'.[23] This gas holder was presumably retained after gas manufacture ceased on site, filled from the public supply during daylight hours and then emptied when lighting was required, thereby reducing the peak demand on the mains system. The original Boulton and Watt gas holder had a nominal capacity of only 2,000 cubic feet (57m³), the largest size which the company offered, so if the reference to a capacity of 3,800 cubic feet is correct, this implies that the original holder had been replaced with a larger one at some stage after 1811. It is unlikely that a larger gas holder could have been accommodated in the original gas holder building and, by around 1816, the small rectangular gas holders which Boulton and Watt and Samuel Clegg supplied for their early gasworks had been superseded by circular designs. It is possible, therefore, that a small circular gas holder was built somewhere in the yard near the Gas House.

Attempts to persuade the Shrewsbury Gas Light Company to lay larger mains evidently failed and in 1835 a larger gas holder was built

at the mill: the accounts for that year contain an entry for a 'new gasometer, gas pit and pipes, Salop' at a cost of £1,009.[24] This is the gas holder at the northern end of the site shown on the 1849 plan (see Fig 8.3). The plans suggest this gas holder had a diameter of around 10.8m, and therefore a volume of something in excess of 20,000 cubic feet (566m³), a substantial increase over the previous on-site gas storage capacity. The plan shows the gas pipes to the gas holder and to the mill emerging from a small Meter House, located between the Fire Engine House and the Waste Room, which is probably where the incoming public supply entered the mill's gas supply system.

The journal of 1834 contains no further references to difficulties with the gas supply but it would appear that the erection of the new larger gas holder did not solve the mill's problems of inadequate gas pressure as a new private gasworks was later erected. The accounts for 1842 include the modest sum of £393 for 'new gas house retorts etc.'[25] The new gasworks buildings were constructed at the

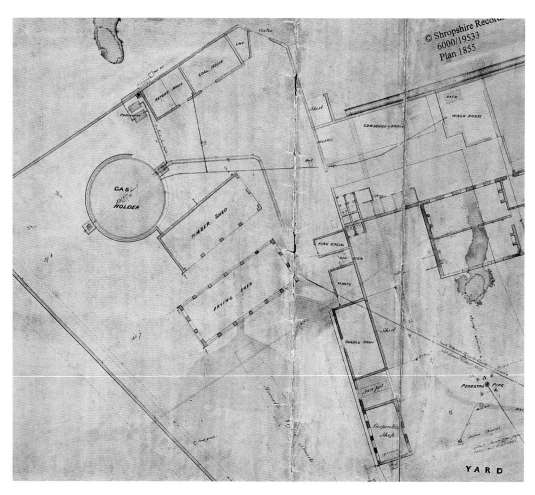

Fig 8.5
The Ditherington Mill gasworks in 1855. The Retort House and Coal House are sited against the northern boundary of the factory. Gas pipes are shown leading from the gas holder to the different buildings within the mill, although the representation of some of these pipes has been erased after the production of the document.
[Shropshire Archives 6000/19533 (BB016003)]

northern extremity of the site and were shown both on the 1849 plan (*see* Fig 8.3) and more clearly on a plan of 1855 (Fig 8.5). The main rectangular building, measuring approximately 14.5m × 5.2m externally, was in two parts: the western part housed the retorts whilst the eastern portion was the Coal Store. A tower condenser, in which the gas was cooled to remove tar, and a pair of lime purifiers to remove other impurities, were located to the west of the Retort House, with the tar pit apparently located outside the mill's perimeter wall. In the corner of the site, east of the Coal Store, was a shed for storing lime for the purifiers.

It is not known when this gasworks ceased operation but the gas holder is shown on the 1:2500 Ordnance Survey map (SJ4913), published in 1881/2, and it is therefore likely that gas continued to be made on site until the flax mill closed in 1886. The gas holder does not appear on a plan of the site dated 1898 which depicts the new railway siding built when the site became a maltings, although this plan does show the gasworks buildings; it is likely that the gas holder was demolished to facilitate construction of the railway siding.[26] An undated engraving of the mill after its conversion to maltings (*see* Fig 10.2) appears to be roughly contemporaneous with this plan, showing the

new railway siding and not the gas holder; the former Retort House and Coal Store can be seen in the centre foreground. Ordnance Survey maps suggest that these latter buildings were demolished sometime between 1965 and 1977, while the range of buildings which housed the original Boulton and Watt gasworks were demolished sometime between 1954 and 1965.

No above-ground remains relating to the manufacture and use of gas have been found at Ditherington, but the historical evidence places John Marshall and his partners as, if not pioneers, then certainly eager to adopt at a relatively early date what was to become one of the 19th century's most significant technological developments. The sight of the brightly lit Ditherington Mill, many years before gas lighting became widespread, must have been a source of wonder to the townspeople of Shrewsbury. The decision to build a new private gasworks at Ditherington, after abandoning the first one in favour of the public gas supply, was unusual and demonstrates how vital reliable gas lighting was to a mill's operations. For Marshalls, like most textile manufacturers at that time, the substantial investment required was justified by the considerable savings in running cost and by the improved safety which gas offered over oil lamps or candles.

9

The workforce in the 19th century

PAUL BELFORD AND BARRIE TRINDER

For 90 years the business of Ditherington Flax Mill was steered by the Marshall family and, for the first eight years, its partners. The survival of company papers allows the management of the mill to be traced in some detail. The picture which emerges is dominated by processes, machines and accounts. The human side of the mill at work – the story of the men, women and children who maintained and operated the machines, stoked the boilers and kept the steam engines running – is recorded only incidentally. It was, however, of vital importance to the success of the business, since the recruitment of a labour force, wage rates, disputes and welfare all had a discernible impact upon productivity and profitability. This chapter will examine how Marshalls recruited their workforce and will consider the scant evidence for working conditions in the mill. Of particular importance is how labour was secured in the first years of the mill's operation, for this illustrates the special circumstances involved in establishing and running a business in a new location in this period. By the early 19th century, nearly five hundred people worked in the different departments, and by the 1840s there were eight hundred hands, making the factory the town's largest employer.[1]

Recruiting the workforce and the parish apprentice system

John Marshall was accustomed to operating in Leeds, a town with a deeply entrenched engagement in the wool textile industry and, by the last years of the 18th century, with a growing familiarity with factory working and steam-powered operation. It is likely, therefore, that he had little difficulty in recruiting a workforce for his Leeds mill. It is true that the linen industry was relatively new to the town, but it was a strong presence in nearby parts of the West Riding, which might, therefore, offer a pool of labour familiar with the processes involved. Furthermore, the skills required for machine operation may have been transferable from one branch of the textile industry to another. Machines developed for flax preparation and spinning, for example, were based on those first applied to the cotton industry, which again flourished in parts of the West Riding in the late 18th century. Yorkshire, therefore, offered a pool of skilled and unskilled labour upon which Marshall could draw in setting up his new flax mill in Holbeck in 1791.

These conditions appear not to have applied to the same extent in Shrewsbury. Admittedly, the domestic linen industry was important, an account of Shrewsbury manufactures in 1785 stating that 'the linen-yarn manufacture, alone, employs several hundred hands, of both sexes'.[2] The wool textile industry also had a presence in the town although it was not a major employer. Nevertheless, recruitment of a labour force for the new mill was likely to have been difficult. In this connection, it is worth recalling John Marshall's rueful acknowledgement in 1801 that 'the obstacles to the first establishment of any new manufacture are greater than any man can imagine who has not experienced them', citing the disciplining of the workforce as one of the main difficulties; it may have been the recent experience of recruiting for the Ditherington mill which was uppermost in his mind.[3]

Shropshire's involvement in mining and iron founding may have provided a pool of expertise for the more highly skilled mechanical aspects of running the new mill, although in 1800 Marshall and his partners had to advertise for an engineman, 'preferably accustomed to a Boulton & Watt engine'. For the less skilled tasks, familiarity with machine operation in a factory was probably much more limited in Shrewsbury than in Yorkshire by the mid-1790s. The other textile manufacturing firms in

Shrewsbury – Benyon Brothers and Bage at Castlefields, and Paddock & Davies – similarly found it necessary to advertise for weavers. In 1809 Marshalls sought 20 flax dressers for Ditherington, offering piecework terms, and specifying that applicants should belong to the 'Hecklers' Club', presumably an early form of trade union. This may be an indication that even the most ambitious textile entrepreneurs had sometimes to contend with custom, in this case, perhaps, with the traditional practices of the itinerant flax dressers who worked for families who grew and spun their own flax. Custom may also explain why Marshalls' mill in Leeds was in production for 355 days in 1815, while only 323 days were worked at Ditherington.[4]

Although manual heckling, dyeing and bleaching were skilled occupations, most of the labour at Ditherington was devoted to simple tasks or minding machines.[5] The size of the workforce grew as the mill reached full capacity. Numbers in the first years are not known, but there were over 400 employees between 1813 and 1819. Marshalls employed 498 hands in 1821: the 24 bleachers were doubtless based at the Hanwood bleachworks, and the 42 weavers probably worked off site, leaving a total of 432 at the mill itself.[6] The workforce increased to 800 in the early 1840s, but the suggestion that it reached 900 in the 1860s seems exaggerated. About 300 remained when the closure of the mill was announced in 1885.[7] Analysis of the 1851 census enumerators' returns for the areas along and on either side of the main road adjacent to the mill reveal 377 flax workers, all of whom at that date would have been employed by Marshalls. The majority, 207 or 55 per cent, were aged under 20, and 133 or 35 per cent were under 16. Boys and girls were employed in approximately equal numbers up to that age. The proportion of males in the 16–25 age group was lower, but there were more men than women among employees over 30, most of whom were skilled operatives or supervisors.[8]

A significant part of the workforce at Ditherington in the early 19th century consisted of parish apprentices – children, usually orphaned, who were placed with employers by parish overseers. The parish apprentice system was already well established by the later 18th century but expanded with the development of the factory-based textile manufacturing industry.[9] Although the poor were required to be supported by the parish under the terms of the Elizabethan Poor Law, the 18th century saw increasingly differentiated treatment of the 'able poor' and those too old or infirm to work. Since accommodation in workhouses was limited, responsibility for the care of able-bodied children who were orphaned, illegitimate or unsupported by their families was passed to employers. This relieved the parish overseers charged with their care from further responsibility, at least for the term of the apprenticeship.

Many children were apprenticed to factory employers, a theoretically consensual process. Under the apprentice system the factory owner was responsible for the provision of food, clothing and lodging; some non-parish apprentices also received a small wage. It has been argued that during this period the 'practice of factory parish apprenticeship … liberated the industrial labour market'.[10] Certainly the system enabled a number of new textile factories to develop and expand where they may otherwise have struggled to find labour. Apprentice labour was also cheap, an important consideration in the running of a mill.

The parish factory apprenticeship system has been criticised by many labour historians as a mechanism for providing cheap labour to greedy industrialists. It has been argued that many apprenticeships only gave experience at a low skill level and did not equip apprentices with sufficient knowledge of a trade to enable them to escape the ties to their original employer and set up in business themselves.[11] However, it has been shown that in some cases – particularly among larger employers and for female apprentices – the system could provide good knowledge of a trade and perhaps even prospects of advancement. Indeed, simply having knowledge of the factory system itself was arguably an advantage in the rapidly industrialising world of the early 19th century.[12] Many employers preferred to take on those who had already been apprenticed in the trade, for this provided workers with many years' experience of their particular jobs. The limited evidence suggests that many former apprentices remained in the industry to which they had been apprenticed for the remainder of their working lives, and in fact many remained as employees of the same firm, in some cases rising to supervisorial positions – as in the case of two former female apprentices at the Quarry Bank Mill in Cheshire.[13]

For Marshalls and other textiles manufacturers in Shrewsbury, the local labour market was evidently insufficient to provide the workforce which they required. Evidence provided in

1832 to the Committee on the Factories Bill described the situation in the town: 'there are only two mills, one belongs to Mr Benyon, the other to Mr Marshall; [Shrewsbury] was thinly populated at one time, and they got girls and boys from all parts of the country, and as they got out of their time, they took others, and the population got stronger'.[14] Resort was consequently commonly made by the large employers to the parish apprenticeship system. In 1805, when seeking girls aged between 11 and 15 years old to work at his cotton mill, Charles Hulbert specified that parish apprentices would have preference and that he would expect each of them to be provided by the parish overseers with a 4-guinea premium and two suits of clothes.[15] Apprentices were taken on at Shrewsbury's new mills from near and far. The Apprentice Register for Shrewsbury shows that Marshalls took in 21 boys and 35 girls in 1805, 5 girls and 4 boys in 1812 and 7 girls in 1814.[16] Some references in Shropshire parish records demonstrate that they were recruited from within the county. A 12-year-old girl spinner from Alberbury, 14km from Shrewsbury, went to Ditherington in 1800 and in 1809 a 10-year-old male flax dresser came from Fitz, just 6km from the town. There are also records of children from Fitz and Prees (19km away) being apprenticed at the Benyons' Castlefields flax mill.[17]

More, however, came from outside the immediate area, some from neighbouring counties such as Staffordshire and Cheshire and others from Yorkshire and other areas further afield.[18] There were certain advantages to acquiring apprentices from more distant locations. There was less chance of the parish of origin interfering with the details of the employment and, in due course, education provision, and it was more difficult for the children to abscond and return home. Together with the further advantage of a greater pool of potential labour, these benefits meant that parishes in large cities – particularly London – were especially favoured as a source for apprentices. A survey of apprentices articled by 23 London parishes between 1780 and 1820 found that the Benyons employed 15 apprentices, and that Marshalls at Ditherington took on 82. These were the only two flax mills in England – apart from the short-lived concern of Haywood & Palfreyman in Macclesfield – that employed parish apprentices from London. Neither Marshalls nor the Benyons employed them in Yorkshire, nor were any employed in other textile mills in Leeds. Evidence indicates that no cotton spinners in Derby, Leicester, Mansfield or Nottingham took on parish apprentices, and that most of the employers who used them had mills in remote or thinly populated areas.[19]

Fig 9.1
The first Apprentice House was built in 1799 on the main road to the south of the mill. Facing south was the Superintendent's House, in the foreground, and the Apprentice House lay attached to the north, facing the road.
[DP163735]

Shrewsbury may not be considered remote but it and its immediate region were not as populous as the textile area in the West Riding of Yorkshire in the late 18th and early 19th centuries. Both Marshalls and the Benyons (the latter at their Castlefields mill) therefore felt it necessary to build apprentice houses to accommodate the recruits who they brought in from other areas. Marshalls built two apprentice houses, the first in 1799 outside the mill and the second in 1811 within the complex. Both buildings still exist.

The first Apprentice House at Ditherington, financed by John Simpson, was built together with a separate house for the factory manager and perhaps his clerks as well.[20] The two buildings, both constructed from great bricks, were located to the south of the mill complex, prominently sited at the crest of a slight rise in the landscape along the main road to Shrewsbury. The Apprentice House was clearly divided into two architecturally discrete components – accommodation for the apprentices themselves and, at one end, a house for a Superintendent – although the whole structure was united by stylistic traits such as the dentilled eaves cornice and windows with segmented brick arches and stone sills (Fig 9.1). The Superintendent's House was situated at the southern end of the range, oriented at right angles to the main road so that its front faced south. The building was constructed at the highest point of the Castlefields landscape and its impressive three-storey, three-bay front would have been the first visible manifestation of the Marshalls concern to visitors arriving from the town. It is perhaps also significant that it faced away from the mill and the world of the workplace. The attached Apprentice House itself (now Nos 56–59 St Michael's Street) was oriented north–south and was slightly narrower than the Superintendent's House. The original internal arrangement has been lost, but the evidence of the fabric points to a building divided laterally into a northern and southern half separated by the main central chimney. The rear elevation shows evidence of two sets of entrances at ground-floor level (now blocked), one at the southern end of the range and one nearer the centre but to the north of the central chimney. Whether the two entrances indicate segregation of the apprentices by gender, anticipating the requirements of the Factories Act of 1802, is not known.[21]

Adjacent to the Apprentice House, the former Manager's House (now No. 55 St Michael's

Fig 9.2
The Manager's House of 1799, built alongside the first Apprentice House.
[DP163737]

Street) is unpretentious yet solid in style (Fig 9.2). The symmetrical three-bay façade has a central door with rectangular overlight and a simple architrave, and the only real embellishment consists of dentilation to the eaves, carried around all four sides of the house. The central front door gave access to a hallway and stairwell, which in turn accessed the four principal rooms on each floor.

The number of employees at the mill continued to rise during the first two decades of the 19th century and an increasing proportion of them were likely to have been apprentices. In her study of employment in a wide range of textile factories during this period, Katrina Honeyman suggests that more than 70 per cent of the workforce of a textile factory could be made up of parish apprentices.[22] An increase in apprentice numbers and perhaps a desire to house the children within the factory complex may have been the reasons for the construction of a second Apprentice House only 12 years after the first one.

The second Apprentice House is located to the north of the Flax Warehouse and main mill. It was constructed in 1811 at a cost of £3,329.[23] There was some overlap with the earlier Apprentice House, both buildings being in use from 1812–15.[24] It seems likely that moving the apprentices inside the factory boundary was at least in part motivated by a greater desire for control and observation of the workforce, and may be connected with the gradual increase in mechanical heckling in the mill in these years, with the apprentices being set to minding the new machines.[25] John Simpson converted the original Apprentice House building into four terraced houses in 1814–15. These he named 'Ann's Hill', after his daughter.

The style of the new Apprentice House was conservative and in keeping with other buildings within the mill (Fig 9.3). It was built of standard brick and is of three storeys, gabled to east and west; the gables take the form of a pediment framed by a stone band and coping. At eaves level there is a dentilled eaves cornice. Like its predecessor, the building contained two elements, a Superintendent's House to the east and accommodation for the apprentices to the west. The Superintendent's House seems to have been given a greater degree of architectural detail, for the central doorway on the east front has a pedimented doorcase of timber. This doorway opened into a hall giving access to the principal reception rooms to north and south and via the stairs to the upper storeys. The northern room was evidently the principal dining room, serviced by a kitchen to the west. The separation between the house and the accommodation for the apprentices was clearly part of

the original design, being absolute from the cellars to the roof space.

The provision made for the apprentices in the western part of the building may reflect legislative changes made since the first Apprentice House was constructed. In 1802 Parliament had passed the Health and Morals of Apprentices Act (more commonly known as the first Factories Act). This stipulated separate accommodation for male and female children, as well as requiring instruction in reading, writing and arithmetic for the first four years of work and religious education on Sundays.[26] It seems likely that the ground floor of the Apprentice House would have contained a refectory, served by a kitchen in the basement, and perhaps a school room. The upper floors provided dormitory accommodation. Each floor was divided longitudinally into two halves by a central spine wall running east–west, a plan perhaps intended to permit segregation by gender. It is difficult to estimate how many apprentices the building was designed to accommodate, but it is not inconceivable that well over a hundred children were sheltered there.

The parish factory apprentice scheme declined from the 1820s, and was effectively brought to an end in the 1830s. This came about partly as a result of the 1833 Factory Act and the 1834 Poor Law Amendment Act. The Factory Act further curtailed the use of child labour, in particular outlawing the employment of children under 9 years old in the textile industry, stipulating that children between the ages of 9 and 13 could only work 8 hours with an hour lunch break, and requiring 2 hours of education per day. The effect of the Poor Law reform was to improve and extend workhouse provision for the indigent poor, and life in the workhouse rather than in the factory became the more common fate for young indigent children.

Legislation and changing working practices affected the mill at Ditherington. The use of apprentices there declined or ceased after 1820; the mill manager, Peter Horsman, stated in 1833 that the mill had had no apprentices for 12 years.[27] Child labour, however, continued to be significant. As mentioned earlier, analysis of the 1851 census returns for the area shows that even then around a third of the workforce was aged under 16.[28] Many would have benefited from the introduction of half-time education in the mill in 1834.[29] Most must have lived with their families outside the mill, an indication, perhaps, that the Shrewsbury labour market had developed to the

Fig 9.3
The second Apprentice House was built at the north end of the mill in 1810 (see also Fig 4.12). The Superintendent's House occupied the east (far) end and apprentices were accommodated in the remainder of the building. [DP163723]

point where it could fulfil Marshalls' needs.[30] After 1820, therefore, it is likely that the Apprentice House became redundant for its original purpose. By 1842 part of the building, probably the former Superintendent's House, was used as the home of the factory manager.[31]

In the absence of an apprentice child labour force, Marshalls must have recruited both locally and more widely. The firm was helped by economic conditions in other parts of the country. In Gloucestershire the woollen industry was in a depressed state in the 1830s and a scheme of assisted emigration appears to have been initiated by the Poor Law Commission. Some families departed for Australia, but in 1837–8 66 people left the village of Bisley for Shrewsbury. Of these, 18 were taken on at Marshalls' mill.[32]

Census records demonstrate how important the flax mill was as a source of employment in the local community. Successive generations laboured at the mill. In 1841 Edward Blower, aged 20, was a bobbin carver. Ten years later, he worked as an oiler. He died in 1860, and the head of household in 1861 was Ann, his wife, described as a thread reeler. Two of her children also worked at the mill: one was an axle setter, the other a factory operative. Ann died in 1867, but two of her daughters, aged 13 and 11, were operatives at the mill: a son, aged 20, was described as a labourer, and he too may have worked in the factory.[33]

Housing for the workforce

Limited provision of workers' housing had been made from the very beginnings of the operational life of Ditherington Mill. As part of the arrangements for the sale of land, the Marshalls partnership required that the vendor, John Mytton, construct a series of 'cluster' houses on the strip of land between the canal and the main road.[34] These clusters comprised blocks of four houses beneath a hipped roof, and the plan enabled each house to have windows in two sides – in effect rather like a pair of back-to-back semi-detached houses (Figs 9.4). The first four clusters (that is, 16 houses) were leased to Marshalls from March 1797 and another four followed shortly afterwards. The Church Rate books for 1799 refer to 16 'Houses near the Manufactory. They were located [to] either side of the Sultan Inn and were provided with generous gardens'.[35] Although subsequently demolished, these houses appear from the map evidence to be identical to groups of cluster

houses built by Strutt at Belper, also in the 1790s.[36] It is not known who occupied the houses but it is likely that they were built to attract the skilled workers needed in the mill at a time when the local labour market could not supply what was required.

Marshalls did not go on from this modest beginning to create a textile colony – in the classic sense as described by Peter Gaskell and Andrew Ure – of a dependent community of employees whose offspring in successive generations provided a stable and contented labour force.[37] This was no Cromford, Saltaire or New Lanark. Only 35 houses were built for workers by an organisation that employed over 500 people. For the rest, John Marshall was content to let speculators provide the accommodation for his growing workforce, and the growth of Shrewsbury's northern suburb around the mill was gradual but inexorable in the first half of the 19th century (*see* Chapter 3).

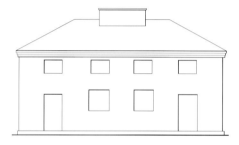

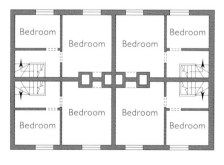

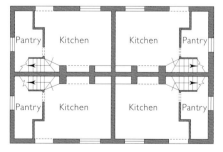

Fig 9.4
Reconstructed plan and elevation of the cluster housing built c 1797 to the north-east of the mill. [Based on drawings attached to the original lease; Shropshire Archives 6001/13323]

Working conditions at Ditherington Mill

The most detailed accounts of the experience of working in Ditherington Mill were provided as part of the inquiry into the need to regulate the employment of children in factories, held in 1832. Two brothers, Samuel and Jonathan Downe, who had worked in the mill some years before, gave a shocking description of conditions there, although it is now impossible to verify whether their accounts were accurate.[38] They stated that children from as young as 6 years old were employed, that a working day of more than 13 hours was the common practice, and that discipline was exercised through brutal treatment of children who made mistakes or who became tired. Children might be beaten with straps or sticks. Jonathan Downe recalled how he had 'seen boys actually knocked down with a strap; they have been called from their work, flogged, and been knocked down on the floor by the blow of the strap, and when they have been on the floor, they have been beaten till they had risen, and when they have risen, they have been flogged to their work again'. A boy might be punished for drowsiness by being ducked in a cistern of water, returning afterwards 'to his work for the remainder of the day; and that boy is to stand, dripping as he is, at his work; he has no chance of drying himself'.

A regime of brutality was allegedly deliberate policy, encouraged particularly by Peter Horsman, the mill manager. Fear prevented recourse to the magistrates, for, it was alleged, dismissal would result and other employment in mills would be impossible to find. A degree of control was also exercised over wages, with a 'truck' system operating in which part of the week's earnings were withheld and paid twice yearly in the form of tokens exchangeable for goods at inflated prices in the town's shops. Answering a question about the extent to which the mill system was severe and tyrannical, Samuel Downe responded: 'Very great, and particularly in Shrewsbury'. The local Conservatives, antagonistic towards the Liberal Marshalls, attempted to make political capital out of the lurid accounts of working conditions in the mill, stating some years later that 'the factory slaves in Shrewsbury are bound, hand and foot, to obey the mandate of the tyrant's lick spittle toady, Mr Horsman'.[39]

Responding to the evidence of the Downe brothers in a letter to the Committee, Peter Horsman denied all the charges and called their evidence into question by besmirching their characters.[40] In some ways, Marshalls were better than other employers, being singled out in 1835 as the only concern in the region to operate a 48-hour week and a 'compulsory schooling shift system' for the apprentices, with a school within the factory.[41] Later, a local newspaper observed that Benjamin Disraeli (1804–81), elected MP for Shrewsbury in 1841, was hooted when making an election speech in The Square in which he addressed Marshalls' workmen as white slaves.[42]

The flax dressers or hecklers comprised the principal bodies of adult male workers at the Ditherington and Castlefields mills, and from time to time displayed corporate solidarity both for and against the management. In 1831 the hands from the two flax mills attended a public meeting en bloc to show their support for the reform of Parliament, and after a pro-Reform MP was elected for Shrewsbury, the flax dressers from both factories, wearing their white aprons, marched two-by-two in support of the new member. The same group in 1842 voiced their protests against the dismissal of 284 fellow employees thrown out of work by progress of machinery, probably by the proliferation of mechanical heckling machines and iron spinning frames.[43]

There is some evidence, in the form of the establishment of a Mill Club, for the existence of mutual help among the workers at the mill. The Club published its Rules and Regulations in 1849, describing its constitution and governance. The Rules set out the subscriptions payable by members, on a scale proportionate to earnings, and the sickness benefits to which they were entitled: a worker earning between 13s and 16s, for example, paid 2d per week and would qualify for a sickness allowance of 10s per week. Funeral expenses were also provided by the Club. The wording of the Rules is not absolutely clear but might be interpreted as indicating that the Club was open only to adult males. It is also not clear whether the employers (Marshalls) were responsible for the establishment of the Club or whether this was a genuine example of unassisted self-help by the workforce.[44]

In later decades the cohesion of the workforce was fostered by railway excursions organised by the manager, Edward Parry. In 1858 the band of the Yeomanry Cavalry led 500 employees and their families on a 20-carriage excursion to Llangollen. The mayor of Shrewsbury accompanied

700 passengers to Liverpool in 1871, about 600 went on a similar excursion the following year and 800, including work-people from Hanwood, in 1873. Many of the 500 who travelled to Liverpool in 1882 crossed the Mersey by steamboat to New Brighton.[45]

The closure of Ditherington Flax Mill in 1886 was a severe blow both to employees and to the local economy.[46] The impact of closure was exaggerated for political effect by the Revd W G D Fletcher, the rabidly Tory vicar of St Michael's parish, in which Ditherington lay. Immediately before the general election of 1906 he attempted to persuade voters that the closure of the factory 20 years previously was caused by the imposition of tariff duties in the United States and that, by implication, a protectionist fiscal policy should be adopted in the United Kingdom. Fletcher alleged that 400 people had been made jobless by the closure of the mill, that many Ditherington people in the winter of 1886–7 were in a state of semi-starvation, and that the district's small shop-keepers were ruined. Former managers and employees of the flax mill responded that Marshalls had closed the business for family reasons, that not more than 200 were employed there at the time of closure, that about 60 per cent of them were lowly paid women and girls, that only one shop ceased trading because of the closure and that the number of shops in the area had subsequently increased. Fletcher was forced ignominiously to withdraw.[47]

While Marshalls had undoubtedly been important to the economic life of Shrewsbury and gave a livelihood to generations of employees, the family never engaged as closely with the town and the workforce as it did with Leeds. The contrast is seen in the provisions made for the communities in the two places. John Marshall was known in Leeds as 'the ready promoter of improvements, and especially of all institutions designed for the intellectual and moral advantage of the bulk of the people … a founder and most liberal supporter of the Lancastrian [sic.] School, the Leeds Philosophical and Literary Society, and the Mechanic's Institution'. In 1832 he built an Infants' school within the mill at Holbeck.[48] The Marshall family went further, establishing

excellent day schools, in which upwards of 1200 children are taught, and a valuable library for the benefit of their workpeople; besides which they erected and endowed a few years ago (in 1850), a beautiful church (in the early English style), for the advancement of the spiritual interests of the inhabitants of the densely populated district in which their factories are situated.

There is little evidence of a similar attachment to Shrewsbury. None of the sons or grandsons lived locally and the family was not listed in trade directories among the town's principal residents. James Marshall must have visited the factory at Ditherington regularly but he did not set up house in Shrewsbury: he is described in directories as living in Headingley, the best of the Leeds suburbs.[49] Within the mill a sickness and death benefit club was formed and allotments were set out at the north end of the property, but that was the extent of the company's benevolence: no institutes, chapels, schools or parks adorned the suburban landscape around the mill at Ditherington.[50] In 1886 Marshalls left an empty factory but little else to mark their long association with the town.

10

Mill into maltings

BARRIE TRINDER

The factory at Ditherington served as a flax mill for about 90 years. It then stood empty for a decade before being adapted to work as a maltings, fulfilling that purpose, with a five-year intermission, for another 90 years. It is therefore unsurprising that the site is more frequently known to Salopians as 'the maltings' than as 'the flax mill', and that some aspects of its history in this later period have become entangled in the popular memory with its earlier role. The purpose of this chapter is to examine the history of the Ditherington complex from the cessation of flax working in 1886 until malting came to an end 101 years later (Fig 10.1).

The end of Marshalls at Ditherington Mill

The closure of Ditherington Mill in October 1886 prompted the disposal of the mill's contents and the property, including buildings and land. The Dundee auctioneer George H Lord sold most of the contents of the Ditherington Thread Works on 2–3 November 1886, a sale which realised £2,640. The stock at the Hanwood bleachworks was auctioned on 4 November. The cover of the catalogue announced that the sale would include 'flax preparing, spinning, twisting, thread polishing and spooling machinery', but while there was plant for drawing, spreading and roving, no spinning machinery is listed, nor are any heckling machines included, apart from eight pairs of rougher and finisher hand-heckles.[1] A sale of sundries by the Shrewsbury auctioneers Hall, Wateridge & Owen realised £185 on 20 December 1886.[2]

The premises at Ditherington, including the two Corliss engines and their boilers, together with the Hanwood property, were put on the market by the Guisborough estate agent J W Clarke. The sale plan in the Marshall archive includes notes of the buyers and the prices paid for plots at Hanwood, but there are no similar annotations for the Ditherington site, which, it appears, failed to find a purchaser. The two fields north of the mill, purchased in 1796–7 but never built on, were offered as separate lots.[3]

After the closure of the Marshalls business, an attempt appears to have been made to reopen the flax mill. The only evidence for this initiative comes from some disconnected reports in local newspapers in the late 1880s, and comments made in 1906 during the controversy provoked by the Revd W G D Fletcher (*see* Chapter 9). Those who tried to revive the factory probably intended to use heckling and spinning machinery omitted from the sale in November 1886. A certain S Jackson, probably Samuel Jackson, manager of the Shrewsbury branch of the National Provincial Bank, described himself as one of those who 'met and tried to start the business'. In March 1888 the borough council discussed the supply of water to the premises, and whether it would be available on the same terms that Marshalls had enjoyed. One councillor remarked that he would regret anything that would prevent the factory being reopened, but only a week later a sale was announced of machinery, including a vertical steam engine, by the 'Shrewsbury Spinning Co Works, The Factory, Castle Foregate'. It seems that some machinery was retained for a revival of manufacturing, but that the mill never actually went back into production.[4]

The purchase of Ditherington Mill by William Jones

After lying idle for over a decade, the mill at Ditherington was purchased by a prominent maltster, William Jones of Shrewsbury (1832–1923). In April 1897 the Revd Fletcher said that he understood that Marshalls' factory had been

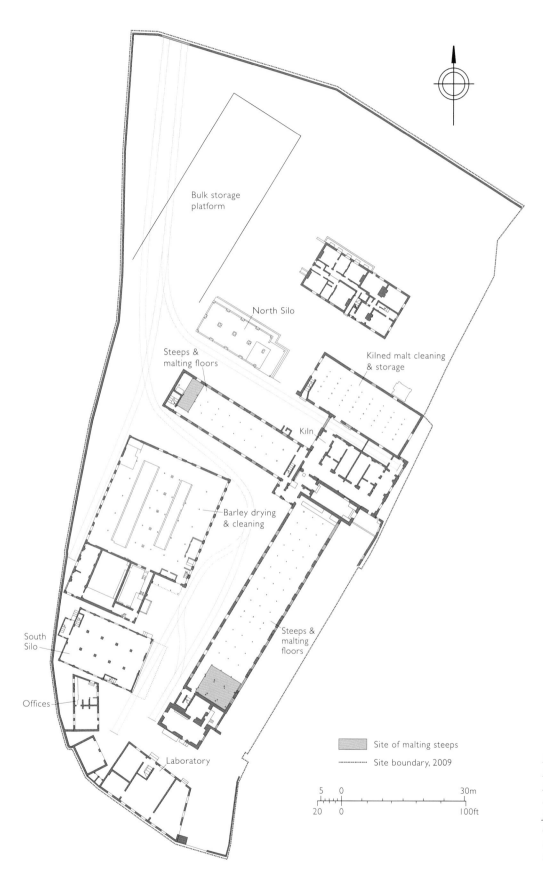

Bulk storage
platform

North Silo

Steeps &
malting floors

Kilned malt cleaning
& storage

Kiln

Barley drying
& cleaning

South
Silo

Steeps &
malting
floors

Offices

Laboratory

Site of malting steeps

Site boundary, 2009

5   0   30m
20   0   100ft

Fig 10.1
Ditherington Mill in the late
20th century, also showing
earlier structures. Most of the
flax industry buildings were
adapted for new uses during
the maltings conversion of
the early 1890s.

121

sold to a firm of maltsters, and regretted that the new owners would not create many jobs. A trade directory published in the same year recorded in its entry for William Jones & Sons that 'the large building formerly known as the "Old Thread Factory" lately acquired ... will hereafter be known as the Shropshire Maltings'. Evidence that the conversion of the buildings took place at about this time is provided by the inscription '1898' on one of the pillars flanking the outer end of the works' railway siding.[5]

William Jones was a magistrate and one of Shrewsbury's most influential citizens. He was born at Llanbrynmair, Montgomeryshire, but in 1857 emigrated with his wife to Gomer, Ohio, a Welsh community founded in 1833. It appears, however, that he and his fellow migrants were frustrated in their hopes of establishing a prosperous farming community in the region by the outbreak of the American Civil War, and Jones returned to Britain.[6] He settled in Shrewsbury where he began a malting business in 1869. Two years later, when he was living on Claremont Bank, he had just two employees. By 1881 he had made his home at Sutton Lodge, an Italianate villa with a three-storey tower on Betton Street, but still employed no more than four workers. The business expanded rapidly in the 1880s, and by 1897 he had at least eight substantial malthouses or grain warehouses, including The Glen at Frankwell, the largest malting complex in Shrewsbury before the 1880s (probably built by John Gittens in 1829), and buildings elsewhere in Frankwell, as well as in Town Walls, Hill's Lane and Beeches Lane. The growth of Jones's company during the 1880s is indicated by the scale of the headquarters that he built in 1888 – the Belle Vue Maltings – erected on a plot adjacent to his house at Sutton Lodge. By the end of the 1890s, therefore, he was running a major, multi-site business, his entrepreneurial skills largely responsible for the revival of an industry which was present in every Shropshire market town in the early 19th century but which subsequently declined in most of them.[7]

The malting industry changed substantially in the late 19th century, in part as a result of the repeal in 1880 of the Malt Tax, which inhibited the introduction of new technology.[8] The Malt Tax had required the grain to be couched before germination, which necessitated special frames in which the grain could stand. Once the Malt Tax had been lifted, a whole stage in the malting process was eliminated, and the grain could be left to stand in the hopper-bottomed steeps before being emptied directly onto the malting floor. After repeal, malting plants on an unprecedented scale were constructed, most of them using innovative technology and served by several forms of long-distance transport. Some were built by brewing companies, others by firms who concentrated on malting alone. Several large plants were built adjacent to breweries in Burton-on-Trent, Staffordshire, and between 1899 and 1905 the Burton brewers Bass, Ratcliff and Gretton constructed the nine buildings that form the gigantic maltings at Sleaford which provide a striking landmark in the Lincolnshire fen country. The plant of John Crisp & Son alongside the railway at Beccles, Suffolk, included eight kilns and was reputedly the largest in the world at the time of its construction, although it was later surpassed by the maltings at Mistley built by Free, Rodwell & Co. Constructed between 1893 and 1904 the Mistley Maltings (Essex) was conveniently positioned on the banks of the River Stour alongside the branch railway to Harwich. New large plants were also built after 1880 in some of the traditional centres of the malting industry such as Ware (Hertfordshire), Grantham (Lincolnshire) and Newark (Nottinghamshire).[9]

Jones's purchase of the Ditherington premises represented a significant expansion of his business, but whatever his ambitions for the site it was never to rival the scale of the great purpose-built maltings elsewhere. Jones doubtless saw the potential savings offered by the conversion of existing buildings to a maltings, but the process of conversion itself involved considerable investment. Designs for the adaptation of the mill were produced by the contemporary authority on the malting industry, Henry Stopes (1840–1902), who had already designed the Belle Vue complex for Jones. Stopes was the author of *Malt and Malting, Drying Malt practically considered* (1885), the standard work on malting technology, as well as other books and pamphlets on the industry. He had inherited from his father the Eagle Brewery in Colchester, which he rebuilt in 1882 and further extended in 1888, by which time he was managing his own firm of brewery engineers. Stopes was also a renowned geologist, while his wife, Charlotte (née Carmichael, 1841–1929), was a distinguished Shakespearean scholar, and their daughter, Marie Stopes (1880–1958), was to become the celebrated feminist and proponent of birth control. Like

Robert Free of Free, Rodwell & Co, Stopes favoured the policy of improving the efficiency of traditional floor malting rather than adopting methods of pneumatic malting developed by the French engineer Jules Saladin that were increasingly favoured in continental Europe. Stopes, like Free, recommended double-floor kilns and self-emptying hopper-bottomed steeping cisterns, both of which were introduced into the Ditherington complex.[10]

Malting: the process

Malting is the conversion of the starches in grains to sugars, enabling the grains to be used in brewing. The process of floor malting involves steeping barley in a cistern (or steep), couching it in heaps so that it warms, and then spreading it to a depth of a few inches on a malting floor. After some days, the grain begins to sprout, at which point growth is halted by placing the barley in a kiln heated by some form of smokeless fuel, whether charcoal, coke or anthracite. The grain is subsequently dressed or cleaned in order to remove the shrivelled remains of rootlets, before the malt is placed in sacks or in bulk road or railway vehicles for dispatch to the brewery. The characteristic components of a traditional maltings are a barley store, a cleaning and drying plant, a malthouse (generally rectangular in plan, with cisterns at one or both ends for steeping barley),

a kiln, a dressing plant and a malt store, together with facilities for handling incoming grain and outgoing malt.

Converting the mill to a maltings[11]

In April 1897 Henry Stopes produced plans for converting the Ditherington Flax Mill into what was to be called the 'Shropshire Maltings'.[12] An artist's impression of the maltings, undated but certainly of the late 19th century, shows the proposed works from the north, with the town in the background, and a revived railway siding running into the premises (Fig 10.2). Either this was a fanciful creation by an artist not fully aware of Stopes's intentions, or plans were changed during the rebuilding, as this does not reflect the reality of the works as carried out. The view shows three pyramidal kilns at the north end of the Spinning Mill and two at the south end of the Dyehouse, together with a tall round chimney west of the Apprentice House, which is not drawn accurately.[13] In fact, only a single kiln, at the north end of the Spinning Mill, was built and the chimney was never constructed.

Ditherington Flax Mill was eminently suitable for adaptation to a maltings for a number of reasons. The size of the Spinning Mill and Cross Building, both multi-storeyed, offered

Fig 10.2
Undated artist's impression of the proposed maltings conversion, which shows several buildings and other modifications that were not actually built.
[Shropshire Archives PH/S/13/M/11 (BB015975)]

Fig 10.3
The railway sidings were
extended to run alongside
the Cross Building and the
Dyehouse.
[DP026460]

Jones the potential to increase his germinating floor capacity substantially. The only disadvantage was that the columns provided obstructions that had to be negotiated when the grain was being spread, but as long as the barley was moved by hand rather than machine this inconvenience could be overcome by the skill of the maltsters. The fireproof construction of the Spinning Mill, Cross Building and Flax Warehouse was doubtless considered an asset because of the risk of fire from the kiln furnaces, and the brick-arch construction may have been deemed to create a humid atmosphere which promoted germination of grain.[14] The ancillary buildings were useful for the running of the business and, although some areas now show no sign of specific maltings functions, that does not mean that they were unused during the site's maltings phase. In addition to the buildings themselves, the transport connections that had been vital for the flax mill also allowed convenient transportation of grain in and out of the site. Both the railway and the canal facilitated the movement of goods,

although probably by 1897 the former was the more important. When William Jones took over the site the rail sidings were extended, with one branch leading directly to the Kiln and a new branch alongside the western wall of the Dyehouse and the adjacent Stove House (Fig 10.3).[15] Consignments of malt for despatch to distant destinations were sent to the railway companies' warehouses elsewhere in the town. Throughout the 1950s much of the plant's barley was brought in by rail from the light soils of Norfolk, Suffolk and Huntingdonshire and unloaded in standard two-hundredweight (cwt) sacks. A tractor was used to shunt the siding, and particular difficulties were caused when rejected consignments of barley had to be returned to their senders.[16]

Incoming barley was dried and cleaned in the former Dyehouse, which during its conversion was given its distinctive hoist structures. The grain was unloaded from standing railway wagons by way of two hoists extending from the roof space over the siding to the west (Fig 10.4). Three further hoist towers were constructed within the former Dyehouse complex. The most southerly is weather-boarded with a slate roof, while the other two are clad with corrugated iron. Barley was originally dried in a kiln, replaced in the 1950s by four Boby drying drums. The drums, together with a barley screen and a half corn machine that were in the Drying House, were removed in the 1980s (Fig 10.5).

Until the mid-20th century, dried grain was bagged and then stored in a number of places on the site, including the south Engine Houses and the attic floor of the Cross Building: both areas retain hoists used to manoeuvre the grain sacks. It was then taken to the malting floors in the different buildings. Malting floors were created on all five floors of the Spinning Mill and two steeps were installed on the first, second, third and fourth floors, each pair offset from those below so that the barley could be fed directly onto the floor below. The steeps in which barley was soaked have now been removed but are known to have been self-emptying and hopper-bottomed, as recommended by Stopes. Barley for the malting floor in the attic storey was soaked in a flat-bottomed steep on the eastern side of the building. The steeps were fed by chutes from above, remnants of which remain. The installation of the steeps – which, when filled with grain and water added greatly to the loading on the building – necessitated

Fig 10.4
Hoist towers were added to the former Dyehouse for unloading barley from the railway.
[DP163712]

Fig 10.5
Barley drying machinery in the former Dyehouse.
[Shropshire Archives PH/S/13/M/1/5 (BB015974)]

Fig 10.6
The large original windows
in the Spinning Mill were
blocked and replaced by
fewer and smaller windows,
enabling better control of
ventilation for the malting
floors.
[AA022751]

up to 550mm thick at the base of the vaults, with a top screed of cement. This alteration obscured the bases of the cast-iron columns of the flax mill and obliterated evidence for the location of flax-working machinery. One of the major alterations needed to convert the mill into a maltings was to change to the building's fenestration. Barley sprouts most readily in dark conditions but benefits from some ventilation. Consequently the windows of the mill building that had provided as much natural light as possible for flax working were filled in, and smaller windows, with shutters that could be used to adjust the inflow of air, were installed in every third bay (Fig 10.6).

The ground, first, second and third storeys of the Cross Building were adapted for malting in the same way as the Spinning Mill. The floors were covered with concrete screed, the original windows were filled in and a few smaller ones inserted, and steeps with cast-iron hopper-bottoms were installed at the western end. The attic storey, with too low a ceiling height and too many upright iron struts to be used for malting, was used for storing barley until about 1951.

During the spreading stage, barley was laid out on the floors. Originally the piece (batch) system was employed, but with the introduction of strip malting, low boards were inserted down the middle of each floor between the

the removal of substantial areas of the mill floor, and the insertion of numerous round cast-iron columns and steel beams. In order to extend the malting area on the ground floor, the Boiler Houses between the Spinning Mill and the Shrewsbury Canal were demolished and a lean-to structure erected. To provide a smooth surface for germinating the barley, the mill's original flooring, above the brick vaults, was removed and replaced with mass concrete,

Fig 10.7
Top storey of the Spinning
Mill in use as a malt floor.
Significant alterations
continued to be made to the
site in the 1950s and 1960s.
[Shropshire Archives
PH/S/13/M/1/104
(BB015990)]

Spinning Mill's original cruciform cast-iron columns. None of these boards survive, though traces of their positions remain. At the same time, the cross wall in the mill, evidence for the building's phased construction in the last years of the 18th century, was removed, as it interfered with the strip system of barley germination. Once the barley had been spread, it was left to germinate (Fig 10.7). This could take up to fourteen days, during which time the temperature of the barley ranged from 56°F (13°C) to 65°F (15°C) or even 70°F (22°C). As it grew, the rootlets needed to be broken up to ensure even growth and to prevent matting. This was originally done by hand shovel, until ploughs with pronged forks were introduced, replaced in the 20th century by mechanical shovels.[17] The semi-germinated grain was called green malt. When it had reached the necessary stage in the conversion of starch to sugars, it was transferred to the Kiln.

The construction of the Malt Kiln was the major intervention required on the conversion of the site to a maltings. It was built at the north end of the Spinning Mill adjacent to the north Engine House and on the site of a boiler house built in 1811 (Figs 10.8 and 10.9). As was customary with kilns designed by Stopes, it had two floors, both made of perforated tiles, apparently heated by a bank of anthracite-fired furnaces. The Kiln was substantially altered in the mid-20th century when two new burners were installed. The upper floor was stripped of its tiles and removed, and wedge wire replaced the tiles on the lower floor which was divided vertically into two halves, through each of which hot air from one of two new large Suxe anthracite burners was circulated by fans. By the mid-20th century, sprouting barley was conveyed from the malting floors to the Kiln by a series of bucket elevators and worm conveyors. In the antechamber in front of the doors giving access to the Kiln floors were three power shovels and a 'thrower', or kiln-loading machine, that could direct grain into either half of the Kiln. The overhead chute that fed the thrower with grain remains *in situ*.

The kilning process took three or four days, during which time, in temperatures reaching 220°F (105°C), the grain was turned to ensure uniform results – originally by hand, and in later years by machine. Kilning halted germination and the conversion of starch to sugars, gave flavour and colour to the malt, and reduced the moisture content so that the kilned

malt could be safely stored. Until the 1950s kilned malt was conveyed from the Kiln to the former Flax Warehouse in baskets. Thereafter it was moved by chutes. In the Flax Warehouse it was dressed to remove rootlets and then cleaned before being stored – usually for at least a month – in timber bins.

One of the characteristics of the new malting technology of the late 19th century, as

Fig 10.8
The Malt Kiln was the major new addition during the maltings conversion. The arched opening on the left was formerly entered by a railway siding. The Cross Building lies to the right, the former Flax Warehouse to the left.
[DP163683]

Fig 10.9
Ground floor of the Malt Kiln, 2002. The coving allowed hot air from the ground-floor furnaces to rise across the whole of the drying floors.
[AA022810]

Fig 10.10
*The tower added to the
north end of the Spinning
Mill contained the grain
elevators for transferring
sprouting malt from the
malt floors to the Kiln. The
ornamental cresting, which
subsequently became a local
landmark, was probably
supplied by MacFarlanes
of Glasgow.
[AA022763]*

exemplified in Robert Free's plant at Mistley, was the use of powered conveyors to carry grain between floors and between buildings. The use of sacks for moving grain between buildings and of baskets for taking malt away from the Kiln continued at Ditherington until the 1950s and 1960s, but the bucket elevators and worm conveyors that carried sprouting malt from the malting floors to the Kiln were probably part of Stopes's conversion of the building, since the system, operated by means of shafting and belts, was housed in the three-storey wooden-clad tower adjacent to the Kiln. This tower, with its crown of ornamental cast iron, has been a feature of the Shrewsbury skyline for more than a century and is thought to have been erected in 1897 to mark Queen Victoria's Diamond Jubilee (Fig 10.10).[18] The conveyor system was worked in the mid-20th century by electric power, but it is likely that when it was first installed it was operated by a gas engine. William Jones & Sons demolished the factory's

round gasholder of 1842, and thereafter probably town gas was used.

Other buildings on the site were also adapted to the uses of the maltsters. The flax mill's Despatch Warehouse positioned on the western side of the entrance was used, at least for some years during the 20th century, as a laboratory. The adjacent building continued to be used as stables until it was adapted as a garage in the mid-20th century. The Apprentice House may have been used first as offices and a laboratory but was later converted to residential apartments. The ornamental features of the garden adjacent to the Apprentice House when it was the home of the flax mill manager had disappeared by 1900.

The acquisition of the Ditherington site was not the last step in the expansion of William Jones's Shrewsbury empire. Soon afterwards he took over the nearby Castle Mills, a corn mill located just off St Michael's Street, part of which was already used for malting. He ceased milling, and converted the whole site into what he called the Castle Maltings. In the course of the 20th century his company ceased to use their smaller Shrewsbury premises and those in the surrounding district, and concentrated production at the Belle Vue, Castle and Ditherington maltings, all three of which remained in operation until the late 1980s. In 1904 Jones also purchased a malting company at Toowoomba, Queensland, in which he invested over £30,000 during a visit to Australia in 1907. It was operated by his company until he died in 1923.[19]

Ditherington Mill in the 20th century

William Jones & Son went bankrupt in 1933–4, and the business was subsequently administered by the Alliance Insurance Company, but the founder's son Richard Jones (1862–1948) – who began to work for the company in 1880 and was three times mayor of Shrewsbury – was associated with the maltings until 1946. His son and heir had been killed at Ypres during the First World War. In 1948 the company was taken over by its principal customer, Ansells, the Birmingham brewing firm that subsequently became part of Allied Breweries Ltd.[20]

Between 1939 and 1945 the Shropshire Maltings served as a barracks for the basic training of infantry recruits. It is remembered as a billet that offered few comforts. The malting floors were used for sleeping accommodation. There were no sanitary facilities and each morning soldiers had to slop out into large metal tanks that were manhandled down the stairs. There was no electric lighting in the buildings, and the infantry recruits, like the maltsters before them, had to find their way around the site with hurricane lamps. Parts of the buildings were adapted as a NAAFI, a gymnasium and a handicraft room, and morale was sustained by a wall newspaper, the *Maltings Gazette*. The military occupied many buildings in Shrewsbury during the Second World War,

and the maltings was one of the first to be vacated, less than a fortnight after VE Day (Fig 10.11).[21]

In the post-war years malting resumed at Ditherington and significant changes were made to the site. The malting company installed electric lighting by 1952. Some of the major buildings on the site in the last decades of malting relate to changes in the methods of storing grain. A concrete barley silo was built in 1951 opposite the entrance to the Spinning Mill, on the site of the 1852 drying shed. A second concrete silo, this one used to store malt,

Fig 10.11
Ditherington Mill in the 1940s, when most of the 19th-century buildings were still extant and the disused canal clearly visible.
[RAF/540/84 PFFO-0011 SJ 4913/11 29 AUG 1948]

Fig 10.12
Concrete barley silo, built
in 1951.
[AA022772]

Fig 10.13
Concrete malt silo, added
in 1961.
[DP026462]

was constructed near the Kiln in 1961 (Figs 10.12 and 10.13). The malt silo was damaged by an implosion soon after it was completed, but was subsequently repaired.[22]

Changes in the operation of the plant came to a climax in 1963. New strains of malting barley that could be grown in Shropshire, in particular Maris Otter, were developed, and soon the maltings drew all its barley from within an 80km radius of Shrewsbury. Barley and malt came to be handled in bulk rather than in sacks. Both were stored in the new purpose-built silos and were transported by road rather than by rail. The railway siding was taken up in about 1963.[23]

The efficiency of the Shropshire Maltings, along with the Belle Vue and Castle sites, greatly improved between the end of the Second World War and the 1980s. Output per man increased six-fold during that period, and the time that barley had to be laid out on the malting floors was reduced from 11 days to 4 or 5. The injection of new capital enabled many aspects of the operation to be modernised, and the company benefited from scientific advances, in particular the development of new strains of barley.[24]

Nevertheless, traditional floor malting operations came under increasing challenge from modern factories such as that at Bury St Edmunds making malt in drums using technology derived from that developed by Jules Saladin. The structural consolidation of breweries during this era, with numerous mergers and takeovers, led the large horizontally integrated breweries to integrate vertically as well, setting up purpose-built maltings facilities. Once a state-of-the-art works, reputed to be among the largest floor maltings in the country, the Ditherington factory had ageing plant and a constrained site and could not match the giant new generation of malting facilities. In the late 1980s Albrew Maltsters Ltd announced the closure of their entire Shrewsbury operation – the purpose-built complex at Belle Vue as well as the adapted buildings at the Castle and Shrewsbury maltings. The last malt was made at Ditherington in 1987, almost exactly a century after Marshalls ceased to use the site for making linen thread. Following the demolition of Jones's other sites at Belle Vue and the Castle Maltings, the Ditherington complex is the only surviving maltings complex in Shrewsbury and bears testimony to the one-time importance of that industry in the area, and to William Jones's empire in particular.

11

Ditherington rescued

JOHN YATES

When the maltings closed in 1987, the future of Ditherington Mill became uncertain (Fig 11.1). The importance of the site was universally acknowledged and is recognised in the protection of its principal buildings, three of which are listed at Grade I, the highest level of protection. Recognition of significance does not, however, lead inevitably to preservation. The fundamental issue after 1987 was how to secure the mill's future through a programme that would juggle the sometimes conflicting demands of conservation and financial viability. On the one hand, there existed the potential for a large programme of renewal providing a model for the restoration of historic industrial buildings and an opportunity for an exemplary heritage-led regeneration scheme. On the other

hand, as with all complex and protracted projects, global and local market conditions and the costs of restoring the mill had a major influence on what was feasible in terms of renewal and future uses. The history of the site between 1987 and the first decade of the 21st century saw this dialogue played out in a series of schemes which illustrate the challenges involved in achieving successful regeneration: the vicissitudes of the wider economic climate, the devising of solutions to complex conservation problems, the search for a sustainable alternative use, the roles of public- and private-sector agencies and the relationship of the site to its local setting. This chapter will review this story, although at the time of writing (July 2014) the conservation project continues and

Fig 11.1
The derelict maltings in 2006.
[DP026449]

in its most recent incarnation is still in the first stage of what must be regarded as a long-term phased programme.

In the years in which the maltings were running down to closure, Shrewsbury was enjoying a period of steady development. The town centre had largely escaped the attentions of 1970s highway engineers, and was beginning to benefit from recognition of its historic character. Major new retail development, in particular the Pride Hill and Darwin shopping centres, was filling the backlands of the shopping streets, and the town already boasted several high-profile and successful conversions of historic buildings for new uses. Prominent among these were the former Shrewsbury School buildings, converted to the Public Library in 1983, and the former Royal Salop Infirmary, converted to The Parade shopping centre in 1980–3.

The Castle Foregate area and its extension to and beyond Ditherington Mill had seen many changes since the early 20th century (Fig 11.2). Then it had the character of a busy working suburb, with housing lining the main road and a number of industrial sites, including the town gasworks. The Church of St Michael, built in 1829, was set back from the main road, and opposite it a school had been built to serve the community. There was, however, still a great deal of open land behind the road frontages in 1900. The 20th century brought a large increase in housing, filling in much of the vacant land,

and the post-war era in particular saw change to the area's character, with the construction of the town's fire station and, in the immediate vicinity of Ditherington Mill, a bus depot and builders' merchants' yards. The closure of the maltings dealt a serious blow to the vitality of the suburb, removing an important source of employment and creating a vacuum in the heart of the area. St Michael's Church closed as a place of worship, and the school too closed as the population of the area declined; both closures further weakened community cohesion. The local context for the restoration of Ditherington Mill was, therefore, somewhat challenging.

Constant participants in the story of the restoration have been the local councils (until 2009 Shrewsbury and Atcham Borough Council – SABC – thereafter Shropshire Council) and English Heritage, relatively newly created in 1987. There have been a number of private developers, each bringing in expertise in the form of architects and engineers. A further interest, that of the local community, developed during the course of the different proposals and resulted in the formation in 2010 of the Friends of the Flaxmill Maltings. Other partners at different stages of the project included the Regional Development Agency (Advantage West Midlands – AWM), the Homes and Communities Agency (HCA), the Arts Council, the European Regional Development Fund (ERDF) and the Heritage Lottery Fund

Fig 11.2
The recently converted maltings of William Jones & Sons, c 1900. Despite the preservation of the main buildings, Ditherington Mill saw the loss of many smaller structures during the 20th century.
[Shropshire Archives, PH/S/13/M/1]

(HLF). The HLF grant offer of £12 million for conservation of the Spinning Mill and other buildings, together with the provision of community and visitor facilities, was particularly vital. All parties recognised the historic importance of the site and shared the objective of securing Ditherington's future. However, all had different roles to play in the process and came to the restoration project with their own priorities – heritage, conservation, financial, economic and community regeneration, or cultural.

On the closure of the maltings, SABC seriously contemplated buying the site from the owners, Allied Lyons, to convert for use as their own offices, following the then current examples set by Stroud District Council with their purchase of Ebley Mill for conversion to council offices, and the conversion of a dock warehouse for Gloucester City Council. English Heritage offered SABC a grant towards the purchase price (interestingly, a decision taken in the same committee meeting was a much larger grant to Bradford City Council to purchase Salt's Mill at Saltaire). Mill conversion may have been the spirit of the times, but in August 1987 SABC decided not to proceed, and the site was put onto the open market.

In the following years, three successive developers put forward schemes for conversion and regeneration, but for a variety of reasons each scheme foundered. Shropshire Industrial Estates Ltd entered the project in 1987, Millview Consulting Ltd in 1994, and Maltings Development Ltd with Mowlems in 1997. The schemes invariably proposed mixed use for the site as a whole, with permutations of office use, residential, retail, arts, sheltered housing and workshops shared among the different buildings. The cost implications of repair, together with a change of company strategy, caused Mowlems to withdraw in 2002, leaving the future of the site once more in doubt.

After the recurrent failure of these development schemes, which had been mainly led by the private sector, a new approach was required. In 2002 this took the form of the assumption by the public-sector agencies, particularly English Heritage, of a much more active role as enabler and catalyst. This action lay outside English Heritage's normal remit but was seen as an essential way of taking urgent action to arrest the deterioration in the site's condition and of buying time before private-sector interest could revive. It was, therefore, a measure of last resort

and an indicator of the mill's exceptional significance. Urgent works, largely funded by English Heritage, were undertaken to make the site secure from further vandalism and to make the buildings weatherproof (Fig 11.3). A new Steering Group was created, drawing in SABC and Advantage West Midlands, to prepare a new scheme. A vital step was the commissioning of a Masterplan study to provide a vision for the site and the wider area. The Masterplan was delivered in 2004 by Feilden, Clegg, Bradley Architects, responding to the brief for a mixed-use, high-quality heritage-led regeneration of the wider area.

The Masterplan, adopted as Supplementary Planning Guidance by SABC, formed the basis for renewed proposals for the mill. Then, after the owner went into liquidation in 2005 and with support from Advantage West Midlands, English Heritage acquired the freehold of the site, a move reserved only for extraordinary

Fig 11.3
The Spinning Mill was fully scaffolded both inside and out during urgent repair works, and a weatherproof roof covering was installed to prevent further ingress of water.
[DP163698]

One particularly important development at this time was the drawing in of the local community to the partnership. English Heritage opened the buildings to local people during a weekend in mid-2005 and this was followed by a 'Heritage Weekend' opening in September. Some 600 people visited the site, most of them local to Shrewsbury. The exercise was repeated the following year, with the same success. In 2006, after word had spread, the visitors included Second World War veterans who had been stationed at 'The Maltings' when it was a barracks – an unpopular posting because of the rats! The public openings were very rewarding for all concerned, with huge public support being expressed for English Heritage's acquisition of the mill and the proposals for its future, and some volunteers were keen to assist in an oral history project and other activities. English Heritage continued to open the site for Heritage Open Days in the following years, increasingly assisted by volunteers from the local community (Figs 11.4a and 11.4b). Local engagement began to have an impact on the form that conservation might take.

A central question that illustrates the approach to conservation adopted in the project has, from the beginning, concerned the issue of how the regenerated mill should show the two principal industries which it had housed. Should the refurbished mill look like a flax-spinning mill, its purpose during the first

Figs 11.4a (above) and 11.4b (below) Community activities have included an archaeological investigation of the Apprentice House outbuildings, supervised by Oxford Archaeology North, and art and music events in the former Dyehouse, organised by the Friends of the Flaxmill Maltings. [Courtesy Friends of the Flaxmill Maltings]

cases as a last resort. The Steering Group appointed the regeneration specialists Urban Splash to take on the development in 2006, and full design proposals were submitted in 2008, putting flesh on the bones of the Masterplan, which proposed the regeneration of the area around the mill complex and, for the mill itself, mixed-uses, careful conservation and a crisp approach to new design.

90 years of its existence? Or should it look like a maltings, its use in its subsequent history? For the industrial historian, the principal importance of the mill rested in the iron-frame construction of its early buildings; for this audience, the flax mill phase was of paramount importance. Local people, however, remember the mill in or after its maltings phase and would be reluctant to see its character as a former maltings weakened. Two sets of values, therefore, weighed in the balance. The starting point of conservation philosophy for more than a hundred years has been 'conserve as found'. Without demolishing significant buildings such as the Malt Kiln the site could not return to its flax mill condition; and similarly the maltings phase utilised the flax mill buildings, so a great deal of this would survive whatever the verdict. At a general level, renovation would necessarily incorporate elements of both phases.

At a more detailed level, however, the balance is more critical. The design of the Spinning Mill's fenestration illustrates the conundrum, having more than anything else the potential to define the building's historic character and use. In the flax mill phase, the mill had large windows to admit maximum light, but these windows were blocked and reduced in size on conversion to a maltings so that ventilation could be better controlled on the germination floors (Fig 11.5). These small openings (and the bold painted lettering on the road frontage proclaiming its use – 'Albrew Maltsters Limited Shropshire Maltings') defined the appearance of the mill in its life as a maltings. Should the small openings be retained? Or should the fenestration of the flax-spinning mill, which was in fact not entirely understood, be reinstated? Should both styles be combined in some way? Or should a radically new design settle the issue? Design work is ongoing, and the outcome of this debate will determine future generations' perceptions of the mill's historic character.

For a number of reasons, the Spinning Mill has proved to be the most difficult building to conserve. Its 16-bay interior, open from end to end, was an important element of the building's historic character, a major feature of its use during its life as both a linen mill and a maltings. Open-plan office or institutional use could best retain the sense of internal space and therefore the character of an industrial building. One scheme proved unacceptable because of its proposal to divide these open floors into a number of small spaces. However, there was a need to

Fig 11.5
Many of the surviving architectural details of the complex, such as these inserted windows, date from the maltings conversion rather than the earlier use of the site as a flax mill. As with many historic industrial buildings the question arises of which features to preserve – those associated with its original construction or its later changes of use.
[DP026474]

achieve a balance between finding an appropriate solution that respected the historic character of the building but at the same time providing a commercially viable scheme.

More intractable than the issue of subdivision, however, was that of the building's structural condition. Successive engineers found that the Spinning Mill was in an unsound condition, largely as a consequence of deficiencies in the design of its iron frame and the means of securing it within the brick shell of the building. Water ingress over nearly two centuries had caused timber members within the wall – lintels over the windows and the timber pads which secured the iron beams to the walls – to rot, threatening failure of the brick walls. Furthermore, it was discovered that the iron beams themselves showed signs of failure, particularly in areas over the cast-iron columns. Bage's method of joining beams and columns had not allowed for movement, and this had caused the beams to crack in places. When precisely the cracks had appeared, and how seriously they jeopardised the safety of the mill, were not clear: some may have appeared very early in the mill's life.

Whatever the case, a solution was required to give confidence to future users. At one point it was proposed to use carbon-fibre bandages to strengthen the beams at critical points. A trial sample of this treatment was applied and demonstrated to the developers and officials. As an interim measure in 2007, a full supporting scaffold was inserted throughout the Spinning Mill to allow repair of the walls. A long-term solution to the need to support the original frame was devised by the structural engineers Adams Kara Taylor, who proposed the insertion of a complete new steel frame taking the 'live' loads of any new uses down to new foundations, leaving the historic floor frame carrying only its own weight. This solution would have a minimal impact on the historic character of the interior, only steel pilasters against the side walls being visible: otherwise Bage's fireproof structure would remain fully legible. The design had a number of benefits: it would stabilise the building, permit a range of new uses and retain the historic character of the structure, which had been identified as of paramount significance. However, it did require major physical intervention, and a considerable cost.

English Heritage's support for such a radical proposal for a Georgian Grade I listed historic building caused some debate in the conservation world. However, it was soundly based on the philosophical framework set out in *Conservation Principles*, English Heritage's guide to best practice in the planning of change to historic assets.[1] The guide emphasises the central role of the assessment of significance in conservation, based on a range of values placed on a site. In the case of Ditherington, the historic importance was well understood, with an English Heritage research project pulling together over half a century of investigation and providing new insights into the mill's development. In proposals for renovation, the 'Evidential value' of the fabric was retained as far as possible, and 'Historical value' was respected and celebrated in the care taken over the planned interventions into the Spinning Mill and in the generally low level of alteration to all the buildings and the spaces between them. The 'Aesthetic value' was largely fortuitous, stemming in particular from the scale of the buildings and the spatial effect of the forests of slender columns within them, but where there has been a deliberately artistic expression (such as Bage's understated Tuscan in the Warehouse and Cross Building, and the Jubilee Crown over the Spinning Mill) it was to be carefully conserved.

Generating less debate than the remedial works required in the Spinning Mill was the fate of the two concrete silos constructed in the post-war years to store grain and malt. While it is true that they clearly demonstrated changing technology in the malting industry, they lacked all but the most brutal aesthetic value and by their design and structure offered little potential for alternative uses. Their presence could be regarded as an obstacle to successful regeneration of the site and it was widely agreed that their loss was an acceptable price to pay. The demolition of these two structures, carried out after 2010, has been the only instance of removal of major structures within the historic complex.

All conservation projects and wider regeneration programmes are subject to some factors beyond their control, and what begins with good prospects in a climate of economic buoyancy can rapidly founder when conditions change for the worse. This happened at Ditherington, as in so many other places, in 2008 with the onset of the deepest recession in the post-war era. Within months the property business worldwide ground to a halt, and Urban Splash announced that it could no longer finance the Ditherington project. The Steering Group took the lead again, with English Heritage and Shropshire Council (as it became in April 2009) funding the next stage of design. As over twenty years earlier, there were strong hints that local government would become the 'anchor' occupier. In November 2010 the Council granted outline planning permission for the whole project, and a conditional full planning permission and listed building consent for the main buildings, and immediately applied for a substantial grant from the Heritage Lottery Fund. This initial bid was rejected in 2011, a year of particularly strong competition from other major projects with better community credentials. The project was kept alive, however, partly by the Friends of the Flaxmill Maltings, who launched a programme of events that gave a major new impetus to a further application by the Council for HLF funding. This was granted in 2013, as were grants from English Heritage and the ERDF. Meanwhile, it had become clear that Shropshire Council would not, after all, need the space for their own use.

The Friends of the Flaxmill Maltings, chaired by Alan Mosley, have fulfilled a vital role by stimulating interest and enthusiasm in the local and wider community, and have generated much media coverage. They have organised site tours, presentations, open days and exhibitions, carried out important new research and provided significant learning opportunities for schools and colleges. Now a registered charity and company with their own staff and hundreds of supporters, the Friends work closely with the Management Board and will be responsible for the public-facing elements of the project.

At the time of writing (July 2014) the renovation of the mill is in its first major stage. Emergency works have arrested deterioration of the different buildings, and the principal building – the Spinning Mill – is heavily scaffolded both externally and internally (Fig 11.6: *see also* Fig 11.3). Work in this stage of the project is focused on the removal of the 20th century silos and on the repair and renovation of the buildings at the south end of the site – the Stable, Smithy and offices. This will provide a base for the Friends as well as site interpretation for visitors and space for learning and outreach activities. Part of the Spinning Mill will be made accessible for light uses on completion of this phase.

Proceeding beyond the first phase of restoration will rest upon the results of an 'options appraisal'. This will set out alternative solutions for the conservation of the Spinning Mill, Cross Building and Malt Kiln – as the historic 'core' – making the best use of the available funding. The preferred option will need to balance the needs of the HLF as major funder, the structural requirements of the buildings, the conservation 'ethic' and the requirements of potential occupiers. Compromises are inevitable.

The model of a public–private partnership that has successfully secured the future of important historic sites elsewhere, such as Manningham Mills, Bradford, and the historic Naval Dockyards at Devonport, is clearly one which offers potential for Ditherington Mill. But all such partnerships – hitherto at Ditherington and at all other sites – are subject to outside pressures, and much will depend upon the economic climate in which the project progresses. This is inherently unpredictable, a quality inimical to the planning of long-term conservation projects.

Despite this uncertainty and the significant challenges which the renovation of the mill presents, the Ditherington project has many positive aspects. Above all, there is a shared acknowledgement among the agencies involved of the need to retain the site's unique historic character. This determination has been forged

through very close collaboration between public, private and voluntary sectors. For the future, it is important not only that Historic England (the new name of the body responsible for the planning functions of English Heritage), Shropshire Council and other public bodies continue to work together, but also that the local community, represented by the Friends of the Flaxmill Maltings, maintains its role in reaffirming the mill's value at a local level. Bringing the mill back to life will re-invigorate the northern side of Shrewsbury, and this is the inducement which will draw in the private sector and maintain the commitment of volunteers. For developers, the vision of a busy, active mill of exceptional historic character, set in a lively, vibrant area close to the town centre, offers the best prospect of a return on investment. Making this vision a reality will have taken 30 years, but that will be time well spent to rescue this wonderful historic place for future generations.

Many issues relating to the future of Ditherington Mill are yet to be resolved. What is clear, however, is that the site includes buildings of international significance and through its fabric tells a story of industrial enterprise, innovation and adaptation. What the research project has achieved is to establish more clearly Ditherington's place in the development of industrial architecture and the history of the

Fig 11.6
Testing methods of concrete removal without damaging the original structure on the first floor of the Spinning Mill, 2014.
[DP163690]

textile industry. Charles Bage's Spinning Mill of 1796–1800 is a world first and can be seen as the progenitor of the towering steel-framed buildings which dominate the landscape of modern cities. Close analysis of its fabric has deepened understanding of its pioneering nature, for the iron frame not only served to provide a fireproof internal structure but also took into account the arrangement of machines within the building and the means to deliver power to them (Fig 11.7). The design process, therefore, extended beyond structure to consider the practical aspects in the operation of a textile mill. The other early iron-framed buildings within the mill differ in significant details from the form of the Spinning Mill, and as a result Bage's design can be seen as experimental and in some respects flawed, for these later buildings – the Flax Warehouse of *c* 1810 and the Cross Building of 1812 – demonstrate improved methods of construction. They also belong to a family of iron-framed buildings which show similarities in structural forms and raise questions about the dissemination of knowledge among mill builders and the responsibility for design in this crucial short period in industrial architecture.

Ditherington's story has also brought into sharp focus the ways in which a company oper-

ated a mill during this period of industrial expansion and adjusted to advances in technology and changes in markets and products. Like the structural forms adopted in the mill's principal buildings, many of the issues faced by the management of the mill were new and others were on a different scale to those faced by earlier entrepreneurs: setting up a mill and recruiting a large labour force in a location without a long tradition of mechanised factory production and developing new markets were considerable challenges. Furthermore, the atmosphere of fierce competition in the engineering industry is revealed in the early years of the mill's operation in the provision of steam engines: Ditherington's history provides a revealing vignette into this wider issue, which was central to Britain's emergence as a major industrial power. Ditherington can be seen as doing more than exemplifying and contributing to these general historical issues, for it is also possible to identify its impact within Shrewsbury and on the people of the town. In its looming industrial buildings, in its noise and smoke, in its daily routines with hundreds of operatives crowding the area at the beginning and end of their shifts, the mill must have demonstrated very powerfully the meaning of the new world of the factory system.

Fig 11.7
The world's first textile mill with an internal iron frame: a challenge to conservation and an iconic monument of the Industrial Revolution.
[AA022786]

GLOSSARY

Apprentice A term used in early textile factories for children and young adults, often taken from workhouses, who were employed with minimum wages and often lived in 'apprentice houses' within or near to a mill complex.

Beam engine The most common form of early mill engine in which a beam, pivoted in the centre, was worked by an upright cylinder at one end and drove a flywheel via a crank or gear at the other end.

Bevel gears A pair of connected gear wheels with angled teeth which were used to transmit power between two shafts set at right angles, such as between a vertical main shaft and a horizontal line shaft.

Bleaching A stage in textiles production using chemicals or sunlight to whiten yarns and cloth.

Bob wall A transverse masonry wall in a beam engine house used to support the main bearing of the working beam. From the early 19th century, bob walls were replaced by an entablature beam (*see* below). Also an alternative name for 'lever wall'.

Carding The opening and straightening of short-staple textile fibres, such as tow flax, before the next stages of preparation and spinning.

Common brick The standard-sized handmade bricks that were used at Ditherington, from *c* 1810. *See also* 'great brick'.

Condenser The component of a steam engine used for condensing steam after it had exhausted the cylinder, originally patented by James Watt in 1769 (Patent 913). In the early beam engines it comprised an iron cylinder immersed in a cold-water cistern beneath the floor.

Corn Laws Trade laws, operating between 1815 and 1846, designed to protect cereal producers in the United Kingdom of Great Britain and Ireland against competition from foreign imports.

Creel A rectangular frame of wood or metal with numerous pegs for supporting bobbins of yarn.

Cruciform Term used to describe the four-armed cross section of the solid cast-iron columns at Ditherington and other early textile mills.

Double-acting The technique patented by James Watt and used in early steam engines, in which steam was alternately fed to both sides of the piston (Patent 1321, 1782). This required two sets of inlet and exhaust valves, located at the top and bottom of the cylinder.

Doubling The process of merging slivers of textile fibre to produce a single sliver with fewer irregularities; usually combined with drawing. Flax preparation involved several stages of doubling and drawing.

Drafting The carefully controlled stretching of a roving in a spinning machine, which was combined with twisting to produce a yarn of the required characteristics.

Drawing The stretching or attenuation of combined slivers in the preparation stages of flax spinning.

Dressing A general term for the multiple stages of flax heckling. Also refers to the application of size (a glue-like substance) or other chemical to give a stronger smooth finish to linen yarn or thread.

Dyeing The use of natural or synthetic chemicals to produce repeatable colours in yarn, thread or cloth, usually by steeping the textile in heated vats dedicated to each colour.

Entablature beam A heavy cast-iron beam, or a pair of beams, spanning the upper part of a beam-engine house to support the pivot of the main working beam.

Entasis A slight thickening of columns near mid-height, used for aesthetic reasons in Classical architecture.

Factor An agent who buys and sells goods on commission.

Finishing General term for the final stages in the production of yarn, thread or cloth, comprising bleaching, dyeing, drying and related processes such as printing.

Flange The horizontal projections at the base of the web in cast-iron beams, designed to counter the bending of the beam due to the weight of the floors. Later beams also had a top flange.

Flywheel A large, heavily weighted cast-iron wheel mounted on the engine's primary shaft. Its momentum enabled the smooth operation of the valves and piston, creating the regular motion that was essential for the operation of mill shafting.

Gasholder A large iron vessel designed to store coal gas.

Governor A mechanism for maintaining the speed of a steam engine, which used the centrifugal force of a pair of spinning weights to control the steam inlet valve via a system of levers.

Great brick The larger types of handmade brick, made to reduce payments of Brick Tax, which were used at Ditherington until the first decade of the 19th century.

Hackling Alternative term for heckling.

Hank A standard unit of measurement for yarns; the actual length of a hank varied in different textile industries.

Heckling The process of combing raw flax though metal spikes (known as heckles) to clean and straighten the fibre and separate the line flax from different grades of tow flax.

Hopper A funnel-shaped vessel used in a maltings for delivering grain to a cistern or kiln.

Kiln The large oven used in a maltings for the controlled heating of the barley after it has germinated on the malt floor. Often distinguished externally by a pyramidal or mansard roof with prominent ventilators.

Lea A standard measure of the weight and length of flax yarns.

Lever wall Alternative term for a 'bob wall', mainly used in the drawings of the Boulton and Watt Collection.

Line The longest and most valuable grade of flax fibre produced by heckling. Used for the finest yarns and for twisting into thread.

Line shaft Shafting driven by gearing, belts or ropes which was used to transmit power to machinery.

Linen The products derived from flax, including yarn, thread and cloth.

Lye An alkaline chemical, often made from diluted wood ash, used in bleaching.

Malt floor The largest working area of a maltings, on which the barley was spread to dry and germinate after being steeped.

Meniscus A term used at Ditherington Mill for the concave undersides of the early cast-iron floor beams, caused by the contraction of the iron in open-topped moulds in the foundry.

Packing Warehouse The warehouse at Ditherington used for finished thread and yarn, where products were packed before dispatch from the site.

Parallel motion The mechanism in a beam engine, as developed by James Watt in 1784 but not patented, which converted the vertical motion of the piston rod into the curved motion of the working beam.

Piecework A system of production in which the number of items made determines the level of wages, rather than the amount of time worked.

Preparation A term used in a flax mill for the sequence of stages after heckling: the slivers of flax fibre were gradually attenuated and converted into a roving, which was transferred to the spinning machines for the final stage of yarn spinning.

Reeling The process of measuring and cutting spun yarn into fixed lengths, usually measured in hanks. Involved winding the yarn onto a drum, or reel, of known circumference, in which the number of rotations indicated the length of the yarn. Also referred to as 'winding'.

Retort The sealed iron vessel in a gasworks in which coal was heated to produce gas and coke.

Retting The process of softening the flax after harvesting, usually by either spreading the stems on the ground (dew retting) or soaking them in water pits or tanks (water retting).

Roughing The initial cleaning of raw flax by pulling it through metal spikes, prior to heckling.

Roving The final stage of preparation, in which the slivers of flax fibre were drafted further, given a slight twist and wound onto bobbins for transfer to the spinning machines.

Scutching The process of breaking and removing the hard outer parts of flax stems, after the crop had been cut and dried in the field.

Shaft box A square or rectangular cast-iron box containing the bearing of a line shaft or part of an engine, mounted in the wall of a mill or an engine house.

Shrink ring A wrought-iron ring, heated in a furnace and used to join cast-iron floor beams, often by connecting horizontal spigots on the sides of the beams. The ring contracted as it cooled, forming a secure joint.

Silo A term used at Ditherington for a large detached concrete building for the storage of malt or grain.

Skewback Angled bracket of iron or wood fixed to the sides of a beam to act as the springer for a brick-vaulted ceiling. At Ditherington, skewbacks were incorporated into the cross sections of the early cast-iron beams.

Spigot A short cylindrical casting at the foot or top of a column, fitting into a circular housing in a floor beam to join the two components together. Spigots were also used to join floor beams from the early 19th century, using shrink rings.

Spreading table The first stage of flax preparation, which comprised a slowly moving conveyor on which the fibres of hackled flax were combined by hand into a continuous sliver that was fed into a drawing machine.

Steep An iron or brick tank in a maltings in which barley was soaked prior to being spread on the malting floor.

Stove house A building heated by steam or warm air, used for the rapid drying of yarn, thread or cloth after bleaching or dyeing.

Sun-and-planet gear The mechanism used in early Watt engines, which converted the reciprocal motion of the working beam into the rotational motion of the mill shafting (Patent 1306, 1782). The sun gear was fixed to the main flywheel shaft and the planet gear to the connecting rod attached to the working beam. This mechanism was replaced by crankshafts from *c* 1800.

Thread A higher-value product than yarn in the flax industry, which was made by twisting together two or more strands of fine yarn and usually dyed. It became the main product of Ditherington Mill in the early 19th century.

Tie-plate External circular, square or cruciform iron plates used to secure a tie-rod to a wall, the tie-rod being fixed in place either with nuts or metal wedges.

Tie-rod Wrought-iron tension rods connecting the beams in an iron-framed mill, used to support the structure during construction and to counter the lateral thrusts generated by brick-vaulted ceilings.

Tow The shorter-length flax fibres that were separated from the more valuable line flax during the process of heckling. The tow was then graded into different lengths in successive stages of heckling.

Twisting The process of combining two or more yarns to make a thread.

Upright shaft The main drive shaft commonly used to transmit power from an engine or water wheel to the line shafting in the upper floors of a textile mill.

Wagon boiler The type of small, low-pressure boiler that was supplied with the early Boulton and Watt engines, named because of its similarity to a covered wagon. This boiler was gradually improved in the early 19th century but was thereafter replaced by more efficient models producing higher-pressure steam, notably the Cornish and Lancashire boilers.

Web The thin vertical part of the beam rising from the bottom flange in cast-iron beams.

Wet spinning An improved technique for flax spinning that was widely introduced from the early 1820s. The spinning machines included a trough of hot water through which the roving was passed, enabling the production of finer yarns with fewer breakages.

Working beam The reciprocating beam of a beam engine, pivoted roughly in the centre, which was driven by the piston at one end and connected to the flywheel at the other.

Yarn The product of the final stage of spinning in a flax mill. Yarns made of tow were often used for weaving canvas or coarser linens, while those made from line flax could be used for weaving fine linens or for twisting into thread.

NOTES

1 Ditherington Mill: an introduction

1 The term 'Industrial Revolution' has been in and out of fashion since its first coining in the 1880s by Arnold Toynbee. It has endured as a popular label for a particularly important period in British history and was used in the title of a recent account of Britain's industrialisation: *see* Trinder 2013.

2 English Heritage set out a method of assessing significance related to different values: evidential, historical, aesthetic and communal: *see* English Heritage 2008, 27–32.

3 *See* Chapter 5 for a discussion of the degree to which iron-framed buildings could be considered fire resistant: it was found that iron components could fail in intense heat.

4 This perception of importance relates to the 'communal value' identified by English Heritage in its *Conservation Principles*: English Heritage 2008, 31–2.

5 Bannister 1950.

6 Skempton and Johnson 1962.

7 Rimmer 1959; Rimmer 1960.

8 Macleod *et al* 1988; Trinder 1992a.

9 Giles and Goodall 1992; Williams (with Farnie) 1992; Calladine and Fricker 1993; Watson, M 1990.

10 Fitzgerald 1987–8; Falconer 1993a.

11 The Marshall papers are held in Leeds University Library, Special Collections, MS200, hereafter LULSC MS200.

12 SA, Letters from Charles Bage to William Strutt, SAL 6001/2657.

13 *See* Chapter 8 and Chapter 9.

2 The linen industry in Great Britain: history, products, processes and location

1 For more on the stages of flax cultivation *see* Warden 1867, 31–40.

2 Warden 1867, 32.

3 Scutching mills were very numerous in Ireland: in 1835 there were more than 500 in the country: McCutcheon 1980, 240–1.

4 Rimmer 1960, 75.

5 LULSC MS200/7, Flax Accounts 1815–22, 109–64.

6 The Cross Building at Ditherington is described as the flax dressing department in newspaper accounts of the fire in 1811, *ESJ*, 30 October 1811; 6 November 1811; *SC* 25 October 1811.

7 'A Day at a Leeds Flax Mill', *Penny Magazine* XII, December 1843, 504.

8 Rimmer 1960, 84.

9 Brown 1980, 103.

10 Patent 3257, 12 August 1809: inventory evidence is discussed in Chapter 7.

11 The machines may have been in use in another Leeds mill in 1808. Murray later received the gold medal of the Society of Arts for his machine; Rimmer 1960, 84.

12 'A Day at a Leeds Flax Mill', 505–6.

13 Brown 1980, 103.

14 Rimmer 1960, 84–5.

15 Patent Number 1613, 21 June 1787.

16 Patent Number 1752, 22 June 1790 and Number 1971, 15 January 1793.

17 Horner 1920, 253, quoting J G Marshall.

18 Patent Number 2034, William Sellers and Peter Standage, 13 February 1795; Patent Number 3855, Horace Hall, 17 November 1814; Horner 1920, 259–60.

19 Patent Number 5226, 26 July 1825.

20 In England, de Girard's machinery of *c* 1812 was included in Hall's patent of 1814 (*see* Note 18 above) and was the basis of an unsuccessful legal challenge to James Kay's 1825 patent for wet spinning (Patent Number 5226); Horner 1920, 334–9; McCutcheon 1980, 322.

21 Rimmer 1960, 80.

22 Edmund Cartwright invented the first powerloom and patented several improvements from the mid-1780s, but despite numerous attempts in different industries, mostly unsuccessfully, it was not a widespread commercial success until the Lancashire loom was introduced by Richard Roberts in 1822.

23 Bage's weaving mill was in operation from *c* 1817–27; Trinder 1992a, 212.

24 SA 6001/26571/17, Charles Bage to William Strutt, 11 August 1818.

25 Watson 1990, 92; McCutcheon 1980, 305.

26 Giles and Goodall 1992, 15, 201: in 1874 there were only about 3,500 powerlooms in operation in Yorkshire.

27 McCutcheon 1980, 288.

28 On the development of bleaching methods *see* Warden 1867, 717–23.

29 Spufford 1984, 107–15.

30 Yarranton 1677 I.44–5; I.119; II.200.

31 Warden 1864, 690–2; UBD, *see under* Darlington; Defoe 1959, II 248; Angerstein 2000, 238.

32 UBD *see under* Knaresborough; Jennings 1967, *passim*; Mackenzie 1949, *passim*; LULSC MS200/57.

33 Cartwright 1888–9, 43; Angerstein 2000, 287; Ayton 1814–25, 129; LULSC MS200/57, 200/62; Falconer 1993a, 13.

34 Cartwright 1888–9, 11, 210; Whatley 1751, *sub* Manchester; Angerstein 2000, 294; Defoe 1959, 259–60; Campbell 1774, I, 322.

35 Young 1799, 407.

36 Cartwright 1888–9, 96; Shaw 1789, 294; Williams 2006.

37 BPP, 1840, XXIII, 352; Eliot 1861, 3–4; Eliot 1860, 225; Trinder and Cox 2000, 75.

38 Trinder and Cox 1980, 61–4; Trinder and Cox 2000, 73–5; Trinder 1996, 134–6; Young 1932, 162.

39 Durie 1979, 15–8, 29–30, 162–5, the last containing an assessment of the effectiveness of measures to promote the linen industry in Scotland.

40 Information from Mark Watson.

41 Hume 1976, 39; Watson 1990, 11–15; Watson 1992, 230.

42 Cullen 1987, 59–64; Pennant 1883, I, 249; Broster 1782, 25.

43 Young 1780, 105, 188–9, 259; Crawford 1987, 16–17.

44 Rimmer 1960, 5–7; Mitchell and Deane 1962, 201–2.

45 Watson 1990, 11–15; Brown 1980, 105–6.

46 Spackman 1847, 149.

47 LULSC MS200/Add.

48 McCutcheon 1980, 298.

49 McCutcheon 1980, 292.

50 McCutcheon 1980, 293–305; Cullen 1987, 120; Crawford 1987 17–33; Spackman 1847, 149.

51 Jennings 1967, 178–9, 210–11; Giles and Goodall 1992, 203, 207–8.

52 Brown 1980, 92–106.

53 BPP, 1840, XXIII, 350, 373, 411; Ure 1835 74–9; Brown 1980, 92–106; Rimmer 1960, 2–9, 115, 125–34; Giles and Goodall 1992, 209, 222.

54 Pigot & Co 1834, 811; Rimmer 1960, 201.

55 Mackenzie 1949, 6–7; Giles and Goodall 1992, 15, 19, 201. Adoption of linen powerlooms was slow in Yorkshire: only 3,500 were in operation there in 1874. In Barnsley, handloom production continued well into the second half of the 19th century, with over a thousand handloom weavers in the town in 1871.

56 Rimmer 1960, 61; Giles and Goodall 1992, 203, 209–23.

57 In 1862 the employment in linen factories in Britain was: England, 20,305; Scotland, 33,599; Ireland, 33,525. Yorkshire had 12,562 and Shropshire just 656, probably all at Ditherington: Warden 1864, 680–1. Information from Mark Watson.

3 Shrewsbury in the 18th and 19th centuries: industry and culture

1 Mitchell and Deane 1962, 5, 24–7; Phillips 1779, 69.

2 *SC* 17 September 1790.

3 Pigot & Co 1835, 372–3.

4 Skrine 1798, 619; Minshull 1786, *passim*.

5 Minshull 1786, *passim*; Minshull 1803, *passim*.

6 Trinder 2005, 109–10; 121–2.

7 Trinder 1996, 177–80; *SC* 18 March, 25 November 1796, *ESJ* 23 March 1796, 16 November 1796; Hadfield, 1966, 160, 163–6.

8 Trinder 1996, 180–4; Hadfield 1966, 166, 173–4; *ESJ* 3 December 1794, 15 January 1800, 18 May 1803; *Shropshire Conservative*, 24 April 1841; SA, DP 289, *Plan of a Proposed Navigable Canal…*, 1792.

9 Lawson 1980, 1–22; Trinder 1996, 59–60; Trinder 2006, 127–8; *SC* 30 October 1840; Trinder 2000, 106–8; Cambridge University Library, Microfilm Dar 227, section 5:38, p 7. I am grateful to Dr Donald Harris for this information; Skempton 2002, 311.

10 SA 1831/8, Apprenticeship Register of the Shrewsbury Drapers' Company; Mendenhall 1953, *passim*; Probate inventories transcribed by members of Shropshire County Council and University of Birmingham adult classes; Pennant 1883, III, 224; Aikin 1797, 69–84; Owen and Blakeway 1825, 551; *ESJ* 3 December 1794.

11 Minshull 1786, i–xix; SA 665/3/9, *A Poll for the Borough of Shrewsbury* 1796; Pigot & Co 1834a, 690–2; *SC* 1 December 1865.

12 Aikin 1797, 77; *ESJ* 18 February, 3 March, 23 June, 28 July 1824.

13 *ESJ* 18 June 1800; *SC* 15 January 1830; Wood 1791, 13, 20, 29–30.

14 *SC* 2 September 1795, 9 October 1800; Hulbert 1852, 194–5, 222–3; Hulbert 1837, 307–8; Trinder 2006, 82–7.

15 *Chester Chronicle* 3 December 1802; Trinder 1996, 138–40; Trinder 2006, 82–4.

16 Trinder 2006, 144–9; *SC* 30 July 1819.

17 Trinder 2006, 160–1.

18 Fiennes 1947, 226; Trinder 2006, 141, 149–50.

19 LULSC MS200/14/13.

20 Trinder 1992a, 206–8; Trinder 2006, 150–1; *SC* 8 July 1825.

21 SA 6001/2657, Bage–Strutt 26 February 1815–June 1816; 11 Aug 1818; Trinder 1996, 148; Trinder 2006, 87; *SC* 20 October, 22 December 1826, 5 January 1827, 12 October 1827.

22 *SC* 3 January 1823, 20 October and 22 December 1826, 5 January and 12 October 1827.

23 Information from Joanna Layton, Friends of the Flaxmill Maltings Documentary Research Group.

24 Trinder 1992a, 211; Trinder 1996, 146–9; Trinder 2006, 155–7; *SC* 9 August 1805, 23 December 1814, 17 June 1831; Tann 1970, 43.

25 The former Flax Warehouse was eventually adapted as dwellings, now Nos 5–8a Severn Street.

26 *SC* 5 November 1813, 11 May 1821, 3 November 1843; Trinder 1996, 147–9; Trinder 2006, 157: S Bagshaw 1851. *History, Gazetteer and Directory of Shropshire*, 71, quoted in Rimmer 1959, 65.

4 Building the mill

1 Details of John Marshall's early life are taken from LULSC MS200/14/7; Rimmer 1960; LULSC MS200/Add; LULSC MS200/01: John Marshall – Thomas Gataker, 19 November 1801, original in Public Record Office of Northern Ireland. Rimmer 1960, 10, note 2, gives the information that Marshall's 'Sketch of his own life' is a 31-page document compiled *c* 1880, probably by his grandson.

2 LULSC MS200/Add; Rimmer 1960, Chapter 2.

3 SA 1831/8; Minshull 1786, i–xix; SA 665/3/9, *A Poll for the Borough of Shrewsbury* 1796; Minshull 1803, 49; SA 4791/1/2, 230, No. 1389; Rimmer 1960, 58, quoting the respected antiquarian L C Lloyd suggests that the Benyons were apprenticed to a draper, but their apprenticeships are not recorded in the records of the Drapers' Company. They may have been articled to a retailer.

4 Rimmer 1960, 61; LULSC MS 200/1 f.20; LULSC MS200/Add.

5 Swailes 2002a.

6 Gould 1981–2.

7 Charles Bage entry in *Oxford Dictionary of National Biography*.

8 Telford 1838, 682; Trinder 1992a, 193; Lawson 1980, 13–15.

9 LULSC MS200/Add.

10 Pattison 2012; Hughes 2004; Minshull 1803, 12; Trinder 1996, 57–60, 150; Cossons and Trinder 2002, 82–7; *SC* 2 March 1827.

11 Cossons and Trinder 2002, 48–9; Trinder 2005, 34.

12 LULSC MS200/Add; LULSC MS200/01.

13 Pinkerton 1808–14, vol 2, 36; Bray 1777, 226–7; Defoe 1959, vol 2, 156; Derwent Valley Mills Partnership 2000, 93–4; Calladine 1993, 82–99.

14 Calladine 1993, 91; Calladine and Fricker 1993, 29.

15 Trinder 2013, 11.

16 Derwent Valley Mills Partnership 2000, 38–40.

17 Chapman 1981–2, 10.

18 Historic Scotland 2000; Williams (with Farnie) 1992, 50–1. A very few years later mills in Ancoats, Manchester, reached seven and later eight storeys: Williams (with Farnie) 1992, 160–1, 164–5.

19 Father of the celebrated eccentric 'Mad Jack' Mytton of Halston (1796–1834).

20 SA Deed 13322/3, indenture and release, John Mytton to John Marshall, Thomas Benyon, Benjamin Benyon and Charles Bage, 20 September 1796.

21 SA 6001/13323.

22 BWC, Box 6, Bundle B, Marshall and Benyons to Boulton and Watt, 2 May 1796.

23 Trinder 1992a, 195; SA 4791/6, No. 3902, 26.

24 Nowhere in the Marshall archive is the building described as the Spinning Mill: mid-century plans label it simply as 'Mill'. The term Spinning Mill is adopted as a matter of convenience in this account simply to assist identification: the building's principal purpose was the production of linen yarn and thread, although other processes apart from spinning were carried out here, as described in Chapter 7.

25 Fitzgerald pers. comm.

26 SC 1 September 1797.

27 Fitzgerald pers. comm.

28 Skempton and Johnson 1962, 181. *See* note 61, Chapter 6 for the evidence of the existence of the north-end engine in 1800.

29 Rimmer 1959, 51; Minshull 1803, 48; the earliest reference in fire insurance documents dates from 1804: SA, Salop Fire Office Policy Books, 4791/1/5, p 234, policy 2657, 14 January 1804.

30 SA, *Salopian Journal* 30 October 1811.

31 Listed in Salop Fire office Policy Books, SRO 4791/1/5, Policy 2657, 14 January 1804; 1855 site plan, SRO 6000/19533.

32 1855 site plan, ibid.

33 LULSC MS200/47, 1886 Sale Catalogue, 4–6.

34 Rimmer 1959, 67: plan of 1849 (erroneously dated by Rimmer to 1819).

35 The building was demolished to provide space for lorries to turn: SA 7396/26/1–7.

36 Identifying the construction date for the Flax Warehouse is important, since the building is iron-framed and is a significant part of the sequence of innovative structures at Ditherington and elsewhere: the evidence for the date is considered in detail in Chapter 5. For Marshalls' policy on stockpiling flax see Rimmer 1960, 72–4.

37 The bridge was purchased in 1811 for £77: LULSC MS200/1, entry for 6 January 1812. It was used in the fire of October 1811 as an escape route to the Flax Warehouse: Trinder 1992a, 202.

38 LULSC MS200/4, 278.

5 Ditherington and the development of the iron-framed mill: innovation and experimentation

1 Skempton 2002, 'Samuel Wyatt'.

2 Trinder 2013, 231–3, 301–4.

3 Paxton 1975.

4 Trinder 2013, 112–16.

5 Lindsey 2004.

6 Giles and Goodall 1992, 24, 63; Menuge 2006.

7 Swailes 2002b, 670–2.

8 Fitton and Wadsworth 1958, 192–223.

9 Bannister 1950, 235.

10 Fitton and Wadsworth 1958, 203.

11 Johnson and Skempton 1956.

12 Johnson and Skempton noted that this was the first mill in which cast-iron columns rather than timber props had been used, but later research has shown that cast-iron columns were, in fact, used at earlier dates, for example in 1787 at Stanley Mill, Perthshire, Scotland: information from Mark Watson.

13 Skempton and Johnson 1962, 176–8; Johnson and Skempton 1956, 179–205; Fitzgerald 1988, 127–8; Falconer 1993a, 11; Trinder 1992a, 193.

14 Britton and Brayley 1802, vol 3, 364.

15 This statement must be qualified by the admission that it is not known what type of floor covering was employed in the mill. Some early 'fireproof' mills had timber floorboards, but others used brick, stone or tile.

16 Paxton 2002, 689.

17 Letters written by Charles Bage of Shrewsbury to William Strutt of Derby between the years 1802 and 1818, presented (to Shrewsbury Record Office) by Miss Gale of Saffron Walden, Essex, through the Fitzwilliam Museum, Cambridge. Reference 6001/2657. Located with the Bage letters is correspondence from Professor A W Skempton of Imperial College, London, that places a single undated letter from Bage in the range 1795–6.

18 Telford, T 1803 'Some account of the Inland Navigation of the County of Salop' in Plymley, J General View of the Agriculture of Shropshire. London, 284–316. Quoted by Paxton 1975.

19 Powell 2002; VCH 1985, 'Ketley: Economic history' 269–73; Paxton 1975.

20 Alan Baxter & Associates 2006 'Ditherington Flax Mill, Shrewsbury, Structural Engineering Appraisal', Appendices, Drawings 1393/01/13 and 1393/01/14. The remains of additional timber bonding plates, located above the end plates of the beams, were revealed in May 2015. These extended the full length of the walls, strengthening the window heads, but were fully concealed behind the brickwork, maintaining the fireproof qualities of the building.

21 Notes by John Marshall, for example on the benefits of fixing the ends of iron beams, are included in his General Notebook, which he kept between c 1790 and c 1830, LULSC MS200/57, 40. Charles Bage expressed concerns about the expansion of the beams due to changes in temperature in a letter to William Strutt Jnr (undated but estimated to be c 1796–7), SA 6001/26571/2.

22 It has been suggested (Watson 1990, 32) that the holes in the beam flanges are part of an early power transmission system, comprising short upright shafts driving machines in the floors above. This seems unlikely at Ditherington, however, since it is not clear how these shafts could be driven from the main line shafts and the holes in the ground-floor beams are partly covered by the column heads.

23 Charles Bage described the cruciform section as 'doubtless the strongest' in a letter to William Strutt Jnr (undated but estimated to be c 1796–7), SA 6001/26571/2; John Marshall also believed that cruciform columns, wider at mid-height, were the strongest form: General Notebook, between c 1790 and c 1830, LULSC MS200/57, 40–1.

24 Interpretation of the significance of variations in the form of both beams and columns is hindered at the time of writing by the fact that much of the evidence

remains obscured by the alterations made to the mill on its conversion to a maltings. Watson contends that the ground- and third-floor columns are later insertions, when horizontal line shafting replaced vertical shafting, and that the ornamental separately cast capitals of these columns became liable to rust (due to wet spinning followed by damp malt) and have been removed.

25 Menuge 2006.

26 Minshull 1803, 47–8, quoted in Watson 1992, 225.

27 Bage–Strutt 28 October 1811, quoted in Rimmer 1959, 51.

28 Tann 1970, 141–3.

29 Hay and Stell 1986, 86–90.

30 Fitzgerald 1988, 129–30.

31 Skempton 1956.

32 Derby Mercury, 12 January 1803.

33 SA 6001/26571/14 dated Shrewsbury 19 May 1803.

34 SA 6001/26571/13 dated 29 August 1803.

35 Fitzgerald 1988, 127, 131.

36 Falconer 1993a, 21.

37 A good summary of development as understood in the early 1990s is contained in Falconer 1993a, 16–19.

38 A sketch of the Meadow Lane mill roof was drawn by Simon Goodrich in 1804; it shows the iron roof with curved principals similar to those of the North Mill roof: Science Museum Library and Archives, Swindon: Goodrich Papers B Journals and Memoranda vol 6 23 January 1804 to 8 March 1805.

39 SA 6001/26571/13 dated August 29 1803.

40 SA 6001/26571/9.

41 This and the following paragraph are based upon the account given in Falconer 1993a, 16–19.

42 Hay and Stell 1986, 90.

43 Robinson 2002.

44 Fitzgerald 1988, 131–3. East Street Mill, Leeds, has cruciform columns in a mill of c 1825: information from Mark Watson. The mill was built for flax spinning by Atkinson and Hives following their separation from Marshalls in 1823: Rimmer 1960, 115, 125.

45 Information from Dr R S Fitzgerald.

46 For the suggested date of 1805, see Macleod et al 1988, 36: the 1805 insurance policy is found in SA, Salop Fire Insurance Policy Books, 4791/1/6. The 1811 plan prepared by Boulton and Watt is BRL 3147/5/810 c (see Fig 8.1). The construction of the detached Flax Warehouse in c 1810 is suggested by an entry in John Marshall's Personal Account Book, 7 January 1811; LULSC MS200/1, 59–60; see Chapter 7, note 21, for further discussion of the phasing evidence.

47 The former warehouse of the Castlefields Factory, later converted into a row of houses, survives with its cast-iron columns, beams and brick-vaulted ceilings at Severn Street, Shrewsbury; Barracks Mill is described in Falconer 1993a, 12–14, 20–1, 24. See also Watson 1992, 234, 241.

48 Cylindrical columns were in use by the 1790s, and were probably first used in an iron-framed structure at Salford Twist Mill in c 1799. They survive in the fireproof structures of Armley Mills, Leeds, of 1805, and Stanley Mills, Gloucestershire, of 1813: Fitzgerald 1988, 131.

49 The separate upper rafters may have been associated with the former presence of skylights; MacLeod et al 1988, 35.

50 Watson 1992, 241.

51 Cumbria Archive Service, Curwen Collection D/Cu2.

52 A close link between the Dundee and Aberdeen mills is suggested by the fact that very soon after the death of James Brown on 16 January 1811, the two mills went on the market. The sale notice of 1811 for Broadford Mill (*Aberdeen Journal*, 27 February 1811) included mention of mill machinery and a steam engine by Fenton, Murray and Wood of Leeds; Watson 1992, 231–4; the sale notice for West Ward Mill (*Aberdeen Journal,* 6 March 1811) included mention of a steam engine by the same firm.

53 Watson 1992; Falconer 1993a, 16–18.

54 The sale of Barracks Mill in 1853 included a Fenton, Murray and Wood steam engine of 30 horsepower (*Preston Chronicle* 4 June 1853); when Campions Mill, Whitby, was sold in 1843, it contained a Murray engine of 15 horsepower (*Leeds Intelligencer* 26 August 1843); information from Paul Murray Thompson.

55 Swailes and Aja Fernandez de Ret 2004.

56 Hodgkinson 1831; Swailes 1995.

57 Swailes and Aja Fernandez de Ret 2004.

58 Fairbairn 1870, 2–3.

59 For example: Manchester, Beehive Mill, 1824; Chorlton New Mill, c 1814; Hope Mill, c 1829; Chepstow Street Mill, c 1820. *See* Williams (with Farnie) 1992, 62–5. The key breakthrough in roof design in the 1830s was Euston station, where trusses, entirely of wrought iron, had clearly defined compression and tensile members: information from Dr R S Fitzgerald.

60 Report to both Houses of Parliament 'On the fall of the cotton mill at Oldham and part of the prison at Northleach', London, HMSO, 1844.

61 Fitzgerald 1988, 143.

62 Braidwood 1849.

63 Young 1886, Chapter V 'Fireproof Buildings'.

64 Henham 2000.

6 Steam power at Ditherington Mill

1 Well-known examples included Haarlem Mill in Wirksworth, Derbyshire and Shudehill Mill in Manchester; Hills 2008, 31–6.

2 John Marshall noted that J Wrigley (Manchester engineer and millwright) recommended using waterwheels for driving textile mills in c 1790; LULSC MS200/57/2. See also Farey 1827, 444, note a.

3 Patent 913, January 1769.

4 Patent 1432, August 1784.

5 BWC Pf 9A, G & J Robinson 1785.

6 Hills 1970, 155–7, 162; BWC PF 44–5; Chaloner 1954.

7 Hills 1970, 162: the largest of these engines was of 30 horsepower, in a mill in Retford, Nottinghamshire; of the others, 11 were of 10 horsepower or less.

8 Hills 1970, 159; Hills 2006, 64.

9 Patent 1321, July 1782.

10 Evidence of boiler values taken from Stocktaking and Balance Sheets: LULSC MS200/3.

11 Tann 1977–8, 44–6.

12 Dickinson and Jenkins 1981, 197, 257.

13 Dickinson and Jenkins 1981, 277.

14 The list of Leeds steam engines compiled by William Lindley in 1824 shows that in that year Marshalls' had five engines, all by Fenton, Murray and Wood. Of the 129 steam engines listed for Leeds, 77 were by Fenton, Murray and Wood and 7 by Boulton and Watt: LULSC MSS18. Research into the history of the Round Foundry is contained in a number of reports by Structural Perspectives produced during the course of the site's restoration in the early 21st century: see West Yorkshire Archaeology Advisory Service Historic Environment Record. It is worth noting that Fenton, Murray and Wood took integrated production even further than was the case at the new Soho Works: Smiles 1863, 263–4.

15 J Wrigley recommended 'deal' timber for the main upright shaft of Marshalls' Holbeck mill in May 1790; LULSC MS200/57/18 General Notebook. Bolton Museum Service holds some timber shafting in store in its industrial collection. An early example of the use of cast-iron upright shafts was at G & J Robinson's Papplewick Mill, 1785; BWC Pf 9a.

16 Account of Stock in Trade of Marshall and Benyons, 5 January 1795; in Leeds 1793–1804 and 1806, LULSC MS200/2.

17 BWC MS3147/3/435/17 Leeds 2 May 1796.

18 BWC MS3147/2/10/109.

19 Ibid.

20 Advert: *Leeds Intelligencer* **11** July 1117, 96: Murray and Wood
Desire to inform their Friends and the Public in general, That they have erected and opened a Foundry, in Water-Lane, Leeds, for the Purpose of Casting Iron, viz. Engine Work of all Kinds, Ballance Wheels, Joints, Bosses and Steps. Crank and Octagon Wheels, Grate Bars, Bearers, Frames and Doors. Steam and Injection Boxes, Wheels, Segments, Tumbling Shafts, Plumbers Blocks, Coupling Boxes, and Mill Work in general…
Those who please to favour them with their Commands, may depend upon them being well executed on the lowest Terms.
N.B. As they cast twice each Day, any Gentleman may be accommodated with Castings on the shortest Notice, in Cases of Emergency.

21 BWC MS 3147/3/435/18 Leeds 13/5/1796.

22 For the final conveyance, see SA 6001/13323; BWC MS3147/3/416/22.

23 BWC MS3147/3/425/76.

24 BWC MS 3147/3/406/31-40, 10 June 1797 and 16 June 1797, 21-30, 16 February 1797; MS 3147/3/406/31-40, 2 July 1797.

25 BWC MS 3147/3/406/31-40, 11 September 1797.

26 BWC Benyons, Marshall and Bage to Boulton and Watt, 22 May 1797.

27 Trinder 1992a, 195, quoting the *Shropshire Chronicle*, 1 September 1797 and BWC, Benyons, Marshall and Bage correspondence with Boulton and Watt, 3 November 1797 and 10 November 1797.

28 A letter from Benyons, Marshall and Bage dated 22 May 1797, gives measured dimensions of the completed structure, in which the smaller chamber to the east of the cross wall is a foot shorter than was specified in the earlier drawings; BWC.

29 The company's 1796 mill at Holbeck had an engine house of similar design.

30 The Leeds mill drawings are identified as 'Messrs Marshall & Benyons No 2', BWC Pf 136.

31 Typical evidence might include blocked floor traps and indications of wall fixtures for supporting the upright shaft and bevel gearing. Original evidence may have been removed, however, when the maltings steeps and concrete floors were inserted in the 1890s.

32 Watson 1990, 32–3.

33 At North Mill, Belper, circular openings in the brick vaults allowed short upright shafts to rise through the floors: Menuge 1993, 52. At Barracks Mill, Whitehaven, the flag floor has circular holes for belts or shafts: National Monuments Record, BB98/16799. William Fairbairn's Saltaire

Mill (1850–3) has clearly defined slots in the brick ceiling vaults for belt drive through to the floor above: Giles and Goodall 1992, 158.

34 LULSC MS200/37, 23: Notebook of James Marshall, 25 November 1830.

35 Brown 1980, 101.

36 A number of rival engine makers competed with Boulton and Watt in the last decades of the 18th century: Joshua Wrigley, Francis Thompson and Bateman and Sherratt all supplied steam engines to textile firms: Hills 1970, 137–61.

37 Fitzgerald nd, 25.

38 BWC MS3147/3/92.

39 BWC MS3147/3/406/42 of 16 December 1797.

40 BWC MS3147/3/272.

41 Conveyances relating to Murray's (and Marshall's) acquisition of the site that was to become the Round Foundry were examined as part of the legal documentation relating to the site in the present owner's possession. See also WYAS Deeds, Volume DS p 613 no. 683, 19 February 1796; 614 no. 684, 19 February 1796; 614–15 no. 685 19 February 1796.

42 See notes 14 and 20.

43 BWC MS3147/3/412/26 Geo Hawks to Boulton and Watt.

44 BWC MS3147/3/298/15, London 8 November 1797, John Rennie to M R Boulton.

45 BWC MS3147/3/282/60 of 13 November 1797.

46 BWC MS3147/3/46/90 of 6 December 1797, James Watt Jnr to M R Boulton.

47 BWC MS3147/3/47/13 of 10 June 1798. The meaning of 'buckram' in this context is not clear: it might indicate that plans for the engines were less advanced than feared, for one meaning of the word suggests an appearance of false strength: *Oxford English Dictionary*.

48 BWC MS 3147/3/416/23.

49 BWC MS3147/3/92 of 29 March 1798.

50 BWC MS 3147/3/406/43, letter dated 4 June 1798.

51 BWC MS 3147/3/92 of 6 June 1798.

52 BWC MS3147/3/36/5a, M R Boulton to James Watt Jnr, 17 June 1798.

53 BWC MS3147/3/272/44 of 22 November 1797; MS3219/6/1/133 of 30 November 1797.

54 BWC MS3147/3/36/5a.

55 BWC MS3147/3/284/30 of 27 March 1799 James Watt Jnr to Lawson c/o Wormald & Co Leeds.

56 BWC MS3147/3/93 of 22 February 1799 Boulton and Watt to Messrs Benyon, Marshall and Bage.

57 BWC MS3147/3/93 Soho 1 April 1799 James Watt Jnr to Messrs Benyon, Marshall and Bage.

58 BWC MS3147/3/94 of 7 September 1799.

59 BWC MS3147/3/274/50 of 28 November 1799.

60 BWC MS3147/3/51/6-12 of 16 June 1802 to 19 June 1802, James Watt Jnr to M R Boulton, and MS3147/3/40/8 of 16 June 1802 M R Boulton to James Watt Jnr; Dickinson and Jenkins 1927, 273–4; Scott 1928, 13, 38; Boulton and Watt's spy was called Halligan.

61 McCleod et al 1988, 30, referencing a letter from George Lee to James Watt Jnr quoted in Tann 1981, 313–14; in the letter, of July 1800, Lee writes that 'Marshalls at Shrewsbury … use or abuse two Engines of Sixty horses power'; Rimmer 1957, 51, states the engine was by Fenton, Murray and Wood but does not give a reference.

62 The annual inventory of 1821 includes 'Paid on New Engine Account, £2,719', LULSC MS200/3, p 29; plan for installation of gas lighting, Marshall Hives & Co, Shrewsbury, 11th April 1811, BWC, Pf 810 (*see* Fig 8.1).

63 Closer investigation is needed to ascertain if these beams could have been reused from another part of the site.

64 Notebook of James Marshall, 25 November 1830, LULSC MS200/37, 22–3.

65 John Marshall's private ledger, 1791–1840, LULSC MS200/1, 59; the date of 7 January 1811 suggests that the engine must have been installed in 1810.

66 Stocktaking and balance sheets, 1806–51, LULSC MS200/3, entry for 1 July 1811.

67 The introduction of lighter and higher-speed line shafting was a significant stage in the development of early 19th-century power-transmission systems. A well-documented example was at Murray's Mills, Manchester, by Fairbairn and Lillie in 1817; Miller and Wild 2007, 77–8.

68 Murray's engine of 1800 for Ard Walker's mill in Hunslet had many timber components: WYAS Leeds, WYL160/71, Ard Walker's notebook.

69 Trinder 1992a, 199.

70 Fenton, Murray and Wood supplied the larger engine for the Benyons' Castlefields Mill in Shrewsbury, the other initial engine being by Boulton and Watt: BWC, Pf 805. The plan for gas lighting (7 April 1811) clearly marked a Murray engine, and the sale notice for the Mill in the *Salopian Journal* of 16 December 1835 includes mention of a 75-horsepower engine by Fenton, Murray and Wood.

71 James Marshall's sketches (LULSC MS200/37, p 34) show proposed alterations to line shafting in Room 8, the third floor of the Cross Building, 1 November 1831. *See also* Fig 7.5 for Henry Marshall's sketch of machinery and line shafting in 1832.

72 LULSC MS200/37, Notebook of James Marshall 1829, 11, 19 and 29.

73 Accounts, Leeds 1806–71, Shrewsbury 1823–71, LULSC MS200/4, 278; section headed 'New Buildings at Leeds and Salop', entries for new boilers and chimney, 1852–3.

74 Accounts, Leeds 1806–71, Shrewsbury 1823–71, LULSC MS200/4, 278; section headed 'New Buildings at Leeds and Salop', includes cost of the well and pumps in 1837–8. This also lists a separate well for the engine, although the 1855 plan indicates that water pipes still connected both engine houses to the canal.

75 Brown 1980, 96–7. Writing in 1921, Brown describes the addition of bore holes to various Leeds mills in *c* 1820; in December 1829 James Marshall noted that the canal water at Ditherington was about 92°F and 'very hot' in the summer: LULSC MS200/37, 9.

76 Sketch of plunger pumps proposed to be erected for Messrs Marshall & Co Shrewsbury, Benj Hick, Bolton, August 1837, SRO 6000/19536: Sale Catalogues 1886, LULSC MS200/47.

77 Rimmer 1960, 292.

78 LULSC MS200/47. Sale Catalogues 1886.

79 Leeds and Salop machinery stocks, January 1850–January 1884, entry for 1875, LULSC MS200/8, 231–2.

80 Ibid, 237–8; they were probably the multi-tube high-pressure boilers manufactured by J & F Howard of Britannia Works, Bedford, described in *The Engineer*, 17 September 1875, 196.

81 For the contemporary recognition of the integrated nature of the 1797–1800 Spinning Mill's design, see the description of the mill written in 1803, cited in Chapter 5, p 55: Minshull 1803, 47–8, quoted in Watson 1992, 225.

7 Ditherington Mill at work

1 For a discussion of the role of organisation in the industrial revolution, see Berg 1994: for the scale of operations in naval dockyards, see Coad 1989.

2 Marshall *Autobiography*, 14, quoted in Rimmer 1959, 51–2.

3 Rimmer 1960, 65.

4 Rimmer 1960, 66–7.

5 Marshall *Autobiography*, 22, quoted in Rimmer 1959, 57.

6 Rimmer 1960, 115.

7 SC 13 June 1845; Rimmer 1960, 149, 181–2.

8 SAP/257/B/1/8; LULSC MS200/17/50; Rimmer 1959, 52.

9 Rimmer 1960, 279, 296–303.

10 Rimmer 1960, 54.

11 LULSC MS200/17/50, entries for 1796 and 1797.

12 Rimmer 1960, 53–4.

13 Rimmer 1960, 46.

14 LULSC MS200/3, p 2; BWC Pf 810, Messrs Marshall, Hives and Co, 11 April 1811.

15 *See* Rimmer 1959, *passim*, for details of production at Ditherington.

16 Rimmer 1960, 76–8, 319–20; LULSC MS200/Add; LULSC MS200/1.

17 Rimmer 1960, 65, states that, in accordance with the partnership's Articles of Agreement, the Benyons removed both stock and plant from the mills in Leeds and Ditherington.

18 LULSC MS200/3, January 1806 to January 1851.

19 SA 4791/1/5, Salop Fire Office, Policy Books, policy 2657, 14 January 1804.

20 The overall arrangement of processes is indicated in the plan for installation of gas lighting, Marshall Hives & Co, Shrewsbury, 11 April 1811, BWC, Pf 810; the use of the main rooms remained similar in 1829: LULSC MS200/37, 2–6; from the 1850s some thread processes were located on the ground floor of the Spinning Mill but spinning remained on the first floor, LULSC MS200/18/12, newspaper clipping 10 April 1852 and MS200/47, Sale Catalogue 2 November 1886.

21 The early combination of warehousing with heckling, and the dates of the warehouses, is suggested by a variety of primary sources. The Salop Fire Office Policy Books, *c* 1801–5, differentiate between 'stock in trade', stored in the 'Heckling Shop Buildings', and 'manufactured goods', which were stored separately in the warehouse at the south end of the site; for example, SA 4791/1/5, policy 2657, 14 January 1804. A later entry includes 'Heckling Shop and Flax Warehouse', with a description which probably refers to the first Cross Building; SA 4791/1/6, policy 3902, 26 June 1805. The southern warehouse for manufactured goods, also known as the Packing Warehouse, was built and insured by 1801; SA 4791/1/4, policy 2269, 8 December 1801. The site plan for the installation of gas lighting in 1811 indicates that two floors in the Cross Building were used for heckling, one for winding and two more, without gas lighting, were probably for storage; BWC, Pf 810, 11 April 1811. The construction of the detached Flax Warehouse in *c* 1810 is suggested by an entry in John Marshall's Personal Account Book, 7 January 1811 (LULSC MS200/1, 59–60; *see also* Chapter 5). At the Leeds mills, the

combination of warehousing with heckling is indicated by the Account of Stock in Trade of Marshall and Benyons, 2 January 1797; LULSC MS200/2, 26.

22 The early heckling machines were more than three times faster than hand-heckling: Rimmer 1960, 85.

23 LULSC MS200/37, 3.

24 Rimmer 1960, 75.

25 LULSC MS200/3, 11.

26 LULSC MS200/37, 5.

27 Brown 1980, 93. Writing in 1821, Brown considered that 1 horsepower in the Leeds industry drove 64 spindles and the required preparation machines. This referred to the average mill at that time, since Brown did not have access to the much larger mills of John Marshall and the Benyons.

28 Rimmer 1959, 52, 56–7.

29 The Weaving Account, which was only kept from 1813 to 1822, suggests that wages were only paid for 'machine weaving' (powerlooms) from 1816; LULSC MS200/7, 187–216.

30 Inventories from 1814 to 1825 list 'weavers & sundries' but the looms themselves are not itemised, suggesting they were either not owned by the firm or were located offsite; the 'eight old power looms', presumably disused, are listed from 1825. LULSC MS200/3. Joanna Layton, of the Friends of the Flaxmill Maltings Documentary Research Group, has put forward the suggestion that Charles Bage undertook powerloom weaving for Marshalls at his Shrewsbury mill.

31 Giles and Goodall 1992, 90–1, 208; *ESJ* 11 June 1806.

32 Rimmer 1960, 46; Trinder 1992a, 204; Trinder 2006, 154, 161.

33 LULSC MS200/55, Notebook of experiments on bleaching, 1797 to 1802.

34 LULSC MS200/37.

35 LULSC MS200/7, 265.

36 Macleod et al 1988, 14.

37 LULSC MS200/37; 200/38; Trinder 1992a, 199; Rimmer 1959, 57–60; Rimmer 1960, 319–20.

38 Rimmer 1959, 61.

39 LULSC MS200/37, 37–9.

40 LULSC MS200/37, 40.

41 Rimmer 1959, 58.

42 LULSC MS200/37, 6, quoted in Rimmer 1959, 59; Rimmer 1959, 68.

43 LULSC MS200/37, 6 (1829).

44 Rimmer 1959, 60.

45 LULSC MS200/37, 11; the water troughs for wetting the roving are sketched on p 29.

46 LULSC MS200/37, p 4; MS 200/57, 48.

47 LULSC MS200/37, 'Salop. Notes on processes, etc', sketches on pp 4–5.

48 LULSC MS200/37, 33.

49 LULSC MS200/37, 35.

50 LULSC MS200/37, 33–4.

51 LULSC MS200/37, 33.

52 LULSC MS200/7, 189–213; 200/3, 48.

53 LULSC MS200/5 Salop Stock Book, entry for 1828.

54 BWC Pf 8810, 11 April 1811, Plan for installation of gas lighting; SA 6000/19531, Plan of the Old Factory and outbuildings, Messrs Marshall & Co, 1849; LULSC M200/4, 278.

55 Details from LULSC MS200/5, Salop Stock Book, 1828–40.

56 LULSC MS200/37, 30.

57 LULSC MS200/37, ibid; MS200/5, ibid; SA 6000/19531, Plan of the Old Factory and outbuildings, Messrs Marshall & Co, 1849; LULSC MS200/4, 278.

58 Details taken from Hanwood Account 1813–22, LULSC MS200/7.

59 Details taken from Salop Stock Book 1828–40, LULSC MS200/5.

60 'Bleachfields', a small housing development adjacent to the site, commemorates the historic use: information from Joanna Layton, Friends of the Flaxmill Maltings Documentary Research Group.

61 Rimmer 1959, 61.

62 Rimmer 1960, 319.

63 Rimmer 1960, 222, 268–76.

64 Rimmer 1960, 296.

65 Ibid.

66 LULSC MS200/47; *Shoe & Leather Trades Chronicle*, 15 August 1882, 14–18; *British Trade Journal*, 1 March 1883, 169–72.

67 Details taken from catalogue of sale of machinery, 2 November 1886, LULSC MS200/47.

68 Details of machinery layout from 1886 Sale Catalogue; LULSC MS200/47, 4 November 1886.

69 Rimmer 1959, 62.

70 LULSC MS200/47.

71 Rimmer 1959, 62; a figure of 900 was claimed for the mid-1860s, but the accuracy of this estimate is not clear: it comes from the *Salopian Journal* of 28 October 1885, recalling the size of the workforce twenty years earlier.

72 Rimmer 1959, 62.

73 Rimmer 1959, 62–3 makes the point that Ditherington's unprofitability 'was due simply to the fact that Castle Foregate registered losses on goods made at Leeds, a matter of internal accounting practice'.

74 'British Industries: Messrs. Marshall & Col, Linen and Linen-thread Manufacturers', *The British Trade Journal*, 1 March 1883, 171.

75 *ESJ* 13 January 1886; *SC* 15 January 1886; Rimmer 1960, 288.

76 *SC* 6 May 1887.

77 *SC* 2 February 1906, 2 March 1906.

78 *ESJ* 28 October 1885.

79 *ESJ* 27 October 1886.

80 *Commonweal*, 10 July 1886.

81 *Wellington Journal*, 9/16 April 1904.

82 Weiner 1985, 13.

83 *The Shoe & Leather Trade Chronicle*, 15 August 1882, 15.

84 Mitchell and Deane 1962, 202–3; Cullen 1987, 158–9.

8 The gasworks and gas lighting at Ditherington Mill

1 BPP Minutes of evidence taken before the Select Committee on the state of the children employed in the manufactories of the United Kingdom 1816 (397) II 235.

2 Shröder 1969.

3 LULSC MS200/4,3.

4 Pearson 1992, 4–7; Pearson 2004, 37, 153–4.

5 Clegg 1853, 5–15.

6 West 2008, 101–9; BPP 1809 (220).

7 West 2008, 171–86.

8 West 2008, 96–110.

9 West 2008, 84–5.

10 West 2008, 113–17.

11 West 2008, 125–38.

12 BWC 3147/4/5.

13 LULSC MS200/3,113.

14 BWC 3147/3/479/14; Bennett 1997, 12.

15 BWC 3147/5/810 b (erroneously headed 'Marshall Hives') and c.

16 BWC 3147/5/811.

17 The plan of 1811 in the Boulton and Watt archive shows a building on this site connected to the main gas supply pipe for the mill, thus identifying the building as the gasholder.

18 Falconer 1993a, 17, records that the cast-iron trusses from the Gas Retort House of 1811 are now in store at Ironbridge Museum.

19 LULSC MS200/4, 276.

20 West 2008, 196–9.

21 West 2008, 130–1.

22 LULSC MS200/37, 59–61.

23 Ibid.

24 LULSC MS200/4, 26.

25 LULSC MS200/4, 278.

26 SA 6000/19535.

9 The workforce in the 19th century

1 Macleod et al 1988, 14; LULSC MS200/207/7, f259; Rimmer 1959, 62.

2 *Pocket Guide to Shrewsbury* 1785 (later the Salopian Guide by Minshull).

3 LULSC MS200/01, copy of letter John Marshall – Thomas Gataker, 19 November 1801, original in Public Record Office of Northern Ireland.

4 *ESJ* 11 June 1806; *SC* 17 March 1809, 5 November 1813; Rimmer 1959, 54.

5 For the higher wages paid to the skilled trades of bleaching and dyeing, see Rimmer 1959, 62: labour costs were lower in Shropshire than in Leeds, and this helps to explain Marshalls' concentration of these processes at the Shropshire end of their business.

6 LULSC MS200/7, f265.

7 Macleod et al 1988, 14, citing SJ 28 October 1885 for the figure of 900 hands.

8 Analysis of 1851 census enumerators' returns in Trinder 1992a, 209.

9 Much of the background to the description of the parish apprentice system is taken from Honeyman 2007b.

10 Honeyman 2007a, 6.

11 Lees 1998, 56.

12 Snell 1996, 306.

13 Honeyman 2007a, 21.

14 Evidence of Samuel Downe, Minutes of evidence taken before the Committee on the bill to regulate the labour of children. BPP, Industrial Revolution. Children's Employment vol 2 1831–2. Shannon: Irish University Press (1968), 199–201.

15 *SC* 19 August 1805.

16 SA PL2/7/1/1.

17 SA 3920/P/4/20; SA 4195/P/22–23; SA 790/P/5/22/, 256a.

18 Giving evidence to the Committee on the Factories Bill in 1832, Jonathan Downe, formerly employed at Marshalls' mill in Ditherington, stated that some apprentices 'were taken from different parishes; some came from as far as Hull, in Yorkshire; they were bound apprentice to Mr Marshall and Mr Benyon.' Evidence of Jonathan Downe, Minutes of evidence taken before the Committee on the bill to regulate the labour of children. BPP, Industrial Revolution. Children's Employment vol 2 1831–2 Shannon: Irish University Press (1968), 201–8.

19 Chapman 1967, 167; Giles and Goodall 1992, 185; Honeyman 2007a, 7–8. In the 18th century some silk mills in south-west England employed children from London workhouses: Williams 2013, 155–6.

20 Trinder 1992a, 205.

21 Frost 1989.

22 Honeyman 2007a, Table 3 and p13.

23 LULSC MS200/7; 200/1 p59 includes £3,329 for the Apprentice House in January 1812.

24 The use of the first Apprentice House by clerks of the mill in 1814 is documented in SA, Salop Fire Office Registers 4791/1/9, policy 10833, 15 February 1814.

25 Rimmer 1960, 84–5 makes the point that in Marshalls' Leeds mill, the early heckling machines were operated mainly by boys and girls, thus reducing labour costs.

26 Honeyman 2007b, 47–9.

27 LULSC MS200/17/50, letter from Peter Horsman.

28 Trinder 1992a, 209.

29 LULSC MS200/34/51.

30 The brothers Samuel and Jonathan Downes were child workers, not apprentices, at the mill in 1813, their father working there as well: Minutes of evidence taken before the Committee on the bill to regulate the labour of children. BPP, Industrial Revolution. Children's Employment vol 2 1831–2 Shannon: Irish University Press (1968), 199–208.

31 *ESJ* 29 June 1842.

32 Information from Penny Ward, Friends of the Flaxmill Maltings Documentary Research Group.

33 Ibid.

34 Trinder 2006, 154.

35 SA O257/B/1.

36 Menuge 1993, 58–9. It is worth noting that an early form of cluster house is also found at Darley Dale, Derbyshire, where Charles Bage had family connections.

37 Trinder 2013, 578.

38 Evidence of Samuel and Jonathan Downe, Minutes of evidence taken before the Committee on the bill to regulate the labour of children. BPP, Industrial Revolution. Children's Employment vol 2 1831–2. Shannon: Irish University Press (1968), 199–208.

39 *Shropshire Conservative* 10 April 1841.

40 LULSC MS200/17/50.

41 Green 1981, 122; Reports by Inspectors of Factories, BPP, Industrial Revolution. Children's Employment vol 6 1835–41, Shannon: Irish University Press (1969), 5; Rimmer 1960, 105–6 discusses Marshall's promotion of education for children in the neighbourhood of his Leeds mill.

42 *SC* 9 May 1823, 2 December 1842; *Shropshire Conservative* 10 April 1841; LULSC MS200/15/7; *SC* 2 December 1842; SA Watton Colln, vol 10, 28.

43 *ESJ* 23 Mar, 4 May 1831; *SC* 13 May 1842.

44 LULSC MS200/41: Rules and Regulations of Messrs Marshall and Co's Mill Club, Shrewsbury, 1849.

45 *SC* 30 July 1858, 4 August 1871, 2 August 1872, 1 August 1873, 11 August 1882.

46 *ESJ* 27 October 1886.

47 *SC* 26 January, 2 September, 16 February, 2 March 1906.

48 Taylor 1865, 413–14; Giles and Goodall 1992, 194–5.

49 White 1853, 113.

50 LULSC MS200/41; SA, 1851 Tithe Map, P257/T/1/7.

10 Mill into maltings

1 LULSC MS200/47.
2 LULSC MS200/18/17.
3 LULSC MS200/46.
4 *SC* 16/23 March 1888, 2 February 1906, 2 March 1906.
5 *SC* 2 April 1897; Macdonald 1897, 36–7; Trinder 2006, 153.
6 *SC* 16 November 1923, 21 May 1948; National Library of Wales, *Wales–Ohio Project* website (accessed October 2007).
7 Trinder 1996, 47–51.
8 Stopes 1885, 18, 35.
9 Wright 1982, 121; Alderton and Booker 1980, 147–8.
10 Stratton and Trinder 1993, 3–8.
11 The changes made to Ditherington Mill on conversion to a maltings were the subject of a specially commissioned report by Amber Patrick: see Patrick 1999. Much of the following description is taken from this report.
12 Macleod et al 1988, 93.
13 Macdonald 1897, 36–7.
14 Trinder 1992a, 215; Patrick 1999, 2.
15 OS 1:2500 map, 2 edn 1902.
16 Information from Mr W Preen.
17 Patrick, 1999, 9.
18 The ironwork was supplied by Walter MacFarlane and Co of the Saracen Foundry, Glasgow. Macfarlanes were the leading supplier of ornamental cast iron in this period. Information from Mark Watson, Historic Scotland.
19 Trinder 1996, 50–1; Trinder 2006, 87–8, 118; Robinson, Son and Pike 1894, 35; MacDonald 1897, 36–7; *SC* 4 May 1923; *Darling Downs Gazette*, 5 June 1907.
20 *SC* 21 May 1948; information from Mr W Preen.
21 *SC* 18 May, 1 June 1945; information from Mr W Preen. The army's occupation prevented Turpin Bannister, who first drew attention to the mill's historic importance, from getting photographs of the site until after the War; information from Penny Ward, Friends of the Flaxmill Maltings Documentary Research Group.
22 This and the paragraphs that followed are based on Patrick 1999 and on the reminiscences of Mr W Preen who worked at the Shropshire Maltings from 1952 until 1987. Both silos were demolished in 2014.
23 Information from Mr W Preen.
24 Information from Mr W Preen.

11 Ditherington rescued

1 English Heritage 2008.

BIBLIOGRAPHY

Aikin, A 1797 *Journal of a Tour through North Wales*. London: J Johnson

Alderton, D and Booker, J H 1980 *The Batsford Guide to the Industrial Archaeology of East Anglia*. London: Batsford

Angerstein, R R 2000 *R R Angerstein's Illustrated Travel Diary, 1753–1755: Industry in England and Wales from a Swedish Perspective* (trans T and P Berg). London: Science Museum

Ayton, R 1814–25 *A Voyage Round Great Britain Undertaken in the Summer of the Year 1813*. London: Longman

Bannister, T 1950 'The first iron-framed buildings'. *Architectural Review* **107**, 231–46

Bennett, S 1997 'Samuel Clegg: His contribution to the development of the gas industry'. Unpublished manuscript, National Gas Archive

Berg, M 1994 'Factories, workshops and industrial organisation' *in* Floud, R and McCloskey, D *The Economic History of Britain since 1700, volume 1: 1700–1860*. Cambridge: Cambridge University Press, 123–50

Booker, J 1974 *Essex and the Industrial Revolution*. Chelmsford: Essex County Council

Borsay, P (ed) 1990 *The Eighteenth Century Town: A Reader in English Urban History*. London: Longman

Braidwood, J 1849 'On fireproof buildings'. *Minutes of the Proceedings of the Institution of Civil Engineers* **8** (1849), 141–64

Bray, W 1777 'A tour through some of the Midland Counties into Derbyshire and Yorkshire' *in* Mavor, W 1809 *The British Tourist's Companion*. London: Phillips, 207–57

British Parliamentary Papers 1840 XXIII *Handloom Weavers Report of the Assistant Commissioners on Eastern and South-Western England, the West Riding of Yorkshire and Germany*

Britton, J and Brayley, E W 1802 *The Beauties of England and Wales*. London: Vernor and Hood

Broster, P 1782 *The Chester Guide*. London: Longman

Brown, W 1980 (ed J Hume) *Early Days in a Dundee Mill 1819–1823: Extracts from the Diary of William Brown, an Early Dundee Spinner*. Dundee: Abertay Historical Society

Calladine, A 1993 'Lombe's Mill: An exercise in reconstruction'. *Industrial Archaeology Review* **16**, 82–99

Calladine, A and Fricker, J 1993 *East Cheshire Textile Mills*. London: RCHME

Campbell, J 1774 *A Political Survey of Britain*. London: the author

Cartwright, J J (ed) 1888–9 *The Travels through England of the Revd Richard Pococke*. London: Camden Society

Chaloner, W H 1954 'Robert Owen, Peter Drinkwater and the early factory system in Manchester, 1788–1800', *Bulletin of the John Rylands Library*, **37**, 78–102

Chapman, S D 1967 *The Early Factory Masters*. Newton Abbot: David & Charles

Chapman, S D 1972 *The Cotton Industry in the Industrial Revolution*. London: Macmillan

Chapman, S D 1981–2 'The Arkwright mills – Colquhoun's Census of 1781 and archaeological evidence'. *Industrial Archaeology Review*, **6**, 5–27

Clark, C 1998 *The British Malting Industry since 1830*. London: Hambledon

Clegg, Samuel, Jnr 1853 *A Practical Treatise on the Manufacture and Distribution of Coal-Gas*, 2 edn. London: John Weale

Coad, J 1989 *The Royal Dockyards 1690–1850: Architecture and Engineering Works of the Sailing Navy*. Aldershot: Scolar Press for RCHME

Cossons, N 1993 *The BP Book of Industrial Archaeology*, 3 edn. Newton Abbot: David & Charles

Cossons, N and Trinder, B 2002 *The Iron Bridge: Symbol of the Industrial Revolution*, 2 edn. Chichester: Phillimore

Crawford, W H 1987 *The Irish Linen Industry*. Belfast: Ulster Folk & Transport Museum

Cullen L M 1987 *An Economic History of Ireland since 1660*, 2 edn. London: Batsford

Defoe, D 1959 *A Tour through England and Wales*. London: Dent (first published 1724–7)

Derwent Valley Mills Partnership 2000 *Nomination of the Derwent Valley Mills for Inscription on the World Heritage List*. Matlock: Derwent Valley Mills Partnership

Dickinson, H W and Jenkins, R 1981 *James Watt and the Steam Engine*. Ashbourne: Moorland (first published 1927)

Dodd, A H 1933 *The Industrial Revolution in North Wales*. Cardiff: University of Wales Press

Durie, A J 1979 *The Scottish Linen Industry in the Eighteenth Century*. Edinburgh: Donald

Eliot, G 1860 *The Mill on the Floss*. London: Nelson

Eliot, G 1861 *Silas Marner*. London: Harrap

English Heritage 2008 *Conservation Principles: Policies and Guidance*. London: English Heritage

Fairbairn, W 1861 *Iron: Its History, Properties and Processes of Manufacture*. London: A & C Black

Fairbairn, W 1870 *On the Application of Cast and Wrought Iron to Building Purposes*, 4th edn, with additions, London: Longmans, Green and Company

Fairbairn, W 1978 *The Life of Sir William Fairbairn* (completed by W Pole, ed A E Musson). Newton Abbot: David & Charles

Falconer, K A 1980 *Guide to England's Industrial Heritage*. London: Batsford

Falconer, K A 1993a 'Fireproof mills: The widening perspectives'. *Industrial Archaeology Review* **16**, 11–26

Falconer, K A 1993b 'Mills of the Stroud Valley'. *Industrial Archaeology Review* **16**, 62–81

Falconer, K A and Thornes, R 1986 'Industrial archaeology and the RCHME'. *Industrial Archaeology Review* **9**, 24–36

Farey, J 1827 *A Treatise on the Steam Engine, Historical, Practical and Descriptive*. London: Longman, Rees, Orme, Brown and Green

Feilden Clegg Bradley 2004 *A Conservation Plan: Ditherington Flax Mill, Ditherington, Shrewsbury*. Report for English Heritage

Fiennes, C 1947 *The Journeys of Celia Fiennes* (ed C Morris). London: Cresset

Fitton, R S and Wadsworth, A P 1958 *The Strutts and the Arkwrights: 1758–1830*. Manchester: Manchester University Press

Fitzgerald, R S 1987–8 'The development of the cast-iron frame in textile mills to 1850'. *Industrial Archaeology Review* **10**, 127–46

Fitzgerald, R S nd 'Synopsis of the history of the steam engine', typescript prepared for English Heritage

Frost, P 1989 'Ann's Hill, Shrewsbury: A survey and historical evaluation'. Unpublished assessed essay, Ironbridge Institute, University of Birmingham

Giles, C 1993 'Housing the loom, 1790–1850: A study of industrial building and mechanisation in a transitional period'. *Industrial Archaeology Review* **16**, 27–37

Giles, C and Goodall, I H 1992 *Yorkshire Textile Mills: The Buildings of the Yorkshire Textile Industry 1770–1930*. London: HMSO

Gloag, J and Bridgwater, D 1948 *A History of Cast-iron in Architecture*. London: Allen & Unwin

Gould, J 1981–2 'The Lichfield Canal and the Wychnor Ironworks'. *Transactions of the South Staffordshire Archaeological and Historical Society*, **2**, 109–17

Gray, A 1819 *A Treatise on Spinning Machinery*. Edinburgh: Constable and Co

Green, H 1981 'The linen industry of Shropshire'. *Industrial Archaeology Review* **5**, 122–5

Griffiths, J 1992 *The Third Man: The Life and Times of William Murdoch 1754–1839*. London: Andre Deutsch

Hadfield, C 1966 *The Canals of the West Midlands*. Newton Abbot: David & Charles

Hamilton, S B 1940–1 'The use of cast iron in building'. *Transactions of the Newcomen Society* **21**, 139–55

Hay, G and Stell, G 1986 *Monuments of Industry: An Illustrated Historical Record*. Edinburgh: RCHAMS

Henham, B 2000 *True Hero: The Life and Times of James Braidwood, Father of the British Fire Service*. Romford: Braidwood Books

Hills, R L 1970 *Power in the Industrial Revolution*. Manchester: Manchester University Press

Hills, R L 2006 *James Watt, Volume 3, Triumph Through Adversity, 1785–1819*. Ashbourne: Landmark Publishing

Hills, R L 2008 *Development of Power in the Textile Industry from 1700–1930*. Ashbourne: Landmark Publishing

Historic Scotland 2000 *Nomination of New Lanark for Inclusion in the World Heritage List*. Edinburgh: Historic Scotland

Hobbs, J L 1954 *Shrewsbury Street Names*. Shrewsbury: Wilding

Hodgkinson, E 1831 'Theoretical and experimental researches to ascertain the strength and best form of iron beams'. *Memoirs of the Literary and Philosophical Society of Manchester*, **5**, 407–544

Honeyman, K 2007a *The London Parish Apprentice and the Early Industrial Labour Market*. Exeter: Economic History Society Conference

Honeyman, K 2007b *Child Workers in England, 1780–1820: Parish Apprentices and the Making of the Early Industrial Labour Force*. Aldershot: Ashgate

Horner, J 1920 *The Linen Trade of Europe During the Spinning-Wheel Period*. Belfast: M'Caw, Stevenson and Orr

Hughes, S 2004 'Hazeldine, William (1763–1840)' *in Oxford Dictionary of National Biography*, Oxford: Oxford University Press [http://www.oxforddnb.com/view/article/12802, accessed 7 Jan 2014]

Hulbert, C 1837 *History and Description of the County of Salop*. Hadnall: Hulbert

Hulbert, C 1852 *Memoirs of Seventy Years of an Eventful Life*. Hadnall: Hulbert

Hume, J 1976 *The Industrial Archaeology of Scotland, vol 1, The Lowlands and Borders*. London: Batsford

Hume, J 1977 *The Industrial Archaeology of Scotland, vol 2, The Highlands and Islands*. London: Batsford

Hutton, W 1872 *The Life of William Hutton*. London: Warne

Jennings, B (ed) 1967 *A History of Nidderdale*. Huddersfield: Advertiser Press

Johnson, H R and Skempton, A W 1956 'William Strutt's cotton mills 1796–1812'. *Transactions of the Newcomen Society* **30**, 179–205

King-Hall, D 1977 *Doctor of Revolution: The Life and Genius of Erasmus Darwin*. London: Faber

Klingender, F 1972 *Art and the Industrial Revolution* (ed Sir Arthur Elton). London: Paladin

Lawson, J B 1980 'Thomas Telford in Shrewsbury: The metamorphosis of an architect into a civil engineer' *in* Penfold, A (ed) *Thomas Telford: Engineer*. London: Thomas Telford, 1–22

Lees, L H 1998 *The Solidarities of Strangers: The English Poor Law and the People, 1700–1948*. Cambridge: Cambridge University Press

Lindsey, C F 2004 'Hartley, David (1731–1813)' *in Oxford Dictionary of National Biography*, Oxford: Oxford University Press

MacDonald, W C 1897 *An Illustrated Guide to Shrewsbury*. Edinburgh: McDonald

Mackenzie, H J 1949 *The Story of Barnsley Linen*. Barnsley: Hickson, Lloyd & King

Macleod, M, Trinder, B and Worthington, M 1988 *Ditherington Flax Mill, Shrewsbury: A Survey and Historical Evaluation*. Telford: Ironbridge Institute

McCutcheon, W A 1980 *The Industrial Archaeology of Northern Ireland*. Belfast: HMSO

McInnes, A 1988 'The emergence of a leisure town: Shrewsbury 1660–1760'. *Past and Present* **120**, 53–87

Mendenhall, T C 1953 *The Shrewsbury Drapers and the Welsh Woollen Trade in the XVI and XVII Centuries*. Oxford: Oxford University Press

Menuge, A 1993 'The Cotton Mills of the Derbyshire Derwent and its Tributaries'. *Industrial Archaeology Review* **16**, 38–61

Menuge, A 2006 'Boar's Head Mills, Darley Abbey, Derby: A survey and investigation of the cotton mills and ancillary buildings'. English Heritage Research Department Report Series No. 35/2006

Miller, I and Wild, C 2007 *A and G Murray and the Cotton Mills of Ancoats*. Lancaster: Oxford Archaeology North

Minshull, T 1786 *Shrewsbury Visitor's Pocket Companion or Salopian Guide*. Shrewsbury: Pryse

Minshull, T 1795 *Shrewsbury Visitor's Pocket Companion or Salopian Guide*. Shrewsbury: published by the bookseller (unknown)

Minshull, T 1803 *Shrewsbury Visitor's Pocket Companion or Salopian Guide*. Shrewsbury: Hodges

Mitchell, B R and Deane, P 1962 *Abstract of British Historical Statistics*. Cambridge: Cambridge University Press

Owen, H 1808 *Some Account of the Ancient and Present State of Shrewsbury*. Shrewsbury: Sandford

Owen, H and Blakeway, J B 1825 *A History of Shrewsbury*. London: Harding Lepard

Pacey, A 1969 'The earliest cast-iron beams'. *Architectural Review* **145**, 140

Patrick, A 1996 'Establishing a typology for the buildings of the floor malting industry'. *Industrial Archaeology Review* **18**, 180–200

Patrick, A 1999 'William Jones's Shropshire Maltings, The Flax Mill, Ditherington, Shrewsbury'. Report for Blacklay Associates

Pattison, A 2012 'William Hazledine, Shropshire Ironmaster and Millwright: A reconstruction of his life, and his contribution to the development of engineering, 1780–1840'. M.Phil thesis, University of Birmingham

Paxton, R A 1975 'The influence of Thomas Telford (1757–1834) on the use of improved construction materials in civil engineering practice'. MSc thesis, Heriot-Watt University

Paxton, R A 2002 'Thomas Telford' in Skempton, A W (ed) *A Biographical Dictionary of Civil Engineers in Great Britain and Ireland*, vol 1, 1500–1830. London: Thomas Telford

Pearson, R 1992 'Fire insurance – the British textile industries during the Industrial Revolution'. *Business History* **34**(3), 1–19

Pearson, R 2004 *Insuring the Industrial Revolution: Fire Insurance in Great Britain 1700–1850*. Aldershot, Ashgate

Penfold, A (ed) 1980 *Thomas Telford: Engineer*. London: Thomas Telford

Pennant, T 1883 *Tours in Wales* (ed J Rhys). Caernarfon: Humphreys

Phillips, T 1779 *The History and Antiquities of Shrewsbury*. Shrewsbury: Wood

Pigot & Co 1834 *National Commercial Directory: Yorkshire*. London: Pigot

Pigot & Co 1834a *New Commercial Directory for Shropshire, &c.* Manchester: Pigot

Pigot & Co 1835 *National Commercial Directory of Derbyshire, Herefordshire, etc.* London and Manchester: Pigot

Pinkerton, J 1808–14 *A General Collection … of the best and most interesting voyages and travels in all parts of the World*. London: Longman, Hirst, Rees & Orme

Powell J 2002 'William Reynolds' in Skempton, A W (ed) *A Biographical Dictionary of Civil Engineers in Great Britain and Ireland*, vol 1, 1500–1830. London: Thomas Telford, 574–5

Quartermaine, J, Trinder, B and Turner, R 2003 *Thomas Telford's Holyhead Road: The A5 in North Wales*. York: Council for British Archaeology

Rees, A 1819–20 *Rees's Manufacturing Industry*, 1972 edn. Newton Abbot: David & Charles

Reynolds, T S 2003 *Stronger than a Thousand Men: The History of the Vertical Waterwheel*. Baltimore: John Hopkins University Press

Rimmer, W G 1959 'Castle Foregate Flax Mill, Shrewsbury (1797–1886)'. *Transactions of the Shropshire Archaeological Society* **56** (1959), 49–68

Rimmer, W G 1960 *Marshall's of Leeds, Flax-spinners 1788–1886*. Cambridge: Cambridge University Press

Robinson, Son and Pike 1894 *Shrewsbury Illustrated*. Brighton: Robinson, Son and Pike

Robinson, M 2002 'Who built the Catherine Street Mill?'. *Cumbria Industrial History Society Newsletter*, April

Scott, K (ed) 1928 *Matthew Murray, Pioneer Engineer*. Leeds: Edwin Jowett

Shaw, S 1789 *A Tour in the West of England in 1788*. London: Robson & Clark & J Walker

Shröder, M 1969 *The Argand Burner: Its Origin and Development in France and England 1780–1800*. Odense: Odense University Press

Skempton, A W 1956 'The origin of iron beams'. *Actes du 8ieme Congres International des Sciences* **3**, 1029–39

Skempton, A W 1980 'Thomas Telford and the design for a new London Bridge' in Penfold, A (ed), *Thomas Telford: Engineer*. London: Thomas Telford, 62–83

Skempton, A W (ed) 2002 *A Biographical Dictionary of Civil Engineers in Great Britain and Ireland*, vol 1, 1500–1830. London: Thomas Telford

Skempton, A W and Johnson, H R 1962 'The first iron-framed buildings'. *Architectural Review* **131**, 175–86

Skrine, H 1798 *Two Successive Tours through the Whole of Wales with Several of the English Counties*. London: Elmsley & Bremner

Snell, K D M 1996 'The apprenticeship system in British history: The fragmentation of a cultural institution'. *History of Education* **25**(4), 303–22

Smiles, S 1863 *Industrial Biography, Iron Workers and Tool Makers*. London: John Murray

Spackman, W 1847 *An Analysis of the Occupations of the People*, 1969 edn. New York: Kelley

Spufford, M 1984 *The Great Reclothing of Rural England: Petty Chapmen and their Wares in the Seventeenth Century*. London: Hambledon Press

Stopes, H 1882 *Drying Malt Practically Considered*. London: F W Lyon

Stopes, H 1885 *Malt and Malting: An Historical, Scientific and Practical Treatise*. London: Brewers' Journal Office

Stratton, M and Trinder, B 1988 'Stanley Mill, Gloucestershire'. *Post-Medieval Archaeology* **22**, 143–80

Stratton, M and Trinder, B 1989 'Industrial monuments in England: The textile industry: A report for English Heritage'. Ironbridge Institute, Telford

Stratton, M and Trinder, B 1993 'Mistley Maltings: A study for English Heritage of maltings 3, 4 and 7 at Mistley Essex'. Ironbridge Institute, Telford

Swailes, T 1995 '19th century cast-iron beams: Their design, manufacture and reliability'. *Proceedings of the Institution of Civil Engineers (Civil Engineering)*, **114**, 25–35

Swailes, T 2002a 'Charles Woolley Bage' in Skempton, A W (ed) *A Biographical Dictionary of Civil Engineers in Great Britain and Ireland*, vol 1, 1500–1830. London: Thomas Telford, 28–9

Swailes, T 2002b 'William Strutt' in Skempton, A W (ed) *A Biographical Dictionary of Civil Engineers in Great Britain and Ireland*, vol 1, 1500–1830. London: Thomas Telford, 670–2

Swailes, T and Aja Fernandez de Ret, E 2004 'The strength of cast-iron columns and the research work of Eaton Hodgkinson (1789–1861)'. *The Structural Engineer* **82**, 18–23, January

Tann, J, 1970 *The Development of the Factory*. London: Cornmarket Press

Tann, J 1977–8 'Boulton and Watt's organisation of steam engine production before the opening of Soho Foundry'. *Transactions of the Newcomen Society* **49**, 41–56

Tann, J 1979 'Arkwright's employment of steam power: A note of some new evidence'. *Business History* **21**, 247–50

Tann, J (ed) 1981 *The Selected Papers of Boulton & Watt*. London: Diploma Press

Taylor, R V (ed) 1865 *The Biographia Leodiensis, or, Biographical Sketches of the Worthies of Leeds*. London: Simpkin and Marshall

Telford, T 1838 *The Life of Thomas Telford* (ed J Rickman). London: J & L G Hansard

Tisdale, T 1875 *Map of the Town and Borough of Shrewsbury*. Shrewsbury: Tisdale

Trinder, B 1980 'The Holyhead Road: An engineering project in its social context' in Penfold, A (ed) *Thomas Telford: Engineer*. London: Thomas Telford, 41–61

Trinder, B (ed) 1984 *Victorian Shrewsbury: Studies in the History of a County Town*. Shrewsbury: Shropshire Libraries

Trinder, B 1992a 'Ditherington Flax Mill, Shrewsbury: A re-evaluation'. *Textile History* **23**, 189–223

Trinder, B (ed) 1992b *The Blackwell Encyclopedia of Industrial Archaeology*. Oxford: Blackwell

Trinder, B 1994 'The textile industry in Shrewsbury in the late eighteenth century' in Clark, P and Corfield, P (eds) *Industry and Urbanisation in Eighteenth Century England*. Leicester: Centre for Urban History, University of Leicester

Trinder, B 1996 *The Industrial Archaeology of Shropshire*. Chichester: Phillimore

Trinder, B 1997 *The Making of the Industrial Landscape*, 3 edn. London: Orion

Trinder, B 2000 *The Industrial Revolution in Shropshire*, 3 edn. Chichester: Phillimore

Trinder, B 2005 *Barges & Bargemen: A Social History of the Upper Severn Navigation 1660–1900*. Chichester: Phillimore

Trinder, B 2006 *Beyond the Bridges: The Suburbs of Shrewsbury 1760–1960*. Chichester: Phillimore

Trinder, B 2013 *Britain's Industrial Revolution*. Lancaster: Carnegie

Trinder, B and Cox, J 1980 *Yeomen and Colliers in Telford: The Probate Inventories of Dawley, Lilleshall, Wellington and Wrockwardine*. Chichester: Phillimore

Trinder, B and Cox, N 2000 *Miners and Mariners of the Severn Gorge: The Probate Inventories of Benthall, Broseley, Little Wenlock and Madeley*. Chichester: Phillimore

Universal British Directory 1791 *The Universal British Directory of Trade, Commerce and Manufactures*. London: Chapman & Whitrow

Ure, A 1835 *The Philosophy of Manufactures*. London: Bohn

VCH Shropshire XI 1985 *The Victoria History of the County of Shropshire*, vol XI. Telford. Oxford: Oxford University Press for the Institute of Historical Research

VCH Shropshire VI 2014 *The Victoria History of the County of Shropshire*, vol VI. Shrewsbury. Woodbridge: Boydell & Brewer

Wakelin, A P 1984 'Historical applications of British fire insurance records'. Unpublished MA thesis, Ironbridge Institute, University of Birmingham

Warden, A J 1864 *The Linen Trade: Ancient and Modern*. London: Longman

Warden, A J 1867 *The Linen Trade: Ancient and Modern*. London: Dundee

Watson, M 1990 *Jute and Flax Mills in Dundee*. Tayport: Hutton Press

Watson, M 1992 'Matthew Murray and the Broadford Works, Aberdeen: Evidence for the earliest iron-framed flax mills'. *Textile History*, **23**, 225–42

Weiner, M J 1985 *English Culture and the Decline of the Industrial Spirit*. Harmondworth: Penguin

West, I 2008 'Light satanic mills – The impact of artificial lighting in early factories'. PhD thesis, School of Archaeology and Ancient History, University of Leicester

Whatley, S 1751 *England's Gazetteer*. London: J & D Knapton

White, W 1853 *Directory of Leeds, Bradford … and the clothing districts of the West Riding of Yorkshire*. Sheffield (facsim edn Newton Abbot: David & Charles 1969)

Williams, M (with Farnie, D A) 1992 *Cotton Mills in Greater Manchester*. Preston: Carnegie

Williams, M 2013 *Textile Mills of South West England*. Swindon: English Heritage

Wood, I 1791 *Some Account of the Shrewsbury House of Industry*. Shrewsbury: Eddowes

Wright, N R 1982 *Lincolnshire Towns and Industry 1700–1914*. Lincoln: History of Lincolnshire Committee

Yarranton, A 1677 *England's Improvement by Sea and Land*. London: Everingham

Young, A 1780 *A Tour in Ireland Made in the Years 1776–8*. London: Cadell

Young, A 1799 *A View of the Corrected Agricultural Survey of Lincolnshire*. London: Board of Agriculture

Young, A 1932 *Tours in England and Wales*. London: LSE

Young, C 1886 *Fires, Fire Engines and Fire Brigades*. London

INDEX